The Editor

William L. Andrews is E. Maynard Adams Professor of English at the University of North Carolina at Chapel Hill. He is the author of *The Literary Career of Charles W. Chesnutt* (1980) and *To Tell a Free Story: The First Century of Afro-American Autobiography, 1760–1865* (1986). He has edited more than a dozen volumes relating to African American literature, among them *Sisters of the Spirit: Three Black Women's Autobiographies of the Nineteenth Century* (1986), Frederick Douglass's *My Bondage and My Freedom* (1987), and *Classic Fiction of the Harlem Renaissance* (1994). He is a co-editor of *The Norton Anthology of African American Literature* (1997), *The Literature of the American South: A Norton Anthology* (1997), and *The Oxford Companion to African American Literature* (1997).

W. W. NORTON & COMPANY, INC.
Also Publishes

THE NORTON ANTHOLOGY OF AFRICAN AMERICAN LITERATURE
edited by Henry Louis Gates Jr. and Nellie Y. McKay et al.

THE NORTON ANTHOLOGY OF AMERICAN LITERATURE
edited by Nina Baym et al.

THE NORTON ANTHOLOGY OF CONTEMPORARY FICTION
edited by R. V. Cassill and Joyce Carol Oates

THE NORTON ANTHOLOGY OF ENGLISH LITERATURE
edited by M. H. Abrams and Stephen Greenblatt et al.

THE NORTON ANTHOLOGY OF LITERATURE BY WOMEN
edited by Sandra M. Gilbert and Susan Gubar

THE NORTON ANTHOLOGY OF MODERN AND CONTEMPORARY POETRY
edited by Jahan Ramazani, Richard Ellmann, and Robert O'Clair

THE NORTON ANTHOLOGY OF POETRY
edited by Margaret Ferguson, Mary Jo Salter, and Jon Stallworthy

THE NORTON ANTHOLOGY OF SHORT FICTION
edited by R. V. Cassill and Richard Bausch

THE NORTON ANTHOLOGY OF THEORY AND CRITICISM
erdited by Vincent B. Leitch et al.

THE NORTON ANTHOLOGY OF WORLD LITERATURE
edited by Sarah Lawall et al.

THE NORTON FACSIMILE OF THE FIRST FOLIO OF SHAKESPEARE
prepared by Charlton Hinman

THE NORTON INTRODUCTION TO LITERATURE
edited by Jerome Beaty, Alison Booth, J. Paul Hunter, and Kelly J. Mays

THE NORTON INTRODUCTION TO THE SHORT NOVEL
edited by Jerome Beaty

THE NORTON READER
edited by Linda H. Peterson, John C. Brereton, and Joan E. Hartman

THE NORTON SAMPLER
edited by Thomas Cooley

THE NORTON SHAKESPEARE, BASED ON THE OXFORD EDITION
edited by Stephen Greenblatt et al.

For a complete list of Norton Critical Editions, visit
www.wwnorton.com/college/english/nce/welcome.htm

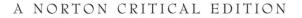

A NORTON CRITICAL EDITION

Booker T. Washington
UP FROM SLAVERY

AUTHORITATIVE TEXT
CONTEXTS AND COMPOSITION HISTORY
CRITICISM

Edited by

WILLIAM L. ANDREWS
UNIVERSITY OF NORTH CAROLINA AT CHAPEL HILL

W • W • NORTON & COMPANY • *New York* • *London*

Printed in the United States of America
First Edition

The text of this book is composed in Electra
with the display set in Bernhard Modern
Composition and manufacturing by Maple-Vail

Library of Congress Cataloging-in-Publication Data

Washington, Booker T., 1856–1915.
Up from slavery : an authoritative text, contexts and composition history, criticism / edited by William L. Andrews.—
p. cm.—(A Norton critical edition)
Includes bibliographical references.
1. Washington, Booker T., 1856–1915. 2. Tuskegee Institute. 3. Afro-Americans—Biography. 4. Educators—United States—Biography. I. Andrews, William, L., 1946– II. Title.
E185.97.W4A3 1995b
370'.92—dc20
[B] 95-1724

ISBN 0-393-96725-5

W. W. Norton & Company, Inc.
500 Fifth Avenue, New York, N.Y. 10110
www.wwnorton.com

W. W. Norton & Company Ltd.
Castle House, 75/76 Wells Street, London W1T 3QT

5 6 7 8 9 0

Contents

swer to such a question. Instead, the contextual materials, reviews, d criticism in this volume have been gathered with an eye toward resenting the range of problems and issues that must be taken into nsideration before such questions can be fairly posed.

n general, the most extreme judgments of Washington, both the pose and the negative, betray a one-sided, superficial understanding of man, his historical situation, his socioeconomic program, his politiagenda, and his sense of the literary traditions that he—as an African erican—had at his disposal. It is crucial to dispel simplistic notions ashington, especially ahistorical ones that superimpose the assump-, values, and goals of today onto a figure who was very much a man s own time. My motive in creating this Norton Critical Edition of *rom Slavery* does not arise from a belief that at this juncture Washn is in need of either tough-minded revision on the one hand or us rehabilitation on the other. What Washington deserves, and over the past three decades he has increasingly received, is a serious g from students of history, culture, and literature. The goal of this n Critical Edition of *Up From Slavery* is to acknowledge the body ful analysis and criticism that Washington's autobiography has l, and by reprinting the most salient commentary from this h and criticism, to encourage more of its kind. I hope this edition th exemplify and justify the idea that what makes *Up From Slav*ortant, if not essential, to an understanding of its author and his the manner in which Washington, a former slave who became st powerful African American of his era, rhetorically converted ilities into assets that, when organized into an autobiographical e, became one of the most compelling personal myths in the of American literature.

Norton Critical Edition of *Up From Slavery* is divided into three he text of Washington's autobiography reproduces exactly the k edition of *Up From Slavery*, published by Doubleday, Page npany in New York in March 1901. Preceding this edition was ed version of *Up From Slavery*, which appeared in *The Outlook* , edited by Hamilton W. Mabie, from November 3, 1900, to 23, 1901. When the serial version of the autobiography was ook publication, the only changes made in the text were the g of the spelling of certain words ("labor" to "labour," "color" ") and the capitalization of the word "Negro," a stylistic point Washington insisted. The index that appends the first book *Up From Slavery* has been retained, although the original bers have been altered to reflect the reset pagination of the itical Edition.

pose of "Contexts and Composition History" is threefold. To on the process by which *Up From Slavery* was written, I have elections from Washington's correspondence that reveal the

Preface

Since his rise to international fame a century ago, I
ton (1856–1915) has remained one of the most co
African American history. Guarded and often eni
were closest to him, conniving and devious to ma
him, Washington liked to represent himself pub
impatient with pretense and show, a straightfor
seeker of consensus, a striver for the common g
time believed implicitly in this Washington an
genuine American hero who had proved himself
black Americans, particularly those in the South
edented progress and harmony between the
assessments of Washington, however, enhance
tions of his private papers in recent years, hav
more complex figure who carefully cultivate
spoken altruist for public consumption wh
scenes as a savvy, sometimes ruthless, politi
ingly, late-twentieth-century views of Was
mixed than those that prevailed after the
applauded autobiography, *Up From Slavery*

Up From Slavery, one of the few Afric
legitimately be termed a classic, does not p
longstanding arguments about who "the r
was. Today's response to Washington's a
that of the nameless protagonist in Ralph I
(1952), as he ponders the meaning of the
freed slave, a statue that has become a
Tuskegee Institute (now University) in A
ton in 1881. In the sculptor's idealized
to be a visionary lifting a veil from th
Ellison's Invisible Man, not unlike ma
today, remains tantalized by the naggi
is really being lifted, or lowered more f
Slavery designed to raise or lower a v
predominantly white audience that I
None of the reviews and criticism tha
Up From Slavery in this Norton Critic

dialogues he had with his publishers about the purpose and style of his autobiography. To suggest the flavor of contemporary reaction to *Up From Slavery*, three reviews of the autobiography are included. The comments from *The Nation* and from the eminent American novelist William Dean Howells, in the *North American Review*, testify to the warm response that *Up From Slavery* received in most of the popular white press. Comparatively few reviews appeared in the African American press, although the observations from *The Colored American Magazine* in 1905 indicate that Washington's black supporters did their best to ensure *Up From Slavery*'s success in the African American reading community. The excerpt from Washington's last autobiography, *My Larger Education* (1911), is included to show how conscious Washington was of Frederick Douglass's prior example and of the inevitable comparisons that would be made between Douglass, the first great African American spokesperson, and himself.

"Criticism" reprints selections from the most original and influential analyses and critical evaluations of *Up From Slavery* in particular and Washington's social, economic, and political program in general. Two standard assessments of Washington by W. E. B. Du Bois and Kelly Miller open the discussion. Du Bois's "Of Mr. Booker T. Washington and Others," arguably the most famous essay in *The Souls of Black Folk* (1903), marked a turning point in the popular reception of the Washington myth as retailed in *Up From Slavery*. Until Du Bois's 1903 critique, Washington's program had received the tacit, if not always the emphatic, endorsement of the large majority of African American intellectuals—indeed, in July 1901, when Du Bois first reviewed *Up From Slavery* for *The Dial*, he too had been careful to modulate his doubts about the wisdom of Washington's methods. But with "Of Mr. Booker T. Washington and Others" Du Bois fired the salvo that split African American leadership into two camps, the civil rights militants, marshalled by Du Bois, and the conservative "Bookerites," who defended their embattled chief to his death. In 1908 Kelly Miller, a professor and dean at Howard University, epitomized the differences between the two groups in his judicious essay, "Radicals and Conservatives," which was one of the first studies of Washington to contrast him systematically to Frederick Douglass.

A cursory look at the "Criticism" section of this edition will reveal a large historical hiatus between the turn-of-the-century assessments of Washington by Du Bois and Miller and the selections from the writings of August Meier and Louis R. Harlan in the 1960s and 1970s. Several books about Washington were published between his death in 1915 and the onset of the work of Meier and Harlan, among them Emmett J. Scott and Lyman Beecher Stowe's *Booker T. Washington: Builder of a Civilization* (1917), which Washington commissioned shortly before his death, and Basil Mathews's *Booker T. Washington, Educator and Inter-*

racial Interpreter (1948), the first attempt at a scholarly biography. But until the work of Meier and Harlan, no scholar had examined Washington systematically and dispassionately in the context of the racial ideologies of his era. This is one of the main reasons why Meier's "Booker T. Washington: An Interpretation" was a milestone in the historical assessment of Washington's significance. Although Harlan's definitive two-volume biography of Washington cannot be excerpted in any satisfying way, his seminal essay, "Booker T. Washington in Biographical Perspective," affords a reader a remarkably intimate glimpse at the man behind the autobiographical mask.

The final four critical estimates of *Up From Slavery* in this edition, by Sidonie Smith, James M. Cox, Houston A. Baker, Jr., and William L. Andrews, represent some of the more productive approaches that recent literary critics and literary historians have taken in reevaluating a text that for so long was regarded as simple, self-evident, and artless. In addition to pointing out multiple affinities between *Up From Slavery* and the *Autobiography of Benjamin Franklin*, Smith was among the first literary critics to detect Washington's strategic adoption of a mask, especially that of Christian self-abnegation, and to argue the constraints that such a mask placed on him as an African American autobiographer. Cox's thoughtful analysis, "Autobiography and Washington," is perhaps the most sensitive study of the style of *Up From Slavery*, "inertial" and infelicitous in many respects and yet profoundly expressive of Washington's sense of himself as a black man attempting to build a power base for himself in the South. Baker's incisive comments on Washington from *Modernism and the Harlem Renaissance* call attention to the importance of Washington's exploitation of the minstrel mask in his autobiography and to the import of his text as a literary herald of African American modernism. Andrews's examination of Washington's crucial revision of the image of slavery in *Up From Slavery* helps to identify his role in establishing a peculiar brand of realism, yet another major mode of late-nineteenth- and early-twentieth-century African American literature that owes much to Washington's autobiographical experiment.

Although the bibliography that concludes this edition lists a number of texts basic to a multidisciplinary study of Washington and his autobiography, it would be a mistake to conclude that the existing scholarship on this fascinating figure has exhausted his potential. More attention to the evolution of Washington's various autobiographies and autobiographical personae is needed to complement the recent studies of this topic by Donald B. Gibson. Feminist analysis of Washington's autobiographies is sorely lacking. Washington's influence on African American autobiography in the first half of the twentieth century needs to be traced as carefully as Robert B. Stepto and James Olney have scrutinized Washington's adaptation of earlier forms, such as the nineteenth-century slave narrative. Some of Washington's favorite themes in his autobiographies—such as his idea of the natural, his concept of the agrarian life, his notion of what a fact is, his sense of what is inherently African or Negro, his obsession with order, cleanliness, and self-control—all need unpacking. The more we engage in these kinds of investigations of the mind and art of the author of *Up From Slavery*, the more likely we are to come to terms with the contradictions that made Washington famous as both the Sage of Tuskegee and the Wizard of the Tuskegee Machine.

The Text of UP FROM SLAVERY An Autobiography

UP FROM SLAVERY

AN AUTOBIOGRAPHY

BY

BOOKER T. WASHINGTON

AUTHOR OF "THE FUTURE OF THE AMERICAN NEGRO"

NEW YORK

DOUBLEDAY, PAGE & CO.

1901

This volume is dedicated to my Wife

MRS. MARGARET JAMES WASHINGTON

And to my Brother

MR. JOHN H. WASHINGTON

Whose patience, fidelity, and hard work have gone far to make the work at Tuskegee successful

Preface

This volume is the outgrowth of a series of articles, dealing with incidents in my life, which were published consecutively in the *Outlook*.[1] While they were appearing in that magazine I was constantly surprised at the number of requests which came to me from all parts of the country, asking that the articles be permanently preserved in book form. I am most grateful to the *Outlook* for permission to gratify these requests.

I have tried to tell a simple, straightforward story, with no attempt at embellishment. My regret is that what I have attempted to do has been done so imperfectly. The greater part of my time and strength is required for the executive work connected with the Tuskegee Normal and Industrial Institute, and in securing the money necessary for the support of the institution. Much of what I have said has been written on board trains, or at hotels or railroad stations while I have been waiting for trains, or during the moments that I could spare from my work while at Tuskegee. Without the painstaking and generous assistance of Mr. Max Bennett Thrasher[2] I could not have succeeded in any satisfactory degree.

1. *Up From Slavery* was first published in *Outlook* magazine from November 3, 1900, to February 23, 1901.
2. A researcher and ghostwriter for Washington who helped outline, draft, and edit the final version of *Up From Slavery*.

Contents

Up From Slavery

Chapter I

A Slave among Slaves

I was born a slave on a plantation in Franklin County, Virginia. I am not quite sure of the exact place or exact date of my birth, but at any rate I suspect I must have been born somewhere and at some time. As nearly as I have been able to learn, I was born near a cross-roads post-office called Hale's Ford, and the year was 1858 or 1859.[1] I do not know the month or the day. The earliest impressions I can now recall are of the plantation and the slave quarters—the latter being the part of the plantation where the slaves had their cabins.

My life had its beginning in the midst of the most miserable, desolate, and discouraging surroundings. This was so, however, not because my owners were especially cruel, for they were not, as compared with many others. I was born in a typical log cabin, about fourteen by sixteen feet square. In this cabin I lived with my mother and a brother and sister till after the Civil War, when we were all declared free.

Of my ancestry I know almost nothing. In the slave quarters, and even later, I heard whispered conversations among the coloured people of the tortures which the slaves, including, no doubt, my ancestors on my mother's side, suffered in the middle passage of the slave ship while being conveyed from Africa to America. I have been unsuccessful in securing any information that would throw any accurate light upon the history of my family beyond my mother. She, I remember, had a half-brother and a half-sister. In the days of slavery not very much attention was given to family history and family records—that is, black family records. My mother, I suppose, attracted the attention of a purchaser who was afterward my owner and hers. Her addition to the slave family attracted about as much attention as the purchase of a new horse or cow. Of my father I know even less than of my mother. I do not even know his name. I have heard reports to the effect that he was a white man who lived on one of the near-by plantations. Whoever he was, I never heard of his taking the least interest in me or providing in any way for

1. According to Louis H. Harlan's *Booker T. Washington: The Making of a Black Leader, 1856–1901*, Washington was born in 1856 on a modest tobacco farm belonging to James Burroughs.

my rearing. But I do not find especial fault with him. He was simply another unfortunate victim of the institution which the Nation unhappily had engrafted upon it at that time.

The cabin was not only our living-place, but was also used as the kitchen for the plantation. My mother was the plantation cook. The cabin was without glass windows; it had only openings in the side which let in the light, and also the cold, chilly air of winter. There was a door to the cabin—that is, something that was called a door—but the uncertain hinges by which it was hung, and the large cracks in it, to say nothing of the fact that it was too small, made the room a very uncomfortable one. In addition to these openings there was, in the lower right-hand corner of the room, the "cat-hole,"—a contrivance which almost every mansion or cabin in Virginia possessed during the ante-bellum period. The "cat-hole" was a square opening, about seven by eight inches, provided for the purpose of letting the cat pass in and out of the house at will during the night. In the case of our particular cabin I could never understand the necessity for this convenience, since there were at least a half-dozen other places in the cabin that would have accommodated the cats. There was no wooden floor in our cabin, the naked earth being used as a floor. In the centre of the earthen floor there was a large, deep opening covered with boards, which was used as a place in which to store sweet potatoes during the winter. An impression of this potato-hole is very distinctly engraved upon my memory, because I recall that during the process of putting the potatoes in or taking them out I would often come into possession of one or two, which I roasted and thoroughly enjoyed. There was no cooking-stove on our plantation, and all the cooking for the whites and slaves my mother had to do over an open fireplace, mostly in pots and "skillets." While the poorly built cabin caused us to suffer with cold in the winter, the heat from the open fireplace in summer was equally trying.

The early years of my life, which were spent in the little cabin, were not very different from those of thousands of other slaves. My mother, of course, had little time in which to give attention to the training of her children during the day. She snatched a few moments for our care in the early morning before her work began, and at night after the day's work was done. One of my earliest recollections is that of my mother cooking a chicken late at night, and awakening her children for the purpose of feeding them. How or where she got it I do not know. I presume, however, it was procured from our owner's farm. Some people may call this theft. If such a thing were to happen now, I should condemn it as theft myself. But taking place at the time it did, and for the reason that it did, no one could ever make me believe that my mother was guilty of thieving. She was simply a victim of the system of slavery. I cannot remember having slept in a bed until after our family was declared free by the Emancipation Proclamation. Three children—

John, my older brother, Amanda, my sister, and myself—had a pallet on the dirt floor, or, to be more correct, we slept in and on a bundle of filthy rags laid upon the dirt floor.

I was asked not long ago to tell something about the sports and pastimes that I engaged in during my youth. Until that question was asked it had never occurred to me that there was no period of my life that was devoted to play. From the time that I can remember anything, almost every day of my life has been occupied in some kind of labour; though I think I would now be a more useful man if I had had time for sports. During the period that I spent in slavery I was not large enough to be of much service, still I was occupied most of the time in cleaning the yards, carrying water to the men in the fields, or going to the mill, to which I used to take the corn, once a week, to be ground. The mill was about three miles from the plantation. This work I always dreaded. The heavy bag of corn would be thrown across the back of the horse, and the corn divided about evenly on each side; but in some way, almost without exception, on these trips, the corn would so shift as to become unbalanced and would fall off the horse, and often I would fall with it. As I was not strong enough to reload the corn upon the horse, I would have to wait, sometimes for many hours, till a chance passer-by came along who would help me out of my trouble. The hours while waiting for some one were usually spent in crying. The time consumed in this way made me late in reaching the mill, and by the time I got my corn ground and reached home it would be far into the night. The road was a lonely one, and often led through dense forests. I was always frightened. The woods were said to be full of soldiers who had deserted from the army, and I had been told that the first thing a deserter did to a Negro boy when he found him alone was to cut off his ears. Besides, when I was late in getting home I knew I would always get a severe scolding or a flogging.

I had no schooling whatever while I was a slave, though I remember on several occasions I went as far as the schoolhouse door with one of my young mistresses to carry her books. The picture of several dozen boys and girls in a schoolroom engaged in study made a deep impression upon me, and I had the feeling that to get into a schoolhouse and study in this way would be about the same as getting into paradise.

So far as I can now recall, the first knowledge that I got of the fact that we were slaves, and that freedom of the slaves was being discussed, was early one morning before day, when I was awakened by my mother kneeling over her children and fervently praying that Lincoln and his armies might be successful, and that one day she and her children might be free. In this connection I have never been able to understand how the slaves throughout the South, completely ignorant as were the masses so far as books or newspapers were concerned, were able to keep themselves so accurately and completely informed about the great National questions that were agitating the country. From the time that Garrison, Lovejoy,[2] and others began to agitate for freedom, the slaves throughout the South kept in close touch with the progress of the movement. Though I was a mere child during the preparation for the Civil War and during the war itself, I now recall the many late-at-night whispered discussions that I heard my mother and the other slaves on the plantation indulge in. These discussions showed that they understood the situation, and that they kept themselves informed of events by what was termed the "grape-vine" telegraph.

During the campaign when Lincoln was first a candidate for the Presidency, the slaves on our far-off plantation, miles from any railroad or large city or daily newspaper, knew what the issues involved were. When war was begun between the North and the South, every slave on our plantation felt and knew that, though other issues were discussed, the primal one was that of slavery. Even the most ignorant members of my race on the remote plantations felt in their hearts, with a certainty that admitted of no doubt, that the freedom of the slaves would be the one great result of the war, if the Northern armies conquered. Every success of the Federal armies and every defeat of the Confederate forces was watched with the keenest and most intense interest. Often the slaves got knowledge of the results of great battles before the white people received it. This news was usually gotten from the coloured man who was sent to the post-office for the mail. In our case the post-office was about three miles from the plantation, and the mail came once or twice a week. The man who was sent to the office would linger about the place long enough to get the drift of the conversation from the group of white people who naturally congregated there, after receiving their mail, to discuss the latest news. The mail-carrier on his way back to our master's house would as naturally retail the news that he had secured among the slaves, and in this way they often heard of important events before the white people at the "big house," as the master's house was called.

I cannot remember a single instance during my childhood or early boyhood when our entire family sat down to the table together, and God's blessing was asked, and the family ate a meal in a civilized manner. On the plantation in Virginia, and even later, meals were gotten by the children very much as dumb animals get theirs. It was a piece of bread here and a scrap of meat there. It was a cup of milk at one time and some potatoes at another. Sometimes a portion of our family would eat out of the skillet or pot, while some one else would eat from a tin plate held on the knees, and often using nothing but the hands with

2. William Lloyd Garrison (1805–1879), editor of *The Liberator*, the most uncompromising antislavery newspaper in the antebellum United States and leader of the American Anti-Slavery Society; Elijah P. Lovejoy (1802–1837), an antislavery editor who was murdered while defending his press from a mob in Alton, Illinois.

which to hold the food. When I had grown to sufficient size, I was required to go to the "big house" at meal-times to fan the flies from the table by means of a large set of paper fans operated by a pulley. Naturally much of the conversation of the white people turned upon the subject of freedom and the war, and I absorbed a good deal of it. I remember that at one time I saw two of my young mistresses and some lady visitors eating ginger-cakes, in the yard. At that time those cakes seemed to me to be absolutely the most tempting and desirable things that I had ever seen; and I then and there resolved that, if I ever got free, the height of my ambition would be reached if I could get to the point where I could secure and eat ginger-cakes in the way that I saw those ladies doing.

Of course as the war was prolonged the white people, in many cases, often found it difficult to secure food for themselves. I think the slaves felt the deprivation less than the whites, because the usual diet for the slaves was corn bread and pork, and these could be raised on the plantation; but coffee, tea, sugar, and other articles which the whites had been accustomed to use could not be raised on the plantation, and the conditions brought about by the war frequently made it impossible to secure these things. The whites were often in great straits. Parched corn was used for coffee, and a kind of black molasses was used instead of sugar. Many times nothing was used to sweeten the so-called tea and coffee.

The first pair of shoes that I recall wearing were wooden ones. They had rough leather on the top, but the bottoms, which were about an inch thick, were of wood. When I walked they made a fearful noise, and besides this they were very inconvenient, since there was no yielding to the natural pressure of the foot. In wearing them one presented an exceedingly awkward appearance. The most trying ordeal that I was forced to endure as a slave boy, however, was the wearing of a flax shirt. In the portion of Virginia where I lived it was common to use flax as part of the clothing for the slaves. That part of the flax from which our clothing was made was largely the refuse, which of course was the cheapest and roughest part. I can scarcely imagine any torture, except, perhaps, the pulling of a tooth, that is equal to that caused by putting on a new flax shirt for the first time. It is almost equal to the feeling that one would experience if he had a dozen or more chestnut burrs, or a hundred small pin-points, in contact with his flesh. Even to this day I can recall accurately the tortures that I underwent when putting on one of these garments. The fact that my flesh was soft and tender added to the pain. But I had no choice. I had to wear the flax shirt or none; and had it been left to me to choose, I should have chosen to wear no covering. In connection with the flax shirt, my brother John, who is several years older than I am, performed one of the most generous acts that I ever heard of one slave relative doing for another. On several occasions when I was being forced to wear a new flax shirt, he generously agreed to put it on in my stead and wear it for several days, till it was "broken in." Until I had grown to be quite a youth this single garment was all that I wore.

One may get the idea, from what I have said, that there was bitter feeling toward the white people on the part of my race, because of the fact that most of the white population was away fighting in a war which would result in keeping the Negro in slavery if the South was successful. In the case of the slaves on our place this was not true, and it was not true of any large portion of the slave population in the South where the Negro was treated with anything like decency. During the Civil War one of my young masters was killed, and two were severely wounded. I recall the feeling of sorrow which existed among the slaves when they heard of the death of "Mars' Billy." It was no sham sorrow, but real. Some of the slaves had nursed "Mars' Billy"; others had played with him when he was a child. "Mars' Billy" had begged for mercy in the case of others when the overseer or master was thrashing them. The sorrow in the slave quarter was only second to that in the "big house." When the two young masters were brought home wounded, the sympathy of the slaves was shown in many ways. They were just as anxious to assist in the nursing as the family relatives of the wounded. Some of the slaves would even beg for the privilege of sitting up at night to nurse their wounded masters. This tenderness and sympathy on the part of those held in bondage was a result of their kindly and generous nature. In order to defend and protect the women and children who were left on the plantations when the white males went to war, the slaves would have laid down their lives. The slave who was selected to sleep in the "big house" during the absence of the males was considered to have the place of honour. Any one attempting to harm "young Mistress" or "old Mistress" during the night would have had to cross the dead body of the slave to do so. I do not know how many have noticed it, but I think that it will be found to be true that there are few instances, either in slavery or freedom, in which a member of my race has been known to betray a specific trust.

As a rule, not only did the members of my race entertain no feelings of bitterness against the whites before and during the war, but there are many instances of Negroes tenderly caring for their former masters and mistresses who for some reason have become poor and dependent since the war. I know of instances where the former masters of slaves have for years been supplied with money by their former slaves to keep them from suffering. I have known of still other cases in which the former slaves have assisted in the education of the descendants of their former owners. I know of a case on a large plantation in the South in which a young white man, the son of the former owner of the estate, has become so reduced in purse and self-control by reason of drink that he is a pitiable creature; and yet, notwithstanding the poverty of the coloured people themselves on this plantation, they have for years supplied this young white man with the necessities of life. One sends him a little coffee or sugar, another a little meat, and so on. Nothing that the coloured people possess is too good for the son of "old Mars' Tom," who will perhaps never be permitted to suffer while any remain on the place who knew directly or indirectly of "old Mars' Tom."

I have said that there are few instances of a member of my race betraying a specific trust. One of the best illustrations of this which I know of is in the case of an ex-slave from Virginia whom I met not long ago in a little town in the state of Ohio. I found that this man had made a contract with his master, two or three years previous to the Emancipation Proclamation, to the effect that the slave was to be permitted to buy himself, by paying so much per year for his body; and while he was paying for himself, he was to be permitted to labour where and for whom he pleased. Finding that he could secure better wages in Ohio, he went there. When freedom came, he was still in debt to his master some three hundred dollars. Notwithstanding that the Emancipation Proclamation freed him from any obligation to his master, this black man walked the greater portion of the distance back to where his old master lived in Virginia, and placed the last dollar, with interest, in his hands. In talking to me about this, the man told me that he knew that he did not have to pay the debt, but that he had given his word to his master, and his word he had never broken. He felt that he could not enjoy his freedom till he had fulfilled his promise.

From some things that I have said one may get the idea that some of the slaves did not want freedom. This is not true. I have never seen one who did not want to be free, or one who would return to slavery.

I pity from the bottom of my heart any nation or body of people that is so unfortunate as to get entangled in the net of slavery. I have long since ceased to cherish any spirit of bitterness against the Southern white people on account of the enslavement of my race. No one section of our country was wholly responsible for its introduction, and, besides, it was recognized and protected for years by the General Government. Having once got its tentacles fastened on to the economic and social life of the Republic, it was no easy matter for the country to relieve itself of the institution. Then, when we rid ourselves of prejudice, or racial feeling, and look facts in the face, we must acknowledge that, notwithstanding the cruelty and moral wrong of slavery, the ten million Negroes inhabiting this country, who themselves or whose ancestors went through the school of American slavery, are in a stronger and more hopeful condition, materially, intellectually, morally, and religiously, than is true of an equal number of black people in any other portion of the globe. This is so to such an extent that Negroes in this country, who themselves or whose forefathers went through the school of slavery, are constantly returning to Africa as missionaries to enlighten those who remained in the fatherland. This I say, not to justify slavery—on the other hand, I condemn it as an institution, as we all know that in America it was established for selfish and financial reasons, and not from a missionary motive—but to call attention to a fact, and to show how Providence so often uses men and institutions to accomplish a purpose. When persons ask me in these days how, in the midst of what sometimes seem hopelessly discouraging conditions, I can have such faith in the future of my race in this country, I remind them of the wilderness through which and out of which, a good Providence has already led us.

Ever since I have been old enough to think for myself, I have entertained the idea that, notwithstanding the cruel wrongs inflicted upon us, the black man got nearly as much out of slavery as the white man did. The hurtful influences of the institution were not by any means confined to the Negro. This was fully illustrated by the life upon our own plantation. The whole machinery of slavery was so constructed as to cause labour, as a rule, to be looked upon as a badge of degradation, of inferiority. Hence labour was something that both races on the slave plantation sought to escape. The slave system on our place, in a large measure, took the spirit of self-reliance and self-help out of the white people. My old master had many boys and girls, but not one, so far as I know, ever mastered a single trade or special line of productive industry. The girls were not taught to cook, sew, or to take care of the house. All of this was left to the slaves. The slaves, of course, had little personal interest in the life of the plantation, and their ignorance prevented them from learning how to do things in the most improved and thorough manner. As a result of the system, fences were out of repair, gates were hanging half off the hinges, doors creaked, window-panes were out, plastering had fallen but was not replaced, weeds grew in the yard. As a rule, there was food for whites and blacks, but inside the house, and on the dining-room table, there was wanting that delicacy and refinement of touch and finish which can make a home the most convenient, comfortable, and attractive place in the world. Withal there was a waste of food and other materials which was sad. When freedom came, the slaves were almost as well fitted to begin life anew as the master, except in the matter of book-learning and ownership of property. The slave owner and his sons had mastered no special industry. They unconsciously had imbibed the feeling that manual labour was not the proper thing for them. On the other hand, the slaves, in many cases, had mastered some handicraft, and none were ashamed, and few unwilling, to labour.

Finally the war closed, and the day of freedom came. It was a momentous and eventful day to all upon our plantation. We had been expecting it. Freedom was in the air, and had been for months. Deserting soldiers returning to their homes were to be seen every day. Others who had been discharged, or whose regiments had been paroled, were constantly passing near our place. The "grape-vine telegraph" was kept busy night and day. The news and mutterings of great events were swiftly carried from one plantation to another. In the fear of "Yankee" invasions, the silverware and other valuables were taken from the "big house," buried in the woods, and guarded by trusted slaves. Woe be to any one who would have attempted to disturb the buried treasure. The slaves would give the Yankee soldiers food, drink, clothing—anything but that which had been specifically intrusted to their care and honour. As the great day drew nearer, there was more singing in the slave quarters than usual. It was bolder, had more ring, and lasted later into the night. Most of the verses of the plantation songs had some reference to freedom. True, they had sung those same verses before, but they had been careful to explain that the "freedom" in these songs referred to the next world, and had no connection with life in this world. Now they gradually threw off the mask, and were not afraid to let it be known that the "freedom" in their songs meant freedom of the body in this world. The night before the eventful day, word was sent to the slave quarters to the effect that something unusual was going to take place at the "big house" the next morning. There was little, if any, sleep that night. All was excitement and expectancy. Early the next morning word was sent to all the slaves, old and young, to gather at the house. In company with my mother, brother, and sister, and a large number of other slaves, I went to the master's house. All of our master's family were either standing or seated on the veranda of the house, where they could see what was to take place and hear what was said. There was a feeling of deep interest, or perhaps sadness, on their faces, but not bitterness. As I now recall the impression they made upon me, they did not at the moment seem to be sad because of the loss of property, but rather because of parting with those whom they had reared and who were in many ways very close to them. The most distinct thing that I now recall in connection with the scene was that some man who seemed to be a stranger (a United States officer, I presume) made a little speech and then read a rather long paper—the Emancipation Proclamation, I think. After the reading we were told that we were all free, and could go when and where we pleased. My mother, who was standing by my side, leaned over and kissed her children, while tears of joy ran down her cheeks. She explained to us what it all meant, that this was the day for which she had been so long praying, but fearing that she would never live to see.

For some minutes there was great rejoicing, and thanksgiving, and wild scenes of ecstasy. But there was no feeling of bitterness. In fact, there was pity among the slaves for our former owners. The wild rejoicing on the part of the emancipated coloured people lasted but for a brief period, for I noticed that by the time they returned to their cabins there was a change in their feelings. The great responsibility of being free, of having charge of themselves, of having to think and plan for themselves and their children, seemed to take possession of them. It was very much like suddenly turning a youth of ten or twelve years out into the world to provide for himself. In a few hours the great questions with which the Anglo-Saxon race had been grappling for centuries had been thrown upon these people to be solved. These were the questions of a home, a living, the rearing of children, education, citizenship, and the establishment and support of churches. Was it any wonder that within a few hours the wild rejoicing ceased and a feeling of deep gloom seemed to pervade the slave quarters? To some it seemed that, now that they were in actual possession of it, freedom was a more serious thing than they had expected to find it. Some of the slaves were seventy or eighty years old; their best days were gone. They had no strength with which to earn a living in a strange place and among strange people, even if they had been sure where to find a new place of abode. To this class the problem seemed especially hard. Besides, deep down in their hearts there was a strange and peculiar attachment to "old Marster" and "old Missus," and to their children, which they found it hard to think of breaking off. With these they had spent in some cases nearly a half-century, and it was no light thing to think of parting. Gradually, one by one, stealthily at first, the older slaves began to wander from the slave quarters back to the "big house" to have a whispered conversation with their former owners as to the future.

Chapter II

Boyhood Days

After the coming of freedom there were two points upon which practically all the people on our place were agreed, and I find that this was generally true throughout the South: that they must change their names, and that they must leave the old plantation for at least a few days or weeks in order that they might really feel sure that they were free.

In some way a feeling got among the coloured people that it was far from proper for them to bear the surname of their former owners, and a great many of them took other surnames. This was one of the first signs of freedom. When they were slaves, a coloured person was simply called "John" or "Susan." There was seldom occasion for more than the use of the one name. If "John" or "Susan" belonged to a white man by the name of "Hatcher," sometimes he was called "John Hatcher," or as often "Hatcher's John." But there was a feeling that "John Hatcher" or "Hatcher's John" was not the proper title by which to denote a freeman; and so in many cases "John Hatcher" was changed to "John S. Lincoln" or "John S. Sherman," the initial "S" standing for no name, it being simply a part of what the coloured man proudly called his "entitles."

As I have stated, most of the coloured people left the old plantation for a short while at least, so as to be sure, it seemed, that they could leave and try their freedom on to see how it felt. After they had remained away for a time, many of the older slaves, especially, returned to their old homes and made some kind of contract with their former owners by which they remained on the estate.

My mother's husband, who was the stepfather of my brother John and myself, did not belong to the same owners as did my mother. In fact, he seldom came to our plantation. I remember seeing him there perhaps once a year, that being about Christmas time. In some way, during the war, by running away and following the Federal soldiers, it seems, he found his way into the new state of West Virginia. As soon as freedom was declared, he sent for my mother to come to the Kanawha Valley, in West Virginia. At that time a journey from Virginia over the mountains to West Virginia was rather a tedious and in some cases a painful undertaking. What little clothing and few household goods we had were placed in a cart, but the children walked the greater portion of the distance, which was several hundred miles.

I do not think any of us ever had been very far from the plantation, and the taking of a long journey into another state was quite an event. The parting from our former owners and the members of our own race on the plantation was a serious occasion. From the time of our parting till their death we kept up a correspondence with the older members of the family, and in later years we have kept in touch with those who were the younger members. We were several weeks making the trip, and most of the time we slept in the open air and did our cooking over a log fire out-of-doors. One night I recall that we camped near an abandoned log cabin, and my mother decided to build a fire in that for cooking, and afterward to make a "pallet" on the floor for our sleeping. Just as the fire had gotten well started a large black snake fully a yard and a half long dropped down the chimney and ran out on the floor. Of course we at once abandoned that cabin. Finally we reached our destination—a little town called Malden, which is about five miles from Charleston, the present capital of the state.

At that time salt-mining was the great industry in that part of West Virginia, and the little town of Malden was right in the midst of the salt-furnaces. My stepfather had already secured a job at a salt-furnace, and he had also secured a little cabin for us to live in. Our new house was no better than the one we had left on the old plantation in Virginia. In fact, in one respect it was worse. Notwithstanding the poor condition of our plantation cabin, we were at all times sure of pure air. Our new home was in the midst of a cluster of cabins crowded closely together, and as there were no sanitary regulations, the filth about the cabins was often intolerable. Some of our neighbours were coloured people, and some were the poorest and most ignorant and degraded white people. It was a motley mixture. Drinking, gambling, quarrels, fights, and shock-ingly immoral practices were frequent. All who lived in the little town were in one way or another connected with the salt business. Though I was a mere child, my stepfather put me and my brother at work in one of the furnaces. Often I began work as early as four o'clock in the morning.

The first thing I ever learned in the way of book knowledge was while working in this salt-furnace. Each salt-packer had his barrels marked with a certain number. The number allotted to my stepfather was "18." At the close of the day's work the boss of the packers would come around and put "18" on each of our barrels, and I soon learned to recognize that figure wherever I saw it, and after a while got to the point where I could make that figure, though I knew nothing about any other figures or letters.

From the time that I can remember having any thoughts about anything, I recall that I had an intense longing to learn to read. I determined, when quite a small child, that, if I accomplished nothing else in life, I would in some way get enough education to enable me to read common books and newspapers. Soon after we got settled in some manner in our new cabin in West Virginia, I induced my mother to get hold of a book for me. How or where she got it I do not know, but in some way she procured an old copy of Webster's "blue-back" spelling-book, which contained the alphabet, followed by such meaningless words as "ab," "ba," "ca," "da." I began at once to devour this book, and I think that it was the first one I ever had in my hands. I had learned from somebody that the way to begin to read was to learn the alphabet, so I tried in all the ways I could think of to learn it,—all of course without a teacher, for I could find no one to teach me. At that time there was not a single member of my race anywhere near us who could read, and I was too timid to approach any of the white people. In some way, within a few weeks, I mastered the greater portion of the alphabet. In all my efforts to learn to read my mother shared fully my ambition, and sympathized with me and aided me in every way that she could. Though she was totally ignorant, so far as mere book knowledge was concerned, she had high ambitions for her children, and a large fund of good, hard, common sense which seemed to enable her to meet and master every situation. If I have done anything in life worth attention, I feel sure that I inherited the disposition from my mother.

In the midst of my struggles and longing for an education, a young coloured boy who had learned to read in the state of Ohio came to Malden. As soon as the coloured people found out that he could read, a newspaper was secured, and at the close of nearly every day's work this young man would be surrounded by a group of men and women who were anxious to hear him read the news contained in the papers. How I used to envy this man! He seemed to me to be the one young man in all the world who ought to be satisfied with his attainments.

About this time the question of having some kind of a school opened for the coloured children in the village began to be discussed by members of the race. As it would be the first school for Negro children that had ever been opened in that part of Virginia, it was, of course, to be a great event, and the discussion excited the widest interest. The most perplexing question was where to find a teacher. The young man from Ohio who had learned to read the papers was considered, but his age was against him. In the midst of the discussion about a teacher, another young coloured man from Ohio, who had been a soldier, in some way found his way into town. It was soon learned that he possessed considerable education, and he was engaged by the coloured people to teach their first school. As yet no free schools had been started for coloured people in that section, hence each family agreed to pay a certain amount per month, with the understanding that the teacher was to "board 'round"—that is, spend a day with each family. This was not bad for the teacher, for each family tried to provide the very best on the day the teacher was to be its guest. I recall that I looked forward with an anxious appetite to the "teacher's day" at our little cabin.

This experience of a whole race beginning to go to school for the first time, presents one of the most interesting studies that has ever occurred in connection with the development of any race. Few people who were not right in the midst of the scenes can form any exact idea of the intense desire which the people of my race showed for an education. As I have stated, it was a whole race trying to go to school. Few were too young, and none too old, to make the attempt to learn. As fast as any kind of teachers could be secured, not only were day-schools filled, but night-schools as well. The great ambition of the older people was to try to learn to read the Bible before they died. With this end in view, men and women who were fifty or seventy-five years old would often be found in the night-school. Sunday-schools were formed soon after freedom, but the principal book studied in the Sunday-school was the spelling-book. Day-school, night-school, Sunday-school, were always crowded, and often many had to be turned away for want of room.

The opening of the school in the Kanawha Valley, however, brought to me one of the keenest disappointments that I ever experienced. I had been working in a salt-furnace for several months, and my stepfather had discovered that I had a financial value, and so, when the school opened, he decided that he could not spare me from my work. This decision seemed to cloud my every ambition. The disappointment was made all the more severe by reason of the fact that my place of work was where I could see the happy children passing to and from school, mornings and afternoons. Despite this disappointment, however, I determined that I would learn something, anyway. I applied myself with greater earnestness than ever to the mastering of what was in the "blue-back" speller.

My mother sympathized with me in my disappointment, and sought to comfort me in all the ways she could, and to help me find a way to learn. After a while I succeeded in making arrangements with the teacher to give me some lessons at night, after the day's work was done. These night lessons were so welcome that I think I learned more at night than the other children did during the day. My own experiences in the night-school gave me faith in the night-school idea, with which, in after years, I had to do both at Hampton and Tuskegee. But my boyish heart was still set upon going to the day-school, and I let no opportunity slip to push my case. Finally I won, and was permitted to go to the school in the day for a few months, with the understanding that I was to rise early in the morning and work in the furnace till nine o'clock, and return immediately after school closed in the afternoon for at least two more hours of work.

The schoolhouse was some distance from the furnace, and as I had to work till nine o'clock, and the school opened at nine, I found myself in a difficulty. School would always be begun before I reached it, and sometimes my class had recited. To get around this difficulty I yielded to a temptation for which most people, I suppose, will condemn me; but since it is a fact, I might as well state it. I have great faith in the power and influence of facts. It is seldom that anything is permanently gained by holding back a fact. There was a large clock in a little office in the furnace. This clock, of course, all the hundred or more workmen depended upon to regulate their hours of beginning and ending the day's work. I got the idea that the way for me to reach school on time was to move the clock hands from half-past eight up to the nine o'clock mark. This I found myself doing morning after morning, till the furnace "boss" discovered that something was wrong, and locked the clock in a case. I did not mean to inconvenience anybody. I simply meant to reach that schoolhouse in time.

When, however, I found myself at the school for the first time, I also found myself confronted with two other difficulties. In the first place, I found that all of the other children wore hats or caps on their heads, and I had neither hat nor cap. In fact, I do not remember that up to the time of going to school I had ever worn any kind of covering upon my head, nor do I recall that either I or anybody else had even thought anything about the need of covering for my head. But, of course, when I saw how all the other boys were dressed, I began to feel quite uncomfortable. As usual, I put the case before my mother, and she explained to me that she had no money with which to buy a "store hat," which was a rather new institution at that time among the members of my race and was considered quite the thing for young and old to own, but that she would find a way to help me out of the difficulty. She accordingly got two pieces of "homespun" (jeans) and sewed them together, and I was soon the proud possessor of my first cap.

The lesson that my mother taught me in this has always remained with me, and I have tried as best I could to teach it to others. I have always felt proud, whenever I think of the incident, that my mother had strength of character enough not to be led into the temptation of seeming to be that which she was not—of trying to impress my schoolmates and others with the fact that she was able to buy me a "store hat" when she was not. I have always felt proud that she refused to go into debt for that which she did not have the money to pay for. Since that time I have owned many kinds of caps and hats, but never one of which I have felt so proud as of the cap made of the two pieces of cloth sewed together by my mother. I have noted the fact, but without satisfaction, I need not add, that several of the boys who began their careers with "store hats" and who were my schoolmates and used to join in the sport that was made of me because I had only a "homespun" cap, have ended their careers in the penitentiary, while others are not able now to buy any kind of hat.

My second difficulty was with regard to my name, or rather *a* name. From the time when I could remember anything, I had been called simply "Booker." Before going to school it had never occurred to me that it was needful or appropriate to have an additional name. When I heard the school-roll called, I noticed that all of the children had at least two names, and some of them indulged in what seemed to me the extravagance of having three. I was in deep perplexity, because I knew that the teacher would demand of me at least two names, and I had only one. By the time the occasion came for the enrolling of my name, an idea occurred to me which I thought would make me equal to the situation; and so, when the teacher asked me what my full name was, I calmly told him "Booker Washington," as if I had been called by that name all my life; and by that name I have since been known. Later in my life I found that my mother had given me the name of "Booker Taliaferro" soon after I was born, but in some way that part of my name seemed to disappear and for a long while was forgotten, but as soon as I found out about it I revived it, and made my full name "Booker Taliaferro Washington." I think there are not many men in our country who have had the privilege of naming themselves in the way that I have.

More than once I have tried to picture myself in the position of a boy or man with an honoured and distinguished ancestry which I could trace back through a period of hundreds of years, and who had not only inherited a name, but fortune and a proud family homestead; and yet I have sometimes had the feeling that if I had inherited these, and had been a member of a more popular race, I should have been inclined to yield to the temptation of depending upon my ancestry and my colour to do that for me which I should do for myself. Years ago I resolved that because I had no ancestry myself I would leave a record of which my children would be proud, and which might encourage them to still higher effort.

The world should not pass judgment upon the Negro, and especially the Negro youth, too quickly or too harshly. The Negro boy has obstacles, discouragements, and temptations to battle with that are little known to those not situated as he is. When a white boy undertakes a task, it is taken for granted that he will succeed. On the other hand, people are usually surprised if the Negro boy does not fail. In a word, the Negro youth starts out with the presumption against him.

The influence of ancestry, however, is important in helping forward any individual or race, if too much reliance is not placed upon it. Those who constantly direct attention to the Negro youth's moral weaknesses, and compare his advancement with that of white youths, do not consider the influence of the memories which cling about the old family homesteads. I have no idea, as I have stated elsewhere, who my grandmother was. I have, or have had, uncles and aunts and cousins, but I have no knowledge as to where most of them are. My case will illustrate that of hundreds of thousands of black people in every part of our country. The very fact that the white boy is conscious that, if he fails in life, he will disgrace the whole family record, extending back through many generations, is of tremendous value in helping him to resist temptations. The fact that the individual has behind and surrounding him proud family history and connection serves as a stimulus to help him to overcome obstacles when striving for success.

The time that I was permitted to attend school during the day was short, and my attendance was irregular. It was not long before I had to stop attending day-school altogether, and devote all of my time again to work. I resorted to the night-school again. In fact, the greater part of the education I secured in my boyhood was gathered through the night-school after my day's work was done. I had difficulty often in securing a satisfactory teacher. Sometimes, after I had secured some one to teach me at night, I would find, much to my disappointment, that the teacher knew but little more than I did. Often I would have to walk several miles at night in order to recite my night-school lessons. There was never a time in my youth, no matter how dark and discouraging the days might be, when one resolve did not continually remain with me, and that was a determination to secure an education at any cost.

Soon after we moved to West Virginia, my mother adopted into our family, notwithstanding our poverty, an orphan boy, to whom afterward we gave the name of James B. Washington. He has ever since remained a member of the family.

After I had worked in the salt-furnace for some time, work was secured for me in a coal-mine which was operated mainly for the purpose of securing fuel for the salt-furnace. Work in the coal-mine I always dreaded. One reason for this was that any one who worked in a coal-mine was always unclean, at least while at work, and it was a very hard job to get one's skin clean after the day's work was over. Then it was fully a mile from the opening of the coal-mine to the face of the coal, and all, of course, was in the blackest darkness. I do not believe that one ever experiences anywhere else such darkness as he does in a coal-mine. The mine was divided into a large number of different "rooms" or departments, and, as I never was able to learn the location of all these "rooms," I many times found myself lost in the mine. To add to the horror of being lost, sometimes my light would go out, and then, if I did not happen to have a match, I would wander about in the darkness until by chance I found some one to give me a light. The work was not only hard, but it was dangerous. There was always the danger of being blown to pieces by a premature explosion of powder, or of being crushed by falling slate. Accidents from one or the other of these causes were frequently occurring, and this kept me in constant fear. Many children of the tenderest years were compelled then, as is now true I fear, in most coal-mining districts, to spend a large part of their lives in these coal-mines, with little opportunity to get an education; and, what is worse, I have often noted that, as a rule, young boys who begin life in a coal-mine are often physically and mentally dwarfed. They soon lose ambition to do anything else than to continue as a coal-miner.

In those days, and later as a young man, I used to try to picture in my imagination thc feelings and ambitions of a white boy with absolutely no limit placed upon his aspirations and activities. I used to envy the white boy who had no obstacles placed in the way of his becoming a Congressman, Governor, Bishop, or President by reason of the accident of his birth or race. I used to picture the way that I would act under such circumstances; how I would begin at the bottom and keep rising until I reached the highest round of success.

In later years, I confess that I do not envy the white boy as I once did. I have learned that success is to be measured not so much by the position that one has reached in life as by the obstacles which he has overcome while trying to succeed. Looked at from this standpoint, I almost reach the conclusion that often the Negro boy's birth and connection with an unpopular race is an advantage, so far as real life is concerned. With few exceptions, the Negro youth must work harder and must perform his tasks even better than a white youth in order to secure recognition. But out of the hard and unusual struggle through which he is compelled to pass, he gets a strength, a confidence, that one misses whose pathway is comparatively smooth by reason of birth and race.

From any point of view, I had rather be what I am, a member of the Negro race, than be able to claim membership with the most favoured of any other race. I have always been made sad when I have heard members of any race claiming rights and privileges, or certain badges of distinction, on the ground simply that they were members of this or that race, regardless of their own individual worth or attainments. I have been made to feel sad for such persons because I am conscious of the fact that mere connection with what is known as a superior race will not permanently carry an individual forward unless he has individual worth, and mere connection with what is regarded as an inferior race will not finally hold an individual back if he possesses intrinsic, individual merit. Every persecuted individual and race should get much consolation out of the great human law, which is universal and eternal, that merit, no matter under what skin found, is, in the long run, recognized and rewarded. This I have said here, not to call attention to myself as an individual, but to the race to which I am proud to belong.

Chapter III

The Struggle for an Education

One day, while at work in the coal-mine, I happened to overhear two miners talking about a great school for coloured people somewhere in Virginia. This was the first time that I had ever heard anything about any kind of school or college that was more pretentious than the little coloured school in our town.

In the darkness of the mine I noiselessly crept as close as I could to the two men who were talking. I heard one tell the other that not only was the school established for the members of my race, but that opportunities were provided by which poor but worthy students could work out all or a part of the cost of board, and at the same time be taught some trade or industry.

As they went on describing the school, it seemed to me that it must be the greatest place on earth, and not even Heaven presented more attractions for me at that time than did the Hampton Normal and Agricultural Institute in Virginia, about which these men were talking. I resolved at once to go to that school, although I had no idea where it was, or how many miles away, or how I was going to reach it; I remembered only that I was on fire constantly with one ambition, and that was to go to Hampton. This thought was with me day and night.

After hearing of the Hampton Institute, I continued to work for a few months longer in the coal-mine. While at work there, I heard of a vacant position in the household of General Lewis Ruffner, the owner of the salt-furnace and coal-mine. Mrs. Viola Ruffner, the wife of General Ruffner, was a "Yankee" woman from Vermont. Mrs. Ruffner had a reputation all through the vicinity for being very strict with her servants, and especially with the boys who tried to serve her. Few of them had remained with her more than two or three weeks. They all left with the same excuse: she was too strict. I decided, however, that I would rather try Mrs. Ruffner's house than remain in the coal-mine, and so my mother applied to her for the vacant position. I was hired at a salary of $5 per month.

I had heard so much about Mrs. Ruffner's severity that I was almost afraid to see her, and trembled when I went into her presence. I had not lived with her many weeks, however, before I began to understand her. I soon began to learn that, first of all, she wanted everything kept clean about her, that she wanted things done promptly and systematically, and that at the bottom of everything she wanted absolute honesty and frankness. Nothing must be sloven or slipshod; every door, every fence, must be kept in repair.

I cannot now recall how long I lived with Mrs. Ruffner before going to Hampton, but I think it must have been a year and a half. At any rate, I here repeat what I have said more than once before, that the lessons that I learned in the home of Mrs. Ruffner were as valuable to me as any education I have ever gotten anywhere since. Even to this day I never see bits of paper scattered around a house or in the street that I do not want to pick them up at once. I never see a filthy yard that I do not want to clean it, a paling off of a fence that I do not want to put it on, an unpainted or unwhitewashed house that I do not want to paint or whitewash it, or a button off one's clothes, or a grease-spot on them or on a floor, that I do not want to call attention to it.

From fearing Mrs. Ruffner I soon learned to look upon her as one of my best friends. When she found that she could trust me she did so implicitly. During the one or two winters that I was with her she gave me an opportunity to go to school for an hour in the day during a portion of the winter months, but most of my studying was done at night, sometimes alone, sometimes under some one whom I could hire to teach me. Mrs. Ruffner always encouraged and sympathized with me in all my efforts to get an education. It was while living with her that I began to get together my first library. I secured a dry-goods box, knocked out one side of it, put some shelves in it, and began putting into it every kind of book that I could get my hands upon, and called it my "library."

Notwithstanding my success at Mrs. Ruffner's I did not give up the idea of going to the Hampton Institute. In the fall of 1872 I determined to make an effort to get there, although, as I have stated, I had no definite idea of the direction in which Hampton was, or of what it would cost to go there. I do not think that any one thoroughly sympathized with me in my ambition to go to Hampton unless it was my mother, and she was troubled with a grave fear that I was starting out on a "wild-goose chase." At any rate, I got only a half-hearted consent from her that I might start. The small amount of money that I had earned had been consumed by my stepfather and the remainder of the family, with the exception of a very few dollars, and so I had very little with which to buy clothes and pay my travelling expenses. My brother John helped me all that he could, but of course that was not a great deal, for his work was in the coal-mine, where he did not earn much, and most of what he did earn went in the direction of paying the household expenses.

Perhaps the thing that touched and pleased me most in connection with my starting for Hampton was the interest that many of the older coloured people took in the matter. They had spent the best days of their lives in slavery, and hardly expected to live to see the time when they would see a member of their race leave home to attend a boarding-school. Some of these older people would give me a nickel, others a quarter, or a handkerchief.

Finally the great day came, and I started for Hampton. I had only a small, cheap satchel that contained what few articles of clothing I could get. My mother at the time was rather weak and broken in health. I hardly expected to see her again, and thus our parting was all the more sad. She, however, was very brave through it all. At that time there were no through trains connecting that part of West Virginia with eastern Virginia. Trains ran only a portion of the way, and the remainder of the distance was travelled by stage-coaches.

The distance from Malden to Hampton is about five hundred miles. I had not been away from home many hours before it began to grow painfully evident that I did not have enough money to pay my fare to Hampton. One experience I shall long remember. I had been travelling over the mountains most of the afternoon in an old-fashioned stage-coach, when, late in the evening, the coach stopped for the night at a common, unpainted house called a hotel. All the other passengers except myself were whites. In my ignorance I supposed that the little hotel existed for the purpose of accommodating the passengers who travelled on the stage-coach. The difference that the colour of one's skin would make I had not thought anything about. After all the other passengers had been shown rooms and were getting ready for supper, I shyly presented myself before the man at the desk. It is true I had practically no money in my pocket with which to pay for bed or food, but I had hoped in some way to beg my way into the good graces of the landlord, for at that season in the mountains of Virginia the weather was cold, and I wanted to get indoors for the night. Without asking as to whether I had any money, the man at the desk firmly refused to even consider the matter of providing me with food or lodging. This was my first experience in finding out what the colour of my skin meant. In some way I managed to keep warm by walking about, and so got through the night. My whole soul was so bent upon reaching Hampton that I did not have time to cherish any bitterness toward the hotel-keeper.

By walking, begging rides both in wagons and in the cars, in some way, after a number of days, I reached the city of Richmond, Virginia, about eighty-two miles from Hampton. When I reached there, tired, hungry, and dirty, it was late in the night. I had never been in a large city, and this rather added to my misery. When I reached Richmond, I was completely out of money. I had not a single acquaintance in the place, and, being unused to city ways, I did not know where to go. I applied at several places for lodging, but they all wanted money, and that was what I did not have. Knowing nothing else better to do, I walked the streets. In doing this I passed by many foodstands where fried chicken and half-moon apple pies were piled high and made to present a most tempting appearance. At that time it seemed to me that I would have promised all that I expected to possess in the future to have gotten hold of one of those chicken legs or one of those pies. But I could not get either of these, nor anything else to eat.

I must have walked the streets till after midnight. At last I became so exhausted that I could walk no longer. I was tired, I was hungry, I was everything but discouraged. Just about the time when I reached extreme physical exhaustion, I came upon a portion of a street where the board sidewalk was considerably elevated. I waited for a few minutes, till I was sure that no passers-by could see me, and then crept under the sidewalk and lay for the night upon the ground, with my satchel of clothing for a pillow. Nearly all night I could hear the tramp of feet over my head. The next morning I found myself somewhat refreshed, but I was extremely hungry, because it had been a long time since I had had sufficient food. As soon as it became light enough for me to see my surroundings I noticed that I was near a large ship, and that this ship seemed to be unloading a cargo of pig iron. I went at once to the vessel and asked the captain to permit me to help unload the vessel in order to get money for food. The captain, a white man, who seemed to be kind-hearted, consented. I worked long enough to earn money for my breakfast, and it seems to me, as I remember it now, to have been about the best breakfast that I have ever eaten.

My work pleased the captain so well that he told me if I desired I could continue working for a small amount per day. This I was very glad to do. I continued working on this vessel for a number of days. After buying food with the small wages I received there was not much left to add to the amount I must get to pay my way to Hampton. In order to economize in every way possible, so as to be sure to reach Hampton in a reasonable time, I continued to sleep under the same sidewalk that gave me shelter the first night I was in Richmond. Many years after that the coloured citizens of Richmond very kindly tendered me a reception at which there must have been two thousand people present. This reception was held not far from the spot where I slept the first night I spent in that city, and I must confess that my mind was more upon the sidewalk that first gave me shelter than upon the reception, agreeable and cordial as it was.

When I had saved what I considered enough money with which to reach Hampton, I thanked the captain of the vessel for his kindness, and started again. Without any unusual occurrence I reached Hampton, with a surplus of exactly fifty cents with which to begin my education. To me it had been a long, eventful journey; but the first sight of the large, three-story, brick school building seemed to have rewarded me for all that I had undergone in order to reach the place. If the people who gave the money to provide that building could appreciate the influence the sight of it had upon me, as well as upon thousands of other youths, they would feel all the more encouraged to make such gifts. It seemed to me to be the largest and most beautiful building I had ever seen. The sight of it seemed to give me new life. I felt that a new kind of existence had now begun—that life would now have a new meaning. I felt that I had reached the promised land, and I resolved to let no obstacle prevent me from putting forth the highest effort to fit myself to accomplish the most good in the world.

As soon as possible after reaching the grounds of the Hampton Institute, I presented myself before the head teacher for assignment to a class. Having been so long without proper food, a bath, and change of clothing, I did not, of course, make a very favourable impression upon her, and I could see at once that there were doubts in her mind about the wisdom of admitting me as a student. I felt that I could hardly blame her if she got the idea that I was a worthless loafer or tramp. For some time she did not refuse to admit me, neither did she decide in my favour, and I continued to linger about her, and to impress her in all the ways I could with my worthiness. In the meantime I saw her admitting other students, and that added greatly to my discomfort, for I felt, deep down in my heart, that I could do as well as they, if I could only get a chance to show what was in me.

After some hours had passed, the head teacher said to me: "The adjoining recitation-room needs sweeping. Take the broom and sweep it."

It occurred to me at once that here was my chance. Never did I receive an order with more delight. I knew that I could sweep, for Mrs. Ruffner had thoroughly taught me how to do that when I lived with her.

I swept the recitation-room three times. Then I got a dusting-cloth and I dusted it four times. All the woodwork around the walls, every bench, table, and desk, I went over four times with my dusting-cloth. Besides, every piece of furniture had been moved and every closet and corner in the room had been thoroughly cleaned. I had the feeling that in a large measure my future depended upon the impression I made upon the teacher in the cleaning of that room. When I was through, I reported to the head teacher. She was a "Yankee" woman who knew just where to look for dirt. She went into the room and inspected the floor and closets; then she took her handkerchief and rubbed it on the woodwork about the walls, and over the table and benches. When she was unable to find one bit of dirt on the floor, or a particle of dust on any of the furniture, she quietly remarked, "I guess you will do to enter this institution."

I was one of the happiest souls on earth. The sweeping of that room was my college examination, and never did any youth pass an examination for entrance into Harvard or Yale that gave him more genuine satisfaction. I have passed several examinations since then, but I have always felt that this was the best one I ever passed.

I have spoken of my own experience in entering the Hampton Institute. Perhaps few, if any, had anything like the same experience that I had, but about that same period there were hundreds who found their way to Hampton and other institutions after experiencing something of the same difficulties that I went through. The young men and women were determined to secure an education at any cost.

The sweeping of the recitation-room in the manner that I did it seems to have paved the way for me to get through Hampton. Miss Mary F. Mackie, the head teacher, offered me a position as janitor. This, of course, I gladly accepted, because it was a place where I could work out nearly all the cost of my board. The work was hard and taxing, but I stuck to it. I had a large number of rooms to care for, and had to work late into the night, while at the same time I had to rise by four o'clock in the morning, in order to build the fires and have a little time in which to prepare my lessons. In all my career at Hampton, and ever since I have been out in the world, Miss Mary F. Mackie, the head teacher to whom I have referred, proved one of my strongest and most helpful friends. Her advice and encouragement were always helpful and strengthening to me in the darkest hour.

I have spoken of the impression that was made upon me by the buildings and general appearance of the Hampton Institute, but I have not spoken of that which made the greatest and most lasting impression upon me, and that was a great man—the noblest, rarest human being that it has ever been my privilege to meet. I refer to the late General Samuel C. Armstrong.[1]

It has been my fortune to meet personally many of what are called great characters, both in Europe and America, but I do not hesitate to say that I never met any man who, in my estimation, was the equal of General Armstrong. Fresh from the degrading influences of the slave plantation and the coal-mines, it was a rare privilege for me to be permitted to come into direct contact with such a character as General Armstrong. I shall always remember that the first time I went into his presence he made the impression upon me of being a perfect man; I was made to feel that there was something about him that was superhuman. It was my privilege to know the General personally from the time I

1. Samuel Chapman Armstrong (1839–1893), former officer in the Union Army and founder, in 1868, of Hampton Institute, the industrial school on which Washington's Tuskegee Institute was modeled.

entered Hampton till he died, and the more I saw of him the greater he grew in my estimation. One might have removed from Hampton all the buildings, class-rooms, teachers, and industries, and given the men and women there the opportunity of coming into daily contact with General Armstrong, and that alone would have been a liberal education. The older I grow, the more I am convinced that there is no education which one can get from books and costly apparatus that is equal to that which can be gotten from contact with great men and women. Instead of studying books so constantly, how I wish that our schools and colleges might learn to study men and things!

General Armstrong spent two of the last six months of his life in my home at Tuskegee. At that time he was paralyzed to the extent that he had lost control of his body and voice in a very large degree. Notwithstanding his affliction, he worked almost constantly night and day for the cause to which he had given his life. I never saw a man who so completely lost sight of himself. I do not believe he ever had a selfish thought. He was just as happy in trying to assist some other institution in the South as he was when working for Hampton. Although he fought the Southern white man in the Civil War, I never heard him utter a bitter word against him afterward. On the other hand, he was constantly seeking to find ways by which he could be of service to the Southern whites.

It would be difficult to describe the hold that he had upon the students at Hampton, or the faith they had in him. In fact, he was worshipped by his students. It never occurred to me that General Armstrong could fail in anything that he undertook. There is almost no request that he could have made that would not have been complied with. When he was a guest at my home in Alabama, and was so badly paralyzed that he had to be wheeled about in an invalid's chair, I recall that one of the General's former students had occasion to push his chair up a long, steep hill that taxed his strength to the utmost. When the top of the hill was reached, the former pupil, with a glow of happiness on his face, exclaimed, "I am so glad that I have been permitted to do something that was real hard for the General before he dies!" While I was a student at Hampton, the dormitories became so crowded that it was impossible to find room for all who wanted to be admitted. In order to help remedy the difficulty, the General conceived the plan of putting up tents to be used as rooms. As soon as it became known that General Armstrong would be pleased if some of the older students would live in the tents during the winter, nearly every student in school volunteered to go.

I was one of the volunteers. The winter that we spent in those tents was an intensely cold one, and we suffered severely—how much I am sure General Armstrong never knew, because we made no complaints. It was enough for us to know that we were pleasing General Armstrong, and that we were making it possible for an additional number of students to secure an education. More than once, during a cold night, when a stiff gale would be blowing, our tent was lifted bodily, and we would find ourselves in the open air. The General would usually pay a visit to the tents early in the morning, and his earnest, cheerful, encouraging voice would dispel any feeling of despondency.

I have spoken of my admiration for General Armstrong, and yet he was but a type of that Christlike body of men and women who went into the Negro schools at the close of the war by the hundreds to assist in lifting up my race. The history of the world fails to show a higher, purer, and more unselfish class of men and women than those who found their way into those Negro schools.

Life at Hampton was a constant revelation to me; was constantly taking me into a new world. The matter of having meals at regular hours, of eating on a tablecloth, using a napkin, the use of the bathtub and of the tooth-brush, as well as the use of sheets upon the bed, were all new to me.

I sometimes feel that almost the most valuable lesson I got at the Hampton Institute was in the use and value of the bath. I learned there for the first time some of its value, not only in keeping the body healthy, but in inspiring self-respect and promoting virtue. In all my travels in the South and elsewhere since leaving Hampton I have always in some way sought my daily bath. To get it sometimes when I have been the guest of my own people in a single-roomed cabin has not always been easy to do, except by slipping away to some stream in the woods. I have always tried to teach my people that some provision for bathing should be a part of every house.

For some time, while a student at Hampton, I possessed but a single pair of socks, but when I had worn these till they became soiled, I would wash them at night and hang them by the fire to dry, so that I might wear them again the next morning.

The charge for my board at Hampton was ten dollars per month. I was expected to pay a part of this in cash and to work out the remainder. To meet this cash payment, as I have stated, I had just fifty cents when I reached the institution. Aside from a very few dollars that my brother John was able to send me once in a while, I had no money with which to pay my board. I was determined from the first to make my work as janitor so valuable that my services would be indispensable. This I succeeded in doing to such an extent that I was soon informed that I would be allowed the full cost of my board in return for my work. The cost of tuition was seventy dollars a year. This, of course, was wholly beyond my ability to provide. If I had been compelled to pay the seventy dollars for tuition, in addition to providing for my board, I would have been compelled to leave the Hampton school. General Armstrong, however, very kindly got Mr. S. Griffitts Morgan, of New Bedford, Mass., to defray the cost of my tuition during the whole time that I was at Hampton. After I finished the course at Hampton and had entered upon my lifework at Tuskegee, I had the pleasure of visiting Mr. Morgan several times.

After having been for a while at Hampton, I found myself in difficulty because I did not have books and clothing. Usually, however, I got around the trouble about books by borrowing from those who were more fortunate than myself. As to clothes, when I reached Hampton I had practically nothing. Everything that I possessed was in a small hand satchel. My anxiety about clothing was increased because of the fact that General Armstrong made a personal inspection of the young men in ranks, to see that their clothes were clean. Shoes had to be polished, there must be no buttons off the clothing, and no grease-spots. To wear one suit of clothes continually, while at work and in the schoolroom, and at the same time keep it clean, was rather a hard problem for me to solve. In some way I managed to get on till the teachers learned that I was in earnest and meant to succeed, and then some of them were kind enough to see that I was partly supplied with second-hand clothing that had been sent in barrels from the North. These barrels proved a blessing to hundreds of poor but deserving students. Without them I question whether I should ever have gotten through Hampton.

When I first went to Hampton I do not recall that I had ever slept in a bed that had two sheets on it. In those days there were not many buildings there, and room was very precious. There were seven other boys in the same room with me; most of them, however, students who had been there for some time. The sheets were quite a puzzle to me. The first night I slept under both of them, and the second night I slept on top of both of them; but by watching the other boys I learned my lesson in this, and have been trying to follow it ever since and to teach it to others.

I was among the youngest of the students who were in Hampton at that time. Most of the students were men and women—some as old as forty years of age. As I now recall the scene of my first year, I do not believe that one often has the opportunity of coming into contact with three or four hundred men and women who were so tremendously in earnest as these men and women were. Every hour was occupied in study or work. Nearly all had had enough actual contact with the world to teach them the need of education. Many of the older ones were, of course, too old to master the text-books very thoroughly, and it was often sad to watch their struggles; but they made up in earnestness much of what they lacked in books. Many of them were as poor as I was, and, besides having to wrestle with their books, they had to struggle with a poverty which prevented their having the necessities of life. Many of them had aged parents who were dependent upon them, and some of them were men who had wives whose support in some way they had to provide for.

The great and prevailing idea that seemed to take possession of every one was to prepare himself to lift up the people at his home. No one seemed to think of himself. And the officers and teachers, what a rare set of human beings they were! They worked for the students night and day, in season and out of season. They seemed happy only when they were helping the students in some manner. Whenever it is written—and I hope it will be—the part that the Yankee teachers played in the education of the Negroes immediately after the war will make one of the most thrilling parts of the history of this country. The time is not far distant when the whole South will appreciate this service in a way that it has not yet been able to do.

Chapter IV

Helping Others

At the end of my first year at Hampton I was confronted with another difficulty. Most of the students went home to spend their vacation. I had no money with which to go home, but I had to go somewhere. In those days very few students were permitted to remain at the school during vacation. It made me feel very sad and homesick to see the other students preparing to leave and starting for home. I not only had no money with which to go home, but I had none with which to go anywhere.

In some way, however, I had gotten hold of an extra, second-hand coat which I thought was a pretty valuable coat. This I decided to sell, in order to get a little money for travelling expenses. I had a good deal of boyish pride, and I tried to hide, as far as I could, from the other students the fact that I had no money and nowhere to go. I made it known to a few people in the town of Hampton that I had this coat to sell, and, after a good deal of persuading, one coloured man promised to come to my room to look the coat over and consider the matter of buying it. This cheered my drooping spirits considerably. Early the next morning my prospective customer appeared. After looking the garment over carefully, he asked me how much I wanted for it. I told him I thought it was worth three dollars. He seemed to agree with me as to price, but remarked in the most matter-of-fact way: "I tell you what I will do; I will take the coat, and I will pay you five cents, cash down, and pay you the rest of the money just as soon as I can get it." It is not hard to imagine what my feelings were at the time.

With this disappointment I gave up all hope of getting out of the town of Hampton for my vacation work. I wanted very much to go where I might secure work that would at least pay me enough to purchase some much-needed clothing and other necessities. In a few days practically all the students and teachers had left for their homes, and this served to depress my spirits even more.

After trying for several days in and near the town of Hampton, I finally secured work in a restaurant at Fortress Monroe. The wages, however, were very little more than my board. At night, and between meals, I found considerable time for study and reading; and in this direction I improved myself very much during the summer.

When I left school at the end of my first year, I owed the institution sixteen dollars that I had not been able to work out. It was my greatest ambition during the summer to save money enough with which to pay this debt. I felt that this was a debt of honour, and that I could hardly bring myself to the point of even trying to enter school again till it was paid. I economized in every way that I could think of—did my own washing, and went without necessary garments—but still I found my summer vacation ending and I did not have the sixteen dollars.

One day, during the last week of my stay in the restaurant, I found under one of the tables a crisp, new ten-dollar bill. I could hardly contain myself, I was so happy. As it was not my place of business I felt it to be the proper thing to show the money to the proprietor. This I did. He seemed as glad as I was, but he coolly explained to me that, as it was his place of business, he had a right to keep the money, and he proceeded to do so. This, I confess, was another pretty hard blow to me. I will not say that I became discouraged, for as I now look back over my life I do not recall that I ever became discouraged over anything that I set out to accomplish. I have begun everything with the idea that I could succeed, and I never had much patience with the multitudes of people who are always ready to explain why one cannot succeed. I have always had a high regard for the man who could tell me how to succeed. I determined to face the situation just as it was. At the end of the week I went to the treasurer of the Hampton Institute, General J. F. B. Marshall, and told him frankly my condition. To my gratification he told me that I could reënter the institution, and that he would trust me to pay the debt when I could. During the second year I continued to work as a janitor.

The education that I received at Hampton out of the text-books was but a small part of what I learned there. One of the things that impressed itself upon me deeply, the second year, was the unselfishness of the teachers. It was hard for me to understand how any individuals could bring themselves to the point where they could be so happy in working for others. Before the end of the year, I think I began learning that those who are happiest are those who do the most for others. This lesson I have tried to carry with me ever since.

I also learned a valuable lesson at Hampton by coming into contact with the best breeds of live stock and fowls. No student, I think, who has had the opportunity of doing this could go out into the world and content himself with the poorest grades.

Perhaps the most valuable thing that I got out of my second year was an understanding of the use and value of the Bible. Miss Nathalie Lord, one of the teachers, from Portland, Me., taught me how to use and love the Bible. Before this I had never cared a great deal about it, but now I learned to love to read the Bible, not only for the spiritual help which it gives, but on account of it as literature. The lessons taught me in this respect took such a hold upon me that at the present time, when I am at home, no matter how busy I am, I always make it a rule to read a chapter or a portion of a chapter in the morning, before beginning the work of the day.

Whatever ability I may have as a public speaker I owe in a measure to Miss Lord. When she found out that I had some inclination in this direction, she gave me private lessons in the matter of breathing, emphasis, and articulation. Simply to be able to talk in public for the sake of talking has never had the least attraction for me. In fact, I consider that there is nothing so empty and unsatisfactory as mere abstract public speaking; but from my early childhood I have had a desire to do something to make the world better, and then to be able to speak to the world about that thing.

The debating societies at Hampton were a constant source of delight to me. These were held on Saturday evening; and during my whole life at Hampton I do not recall that I missed a single meeting. I not only attended the weekly debating society, but was instrumental in organizing an additional society. I noticed that between the time when supper was over and the time to begin evening study there were about twenty minutes which the young men usually spent in idle gossip. About twenty of us formed a society for the purpose of utilizing this time in debate or in practice in public speaking. Few persons ever derived more happiness or benefit from the use of twenty minutes of time than we did in this way.

At the end of my second year at Hampton, by the help of some money sent me by my mother and brother John, supplemented by a small gift from one of the teachers at Hampton, I was enabled to return to my home in Malden, West Virginia, to spend my vacation. When I reached home I found that the salt-furnaces were not running, and that the coal-mine was not being operated on account of the miners being out on a "strike." This was something which, it seemed, usually occurred whenever the men got two or three months ahead in their savings. During the strike, of course, they spent all that they had saved, and would often return to work in debt at the same wages, or would move to another mine at considerable expense. In either case, my observations convinced me that the miners were worse off at the end of a strike. Before the days of strikes in that section of the country, I knew miners who had considerable money in the bank, but as soon as the professional labour agitators got control, the savings of even the more thrifty ones began disappearing.

My mother and the other members of the family were, of course, much rejoiced to see me and to note the improvement that I had made during my two years' absence. The rejoicing on the part of all classes of the coloured people, and especially the older ones, over my return, was almost pathetic. I had to pay a visit to each family and take a meal with each, and at each place tell the story of my experiences at Hampton. In addition to this I had to speak before the church and Sunday-school, and at various other places. The thing that I was most in search of, though, work, I could not find. There was no work on account of the strike. I spent nearly the whole of the first month of my vacation in an effort to find something to do by which I could earn money to pay my way back to Hampton and save a little money to use after reaching there.

Toward the end of the first month, I went to a place a considerable distance from my home, to try to find employment. I did not succeed, and it was night before I got started on my return. When I had gotten within a mile or so of my home I was so completely tired out that I could not walk any farther, and I went into an old, abandoned house to spend the remainder of the night. About three o'clock in the morning my brother John found me asleep in this house, and broke to me, as gently as he could, the sad news that our dear mother had died during the night.

This seemed to me the saddest and blankest moment in my life. For several years my mother had not been in good health, but I had no idea, when I parted from her the previous day, that I should never see her alive again. Besides that, I had always had an intense desire to be with her when she did pass away. One of the chief ambitions which spurred me on at Hampton was that I might be able to get to be in a position in which I could better make my mother comfortable and happy. She had so often expressed the wish that she might be permitted to live to see her children educated and started out into the world.

In a very short time after the death of my mother our little home was in confusion. My sister Amanda, although she tried to do the best she could, was too young to know anything about keeping house, and my stepfather was not able to hire a housekeeper. Sometimes we had food cooked for us, and sometimes we did not. I remember that more than once a can of tomatoes and some crackers constituted a meal. Our clothing went uncared for, and everything about our home was soon in a tumble-down condition. It seems to me that this was the most dismal period of my life.

My good friend Mrs. Ruffner, to whom I have already referred, always made me welcome at her home, and assisted me in many ways during this trying period. Before the end of the vacation she gave me some work, and this, together with work in a coal-mine at some distance from my home, enabled me to earn a little money.

At one time it looked as if I would have to give up the idea of returning to Hampton, but my heart was so set on returning that I determined not to give up going back without a struggle. I was very anxious to secure some clothes for the winter, but in this I was disappointed, except for a few garments which my brother John secured for me. Notwithstanding my need of money and clothing, I was very happy in the fact that I had secured enough money to pay my travelling expenses back to Hampton. Once there, I knew that I could make myself so useful as a janitor that I could in some way get through the school year.

Three weeks before the time for the opening of the term at Hampton, I was pleasantly surprised to receive a letter from my good friend Miss Mary F. Mackie, the lady principal, asking me to return to Hampton two weeks before the opening of the school, in order that I might assist her in cleaning the buildings and getting things in order for the new school year. This was just the opportunity I wanted. It gave me a chance to secure a credit in the treasurer's office. I started for Hampton at once.

During these two weeks I was taught a lesson which I shall never forget. Miss Mackie was a member of one of the oldest and most cultured families of the North, and yet for two weeks she worked by my side cleaning windows, dusting rooms, putting beds in order, and what not. She felt that things would not be in condition for the opening of school unless every window-pane was perfectly clean, and she took the greatest satisfaction in helping to clean them herself. The work which I have described she did every year that I was at Hampton.

It was hard for me at this time to understand how a woman of her education and social standing could take such delight in performing such service, in order to assist in the elevation of an unfortunate race. Ever since then I have had no patience with any school for my race in the South which did not teach its students the dignity of labour.

During my last year at Hampton every minute of my time that was not occupied with my duties as janitor was devoted to hard study. I was determined, if possible, to make such a record in my class as would cause me to be placed on the "honour roll" of Commencement speakers. This I was successful in doing. It was June of 1875 when I finished the regular course of study at Hampton. The greatest benefits that I got out of my life at the Hampton Institute, perhaps, may be classified under two heads:—

First was contact with a great man, General S. C. Armstrong, who, I repeat, was, in my opinion, the rarest, strongest, and most beautiful character that it has ever been my privilege to meet.

Second, at Hampton, for the first time, I learned what education was expected to do for an individual. Before going there I had a good deal of the then rather prevalent idea among our people that to secure an education meant to have a good, easy time, free from all necessity for manual labour. At Hampton I not only learned that it was not a disgrace to labour, but learned to love labour, not alone for its financial value, but for labour's own sake and for the independence and self-reliance which the ability to do something which the world wants done brings. At that institution I got my first taste of what it meant to live a life of unselfishness, my first knowledge of the fact that the happiest individuals are those who do the most to make others useful and happy.

I was completely out of money when I graduated. In company with other Hampton students, I secured a place as a table waiter in a summer hotel in Connecticut, and managed to borrow enough money with which to get there. I had not been in this hotel long before I found out that I knew practically nothing about waiting on a hotel table. The head waiter, however, supposed that I was an accomplished waiter. He soon gave me charge of a table at which there sat four or five wealthy and rather aristocratic people. My ignorance of how to wait upon them was so apparent that they scolded me in such a severe manner that I became frightened and left their table, leaving them sitting there without food. As a result of this I was reduced from the position of waiter to that of a dish-carrier.

But I determined to learn the business of waiting, and did so within a few weeks and was restored to my former position. I have had the satisfaction of being a guest in this hotel several times since I was a waiter there.

At the close of the hotel season I returned to my former home in Malden, and was elected to teach the coloured school at that place. This was the beginning of one of the happiest periods of my life. I now felt that I had the opportunity to help the people of my home town to a higher life. I felt from the first that mere book education was not all that the young people of that town needed. I began my work at eight o'clock in the morning, and, as a rule, it did not end until ten o'clock at night. In addition to the usual routine of teaching, I taught the pupils to comb their hair, and to keep their hands and faces clean, as well as their clothing. I gave special attention to teaching them the proper use of the tooth-brush and the bath. In all my teaching I have watched carefully the influence of the tooth-brush, and I am convinced that there are few single agencies of civilization that are more far-reaching.

There were so many of the older boys and girls in the town, as well as men and women, who had to work in the daytime but still were craving an opportunity for some education, that I soon opened a night-school. From the first, this was crowded every night, being about as large as the school that I taught in the day. The efforts of some of the men and women, who in many cases were over fifty years of age, to learn, were in some cases very pathetic.

My day and night school work was not all that I undertook. I established a small reading-room and a debating society. On Sundays I taught two Sunday-schools, one in the town of Malden in the afternoon, and the other in the morning at a place three miles distant from Malden. In addition to this, I gave private lessons to several young men whom I was fitting to send to the Hampton Institute. Without regard to pay and with little thought of it, I taught any one who wanted to learn anything that I could teach him. I was supremely happy in the opportunity of being able to assist somebody else. I did receive, however, a small salary from the public fund, for my work as a public-school teacher.

During the time that I was a student at Hampton my older brother, John, not only assisted me all that he could, but worked all of the time in the coal-mines in order to support the family. He willingly neglected his own education that he might help me. It was my earnest wish to help him to prepare to enter Hampton, and to save money to assist him in his expenses there. Both of these objects I was successful in accomplishing. In three years my brother finished the course at Hampton, and he is now holding the important position of Superintendent of Industries at Tuskegee. When he returned from Hampton, we both combined our efforts and savings to send our adopted brother, James, through the Hampton Institute. This we succeeded in doing, and he is now the postmaster at the Tuskegee Institute. The year 1877, which was my second year of teaching in Malden, I spent very much as I did the first.

It was while my home was at Malden that what was known as the "Ku Klux Klan" was in the height of its activity. The "Ku Klux" were bands of men who had joined themselves together for the purpose of regulating the conduct of the coloured people, especially with the object of preventing the members of the race from exercising any influence in politics. They corresponded somewhat to the "patrollers" of whom I used to hear a great deal during the days of slavery, when I was a small boy. The "patrollers" were bands of white men—usually young men—who were organized largely for the purpose of regulating the conduct of the slaves at night in such matters as preventing the slaves from going from one plantation to another without passes, and for preventing them from holding any kind of meetings without permission and without the presence at these meetings of at least one white man.

Like the "patrollers" the "Ku Klux" operated almost wholly at night. They were, however, more cruel that the "patrollers." Their objects, in the main, were to crush out the political aspirations of the Negroes, but they did not confine themselves to this, because schoolhouses as well as churches were burned by them, and many innocent persons were made to suffer. During this period not a few coloured people lost their lives.

As a young man, the acts of these lawless bands made a great impression upon me. I saw one open battle take place at Malden between some of the coloured and white people. There must have been not far from a hundred persons engaged on each side; many on both sides were seriously injured, among them being General Lewis Ruffner, the husband of my friend Mrs. Viola Ruffner. General Ruffner tried to defend the coloured people, and for this he was knocked down and so seriously wounded that he never completely recovered. It seemed to me as I watched this struggle between members of the two races, that there was no hope for our people in this country. The "Ku Klux" period was, I think, the darkest part of the Reconstruction days.

I have referred to this unpleasant part of the history of the South simply for the purpose of calling attention to the great change that has taken place since the days of the "Ku Klux." To-day there are no such organizations in the South, and the fact that such ever existed is almost forgotten by both races. There are few places in the South now where public sentiment would permit such organizations to exist.

Chapter V

The Reconstruction Period

The years from 1867 to 1878 I think may be called the period of Reconstruction. This included the time that I spent as a student at Hampton and as a teacher in West Virginia. During the whole of the Reconstruction period two ideas were constantly agitating the minds of the coloured people, or, at least, the minds of a large part of the race. One of these was the craze for Greek and Latin learning, and the other was a desire to hold office.

It could not have been expected that a people who had spent generations in slavery, and before that generations in the darkest heathenism, could at first form any proper conception of what an education meant. In every part of the South, during the Reconstruction period, schools, both day and night, were filled to overflowing with people of all ages and conditions, some being as far along in age as sixty and seventy years. The ambition to secure an education was most praiseworthy and encouraging. The idea, however, was too prevalent that, as soon as one secured a little education, in some unexplainable way he would be free from most of the hardships of the world, and, at any rate, could live without manual labour. There was a further feeling that a knowledge, however little, of the Greek and Latin languages would make one a very superior human being, something bordering almost on the supernatural. I remember that the first coloured man whom I saw who knew something about foreign languages impressed me at that time as being a man of all others to be envied.

Naturally, most of our people who received some little education became teachers or preachers. While among these two classes there were many capable, earnest, godly men and women, still a large proportion took up teaching or preaching as an easy way to make a living. Many became teachers who could do little more than write their names. I remember there came into our neighbourhood one of this class, who was in search of a school to teach, and the question arose while he was there as to the shape of the earth and how he would teach the children concerning this subject. He explained his position in the matter by saying that he was prepared to teach that the earth was either flat or round, according to the preference of a majority of his patrons.

The ministry was the profession that suffered most—and still suffers, though there has been great improvement—on account of not only ignorant but in many cases immoral men who claimed that they were "called to preach." In the earlier days of freedom almost every coloured man who learned to read would receive "a call to preach" within a few days after he began reading. At my home in West Virginia the process of being called to the ministry was a very interesting one. Usually the "call" came when the individual was sitting in church. Without warning the one called would fall upon the floor as if struck by a bullet, and would lie there for hours, speechless and motionless. Then the news would spread all through the neighbourhood that this individual had received a "call." If he were inclined to resist the summons, he would fall or be made to fall a second or third time. In the end he always yielded to the call. While I wanted an education badly, I confess that in my youth I had a fear that when I had learned to read and write well I would receive one of these "calls"; but, for some reason, my call never came.

When we add the number of wholly ignorant men who preached or "exhorted" to that of those who possessed something of an education, it can be seen at a glance that the supply of ministers was large. In fact, some time ago I knew a certain church that had a total membership of about two hundred, and eighteen of that number were ministers. But, I repeat, in many communities in the South the character of the ministry is being improved, and I believe that within the next two or three decades a very large proportion of the unworthy ones will have disappeared. The "calls" to preach, I am glad to say, are not nearly so numerous now as they were formerly, and the calls to some industrial occupation are growing more numerous. The improvement that has taken place in the character of the teachers is even more marked than in the case of the ministers.

During the whole of the Reconstruction period our people throughout the South looked to the Federal Government for everything, very much as a child looks to its mother. This was not unnatural. The central government gave them freedom, and the whole Nation had been enriched for more than two centuries by the labour of the Negro. Even as a youth, and later in manhood, I had the feeling that it was cruelly wrong in the central government, at the beginning of our freedom, to fail to make some provision for the general education of our people in addition to what the states might do, so that the people would be the better prepared for the duties of citizenship.

It is easy to find fault, to remark what might have been done, and perhaps, after all, and under all the circumstances, those in charge of the conduct of affairs did the only thing that could be done at the time. Still, as I look back now over the entire period of our freedom, I cannot help feeling that it would have been wiser if some plan could have been put in operation which would have made the possession of a certain amount of education or property, or both, a test for the exercise of the franchise, and a way provided by which this test should be made to apply honestly and squarely to both the white and black races.

Though I was but little more than a youth during the period of Reconstruction, I had the feeling that mistakes were being made, and that things could not remain in the condition that they were in then very long. I felt that the Reconstruction policy, so far as it related to my race, was in a large measure on a false foundation, was artificial and forced. In many cases it seemed to me that the ignorance of my race was being used as a tool with which to help white men into office, and that there was an element in the North which wanted to punish the Southern white men by forcing the Negro into positions over the heads of the Southern whites. I felt that the Negro would be the one to suffer for this in the end. Besides, the general political agitation drew the attention of our people away from the more fundamental matters of perfecting themselves in the industries at their doors and in securing property.

The temptations to enter political life were so alluring that I came very near yielding to them at one time, but I was kept from doing so by the feeling that I would be helping in a more substantial way by assisting in the laying of the foundation of the race through a generous education of the hand, head, and heart. I saw coloured men who were members of the state legislatures, and county officers, who, in some cases, could not read or write, and whose morals were as weak as their education. Not long ago, when passing through the streets of a certain city in the South, I heard some brick-masons calling out, from the top of a two-story brick building on which they were working, for the "Governor" to "hurry up and bring up some more bricks." Several times I heard the command, "Hurry up, Governor!" "Hurry up, Governor!" My curiosity was aroused to such an extent that I made inquiry as to who the "Governor" was, and soon found that he was a coloured man who at one time had held the position of Lieutenant-Governor of his state.

But not all the coloured people who were in office during Reconstruction were unworthy of their positions, by any means. Some of them, like the late Senator B. K. Bruce, Governor Pinchback,[1] and many others, were strong, upright, useful men. Neither were all the class designated as carpetbaggers dishonourable men. Some of them, like ex-Governor Bullock,[2] of Georgia, were men of high character and usefulness.

Of course the coloured people, so largely without education, and wholly without experience in government, made tremendous mistakes, just as any people similarly situated would have done. Many of the Southern whites have a feeling that, if the Negro is permitted to exercise his political rights now to any degree, the mistakes of the Reconstruction period will repeat themselves. I do not think this would be true, because the Negro is a much stronger and wiser man than he was thirty-five years ago, and he is fast learning the lesson that he cannot afford to act in a manner that will alienate his Southern white neighbours from him. More and more I am convinced that the final solution of the political end of our race problem will be for each state that finds it necessary to change the law bearing upon the franchise to make the law apply with absolute honesty, and without opportunity for double dealing or evasion, to both races alike. Any other course my daily observation in the South convinces me, will be unjust to the Negro, unjust to the white man, and unfair to the rest of the states in the Union, and will be, like slavery, a sin that at some time we shall have to pay for.

In the fall of 1878, after having taught school in Malden for two years, and after I had succeeded in preparing several of the young men and women, besides my two brothers, to enter the Hampton Institute, I decided to spend some months in study at Washington, D.C.[3] I remained there for eight months. I derived a great deal of benefit from the studies which I pursued, and I came into contact with some strong men and women. At the institution I attended there was no industrial training given to the students, and I had an opportunity of comparing the influence of an institution with no industrial training with that of one like the Hampton Institute, that emphasized the industries. At this school I found the students, in most cases, had more money, were better dressed, wore the latest style of all manner of clothing, and in some cases were more brilliant mentally. At Hampton it was a standing rule that, while the institution would be responsible for securing some one to pay the tuition for the students, the men and women themselves must provide for their own board, books, clothing, and room wholly by work, or partly by work and partly in cash. At the institution at which I now was, I found that a large proportion of the students by some means

1. Blanche Kelso Bruce (1841–1898), United States senator from Mississippi from 1875 to 1881; Pinkney Benton Stewart Pinchback (1837–1921), lieutenant-governor of Louisiana from 1871 to 1873.
2. Rufus B. Bullock (1834–1907), governor of Georgia from 1868 to 1871.
3. Washington studied at Wayland (Baptist) Seminary in Washington, D.C.

had their personal expenses paid for them. At Hampton the student was constantly making the effort through the industries to help himself, and that very effort was of immense value in character-building. The students at the other school seemed to be less self-dependent. They seemed to give more attention to mere outward appearances. In a word, they did not appear to me to be beginning at the bottom, on a real, solid foundation, to the extent that they were at Hampton. They knew more about Latin and Greek when they left school, but they seemed to know less about life and its conditions as they would meet it at their homes. Having lived for a number of years in the midst of comfortable surroundings, they were not as much inclined as the Hampton students to go into the country districts of the South, where there was little of comfort, to take up work for our people, and they were more inclined to yield to the temptation to become hotel waiters and Pullman-car porters as their life-work.

During the time I was a student in Washington the city was crowded with coloured people, many of whom had recently come from the South. A large proportion of these people had been drawn to Washington because they felt that they could lead a life of ease there. Others had secured minor government positions, and still another large class was there in the hope of securing Federal positions. A number of coloured men—some of them very strong and brilliant—were in the House of Representatives at that time, and one, the Hon. B. K. Bruce, was in the Senate. All this tended to make Washington an attractive place for members of the coloured race. Then, too, they knew that at all times they could have the protection of the law in the District of Columbia. The public schools in Washington for coloured people were better then than they were elsewhere. I took great interest in studying the life of our people there closely at that time. I found that while among them there was a large element of substantial, worthy citizens, there was also a superficiality about the life of a large class that greatly alarmed me. I saw young coloured men who were not earning more than four dollars a week spend two dollars or more for a buggy on Sunday to ride up and down Pennsylvania Avenue in, in order that they might try to convince the world that they were worth thousands. I saw other young men who received seventy-five or one hundred dollars per month from the Government, who were in debt at the end of every month. I saw men who but a few months previous were members of Congress, then without employment and in poverty. Among a large class there seemed to be a dependence upon the Government for every conceivable thing. The members of this class had little ambition to create a position for themselves, but wanted the Federal officials to create one for them. How many times I wished then, and have often wished since, that by some power of magic I might remove the great bulk of these people into the country districts and plant them upon the soil, upon the solid and never deceptive foundation of Mother Nature, where all nations and races that have ever succeeded have gotten their start,—a start that at first may be slow and toilsome, but one that nevertheless is real.

In Washington I saw girls whose mothers were earning their living by laundrying. These girls were taught by their mothers, in rather a crude way it is true, the industry of laundrying. Later, these girls entered the public schools and remained there perhaps six or eight years. When the public-school course was finally finished, they wanted more costly dresses, more costly hats and shoes. In a word, while their wants had been increased, their ability to supply their wants had not been increased in the same degree. On the other hand, their six or eight years of book education had weaned them away from the occupation of their mothers. The result of this was in too many cases that the girls went to the bad. I often thought how much wiser it would have been to give these girls the same amount of mental training—and I favour any kind of training, whether in the languages or mathematics, that gives strength and culture to the mind—but at the same time to give them the most thorough training in the latest and best methods of laundrying and other kindred occupations.

Chapter VI

Black Race and Red Race

During the year that I spent in Washington, and for some little time before this, there had been considerable agitation in the state of West Virginia over the question of moving the capital of the state from Wheeling to some other central point. As a result of this, the Legislature designated three cities to be voted upon by the citizens of the state as the permanent seat of government. Among these cities was Charleston, only five miles from Malden, my home. At the close of my school year in Washington I was very pleasantly surprised to receive, from a committee of white people in Charleston, an invitation to canvass the state in the interests of that city. This invitation I accepted, and spent nearly three months in speaking in various parts of the state. Charleston was successful in winning the prize, and is now the permanent seat of government.

The reputation that I made as a speaker during this campaign induced a number of persons to make an earnest effort to get me to enter political life, but I refused, still believing that I could find other service which would prove of more permanent value to my race. Even then I had a strong feeling that what our people most needed was to get a foundation in education, industry, and property, and for this I felt that they could better afford to strive than for political preferment. As for my individual self, it appeared to me to be reasonably certain that I could succeed in political life, but I had a feeling that it would be a rather selfish kind of success—individual success at the cost of failing to do my duty in assisting in laying a foundation for the masses.

At this period in the progress of our race a very large proportion of the young men who went to school or to college did so with the expressed determination to prepare themselves to be great lawyers, or Congressmen, and many of the women planned to become music teachers; but I had a reasonably fixed idea, even at that early period in my life, that there was need for something to be done to prepare the way for successful lawyers, Congressmen, and music teachers.

I felt that the conditions were a good deal like those of an old coloured man, during the days of slavery, who wanted to learn how to play on the guitar. In his desire to take guitar lessons he applied to one of his young masters to teach him; but the young man, not having much faith in the ability of the slave to master the guitar at his age, sought to discourage him by telling him: "Uncle Jake, I will give you guitar lessons; but, Jake, I will have to charge you three dollars for the first lesson, two dollars for the second lesson, and one dollar for the third lesson. But I will charge you only twenty-five cents for the last lesson."

Uncle Jake answered: "All right, boss, I hires you on dem terms. But, boss! I wants yer to be sure an' give me dat las' lesson first."

Soon after my work in connection with the removal of the capital was finished, I received an invitation which gave me great joy and which at the same time was a very pleasant surprise. This was a letter from General Armstrong, inviting me to return to Hampton at the next Commencement to deliver what was called the "post-graduate address." This was an honour which I had not dreamed of receiving. With much care I prepared the best address that I was capable of. I chose for my subject "The Force That Wins."

As I returned to Hampton for the purpose of delivering this address, I went over much of the same ground—now, however, covered entirely by railroad—that I had traversed nearly six years before, when I first sought entrance into Hampton Institute as a student. Now I was able to ride the whole distance in the train. I was constantly contrasting this with my first journey to Hampton. I think I may say, without seeming egotism, that it is seldom that five years have wrought such a change in the life and aspirations of an individual.

At Hampton I received a warm welcome from teachers and students. I found that during my absence from Hampton the institute each year had been getting closer to the real needs and conditions of our people; that the industrial teaching, as well as that of the academic department, had greatly improved. The plan of the school was not modelled after that of any other institution then in existence, but every improvement was made under the magnificent leadership of General Armstrong solely with the view of meeting and helping the needs of our people as they presented themselves at the time. Too often, it seems to me, in missionary and educational work among undeveloped races, people yield to the temptation of doing that which was done a hundred years before, or is being done in other communities a thousand miles away. The temptation often is to run each individual through a certain educational mould, regardless of the condition of the subject or the end to be accomplished. This was not so at Hampton Institute.

The address which I delivered on Commencement Day seems to have pleased every one, and many kind and encouraging words were spoken to me regarding it. Soon after my return to my home in West Virginia, where I had planned to continue teaching, I was again surprised to receive a letter from General Armstrong, asking me to return to Hampton partly as a teacher and partly to pursue some supplementary studies. This was in the summer of 1879. Soon after I began my first teaching in West Virginia I had picked out four of the brightest and most promising of my pupils, in addition to my two brothers, to whom I have already referred, and had given them special attention, with the view of having them go to Hampton. They had gone there, and in each case the teachers had found them so well prepared that they entered advanced classes. This fact, it seems, led to my being called back to Hampton as a teacher. One of the young men that I sent to Hampton in this way is now Dr. Samuel E. Courtney, a successful physician in Boston, and a member of the School Board of that city.

About this time the experiment was being tried for the first time, by General Armstrong, of educating Indians at Hampton. Few people then had any confidence in the ability of the Indians to receive education and to profit by it. General Armstrong was anxious to try the experiment systematically on a large scale. He secured from the reservations in the Western states over one hundred wild and for the most part perfectly ignorant Indians, the greater proportion of whom were young men. The special work which the General desired me to do was to be a sort of "house father" to the Indian young men—that is, I was to live in the building with them and have the charge of their discipline, clothing, rooms, and so on. This was a very tempting offer, but I had become so much absorbed in my work in West Virginia that I dreaded to give it up. However, I tore myself away from it. I did not know how to refuse to perform any service that General Armstrong desired of me.

On going to Hampton, I took up my residence in a building with about seventy-five Indian youths. I was the only person in the buildin[g] who was not a member of their race. At first I had a good deal of do[ubt] about my ability to succeed. I knew that the average Indian felt hi[mself] above the white man, and, of course, he felt himself far ab[ove the] Negro, largely on account of the fact of the Negro having su[b-] slavery—a thing which the Indian would never do. The Indians, in the Indian Territory,[1] owned a large number of slaves during the days of slavery. Aside from this, there was a general feeling that the attempt to educate and civilize the red men at Hampton would be a failure. All this made me proceed very cautiously, for I felt keenly the great responsibility. But I was determined to succeed. It was not long before I had the complete confidence of the Indians, and not only this, but I think I am safe in saying that I had their love and respect. I found that they were about like any other human beings; that they responded to kind treatment and resented ill-treatment. They were continually planning to do something that would add to my happiness and comfort. The things that they disliked most, I think, were to have their long hair cut, to give up wearing their blankets, and to cease smoking; but no white American ever thinks that any other race is wholly civilized until he wears the white man's clothes, eats the white man's food, speaks the white man's language, and professes the white man's religion.

When the difficulty of learning the English language was subtracted, I found that in the matter of learning trades and in mastering academic studies there was little difference between the coloured and Indian students. It was a constant delight to me to note the interest which the coloured students took in trying to help the Indians in every way possible. There were a few of the coloured students who felt that the Indians ought not to be admitted to Hampton, but these were in the minority. Whenever they were asked to do so, the Negro students gladly took the Indians as room-mates, in order that they might teach them to speak English and to acquire civilized habits.

I have often wondered if there was a white institution in this country whose students would have welcomed the incoming of more than a hundred companions of another race in the cordial way that these black students at Hampton welcomed the red ones. How often I have wanted to say to white students that they lift themselves up in proportion as they help to lift others, and the more unfortunate the race, and the lower in the scale of civilization, the more does one raise one's self by giving the assistance.

This reminds me of a conversation which I once had with the Hon. Frederick Douglass.[2] At one time Mr. Douglass was travelling in the ...lvania, and was forced, on account of his colour, to ride ... of the fact that he had paid the same price ... assengers had paid. When some of the ... baggage-car to console Mr. Douglass, ... I am sorry, Mr. Douglass, that you have

...oma was set aside as a reservation for American Indians ... states.

...editor, and author, Douglass (1818–1895) was the most ...neteenth century.

been degraded in this manner," Mr. Douglass straightened himself up on the box upon which he was sitting, and replied: "They cannot degrade Frederick Douglass. The soul that is within me no man can degrade. I am not the one that is being degraded on account of this treatment, but those who are inflicting it upon me."

In one part of our country, where the law demands the separation of the races on the railroad trains, I saw at one time a rather amusing instance which showed how difficult it sometimes is to know where the black begins and the white ends.

There was a man who was well known in his community as a Negro, but who was so white that even an expert would have hard work to classify him as a black man. This man was riding in the part of the train set aside for the coloured passengers. When the train conductor reached him, he showed at once that he was perplexed. If the man was a Negro, the conductor did not want to send him into the white people's coach; at the same time, if he was a white man, the conductor did not want to insult him by asking him if he was a Negro. The official looked him over carefully, examining his hair, eyes, nose, and hands, but still seemed puzzled. Finally, to solve the difficulty, he stooped over and peeped at the man's feet. When I saw the conductor examining the feet of the man in question, I said to myself, "That will settle it;" and so it did, for the trainman promptly decided that the passenger was a Negro, and let him remain where he was. I congratulated myself that my race was fortunate in not losing one of its members.

My experience has been that the time to test a true gentleman is to observe him when he is in contact with individuals of a race that is less fortunate than his own. This is illustrated in no better way than by observing the conduct of the old-school type of Southern gentleman when he is in contact with his former slaves or their descendants.

An example of what I mean is shown in a story told of George Washington, who, meeting a coloured man in the road once, who politely lifted his hat, lifted his own in return. Some of his white friends who saw the incident criticised Washington for his action. In reply to their criticism George Washington said: "Do you suppose that I am going to permit a poor, ignorant, coloured man to be more polite than I am?"

While I was in charge of the Indian boys at Hampton, I had one or two experiences which illustrate the curious workings of caste in America. One of the Indian boys was taken ill, and it became my duty to take him to Washington, deliver him over to the Secretary of the Interior, and get a receipt for him, in order that he might be returned to his Western reservation. At that time I was rather ignorant of the ways of the world. During my journey to Washington, on a steamboat, when the bell rang for dinner, I was careful to wait and not enter the dining room until after the greater part of the passengers had finished their meal. Then, with my charge, I went to the dining saloon. The man in charge politely informed me that the Indian could be served, but that I could not. I never could understand how he knew just where to draw the colour line, since the Indian and I were of about the same complexion. The steward, however, seemed to be an expert in this matter. I had been directed by the authorities at Hampton to stop at a certain hotel in Washington with my charge, but when I went to this hotel the clerk stated that he would be glad to receive the Indian into the house, but said that he could not accommodate me.

An illustration of something of this same feeling came under my observation afterward. I happened to find myself in a town in which so much excitement and indignation were being expressed that it seemed likely for a time that there would be a lynching. The occasion of the trouble was that a dark-skinned man had stopped at the local hotel. Investigation, however, developed the fact that this individual was a citizen of Morocco, and that while travelling in this country he spoke the English language. As soon as it was learned that he was not an American Negro, all the signs of indignation disappeared. The man who was the innocent cause of the excitement, though, found it prudent after that not to speak English.

At the end of my first year with the Indians there came another opening for me at Hampton, which, as I look back over my life now, seems to have come providentially, to help to prepare me for my work at Tuskegee later. General Armstrong had found out that there was quite a number of young coloured men and women who were intensely in earnest in wishing to get an education, but who were prevented from entering Hampton Institute because they were too poor to be able to pay any portion of the cost of their board, or even to supply themselves with books. He conceived the idea of starting a night-school in connection with the Institute, into which a limited number of the most promising of these young men and women would be received, on condition that they were to work for ten hours during the day, and attend school for two hours at night. They were to be paid something above the cost of their board for their work. The greater part of their earnings was to be reserved in the school's treasury as a fund to be drawn on to pay their board when they had become students in the day-school, after they had spent one or two years in the night-school. In this way they would obtain a start in their books and a knowledge of some trade or industry, in addition to the other far-reaching benefits of the institution.

General Armstrong asked me to take charge of the night-school, and I did so. At the beginning of this school there were about twelve strong, earnest men and women who entered the class. During the day the greater part of the young men worked in the school's sawmill, and the young women worked in the laundry. The work was not easy in either place, but in all my teaching I never taught pupils who gave me such genuine satisfaction as these did. They were good students, and mastered their work thoroughly. They were so much in earnest that only the ringing of the retiring-bell would make them stop studying, and often they would urge me to continue the lessons after the usual hour for going to bed had come.

These students showed so much earnestness, both in their hard work during the day, as well as in their application to their studies at night, that I gave them the name of "The Plucky Class"—a name which soon grew popular and spread throughout the institution. After a student had been in the night-school long enough to prove what was in him, I gave him a printed certificate which read something like this:—

"This is to certify that James Smith is a member of The Plucky Class of the Hampton Institute, and is in good and regular standing."

The students prized these certificates highly, and they added greatly to the popularity of the night-school. Within a few weeks this department had grown to such an extent that there were about twenty-five students in attendance. I have followed the course of many of these twenty-five men and women ever since then, and they are now holding important and useful positions in nearly every part of the South. The night-school at Hampton, which started with only twelve students, now numbers between three and four hundred, and is one of the permanent and most important features of the institution.

Chapter VII

Early Days at Tuskegee

During the time that I had charge of the Indians and the night-school at Hampton, I pursued some studies myself, under the direction of the instructors there. One of these instructors was the Rev. Dr. H. B. Frissell, the present Principal of the Hampton Institute, General Armstrong's successor.

In May, 1881, near the close of my first year in teaching the night-school, in a way that I had not dared expect, the opportunity opened for me to begin my life-work. One night in the chapel, after the usual chapel exercises were over, General Armstrong referred to the fact that he had received a letter from some gentlemen in Alabama asking him to recommend some one to take charge of what was to be a normal school for the coloured people in the little town of Tuskegee in that state. These gentlemen seemed to take it for granted that no coloured man suitable for the position could be secured, and they were expecting the General to recommend a white man for the place. The next day General Armstrong sent for me to come to his office, and, much to my surprise, asked me if I thought I could fill the position in Alabama. I told him that I would be willing to try. Accordingly, he wrote to the people who had applied to him for the information, that he did not know of any white man to suggest, but if they would be willing to take a coloured man, he had one whom he could recommend. In this letter he gave them my name.

Several days passed before anything more was heard about the matter. Some time afterward, one Sunday evening during the chapel exercises, a messenger came in and handed the General a telegram. At the end of the exercises he read the telegram to the school. In substance, these were its words: "Booker T. Washington will suit us. Send him at once."

There was a great deal of joy expressed among the students and teachers, and I received very hearty congratulations. I began to get ready at once to go to Tuskegee. I went by way of my old home in West Virginia, where I remained for several days, after which I proceeded to Tuskegee. I found Tuskegee to be a town of about two thousand inhabitants, nearly one-half of whom were coloured. It was in what was known as the Black Belt of the South. In the county in which Tuskegee is situated the coloured people outnumbered the whites by about three to one. In some of the adjoining and near-by counties the proportion was not far from six coloured persons to one white.

I have often been asked to define the term "Black Belt." So far as I can learn, the term was first used to designate a part of the country which was distinguished by the colour of the soil. The part of the country possessing this thick, dark, and naturally rich soil was, of course, the part of the South where the slaves were most profitable, and consequently they were taken there in the largest numbers. Later, and especially since the war, the term seems to be used wholly in a political sense—that is, to designate the counties where the black people outnumber the white.

Before going to Tuskegee I had expected to find there a building and all the necessary apparatus ready for me to begin teaching. To my disappointment, I found nothing of the kind. I did find, though, that which no costly building and apparatus can supply,—hundreds of hungry, earnest souls who wanted to secure knowledge.

Tuskegee seemed an ideal place for the school. It was in the midst of the great bulk of the Negro population, and was rather secluded, being five miles from the main line of railroad, with which it was connected by a short line. During the days of slavery, and since, the town had been a centre for the education of the white people. This was an added advantage, for the reason that I found the white people possessing a degree of culture and education that is not surpassed by many localities. While the coloured people were ignorant, they had not, as a rule, degraded and weakened their bodies by vices such as are common to the lower class of people in the large cities. In general, I found the relations between the two races pleasant. For example, the largest, and I think at that time the only hardware store in the town was owned and operated jointly by a coloured man and a white man. This copartnership continued until the death of the white partner.

I found that about a year previous to my going to Tuskegee some of the coloured people who had heard something of the work of education being done at Hampton had applied to the state Legislature, through their representatives, for a small appropriation to be used in starting a normal school in Tuskegee. This request the Legislature had complied with to the extent of granting an annual appropriation of two thousand dollars. I soon learned, however, that this money could be used only for the payment of the salaries of the instructors, and that there was no provision for securing land, buildings, or apparatus. The task before me did not seem a very encouraging one. It seemed much like making bricks without straw. The coloured people were overjoyed, and were constantly offering their services in any way in which they could be of assistance in getting the school started.

My first task was to find a place in which to open the school. After looking the town over with some care, the most suitable place that could be secured seemed to be a rather dilapidated shanty near the coloured Methodist church, together with the church itself as a sort of assembly-room. Both the church and the shanty were in about as bad condition as was possible. I recall that during the first months of school that I taught in this building it was in such poor repair that, whenever it rained, one of the older students would very kindly leave his lessons and hold an umbrella over me while I heard the recitations of the others. I remember, also, that on more than one occasion my landlady held an umbrella over me while I ate breakfast.

At the time I went to Alabama the coloured people were taking considerable interest in politics, and they were very anxious that I should become one of them politically, in every respect. They seemed to have a little distrust of strangers in this regard. I recall that one man, who seemed to have been designated by the others to look after my political destiny, came to me on several occasions and said, with a good deal of earnestness: "We wants you to be sure to vote jes' like we votes. We can't read de newspapers very much, but we knows how to vote, an' we wants you to vote jes' like we votes." He added: "We watches de white man, and we keeps watching de white man till we finds out which way de white man's gwine to vote; an' when we finds out which way de white man's gwine to vote, den we votes 'xactly de other way. Den we knows we's right."

I am glad to add, however, that at the present time the disposition to vote against the white man merely because he is white is largely disappearing, and the race is learning to vote from principle, for what the voter considers to be for the best interests of both races.

I reached Tuskegee, as I have said, early in June, 1881. The first month I spent in finding accommodations for the school, and in travelling through Alabama, examining into the actual life of the people, especially in the country districts, and in getting the school advertised among the class of people that I wanted to have attend it. The most of my travelling was done over the country roads, with a mule and a cart or a mule and a buggy wagon for conveyance. I ate and slept with the people, in their little cabins. I saw their farms, their schools, their churches. Since, in the case of the most of these visits, there had been no notice given in advance that a stranger was expected, I had the advantage of seeing the real, everyday life of the people.

In the plantation districts I found that, as a rule, the whole family slept in one room, and that in addition to the immediate family there sometimes were relatives, or others not related to the family, who slept in the same room. On more than one occasion I went outside the house to get ready for bed, or to wait until the family had gone to bed. They usually contrived some kind of a place for me to sleep, either on the floor or in a special part of another's bed. Rarely was there any place provided in the cabin where one could bathe even the face and hands, but usually some provision was made for this outside the house, in the yard.

The common diet of the people was fat pork and corn bread. At times I have eaten in cabins where they had only corn bread and "black-eye peas" cooked in plain water. The people seemed to have no other idea than to live on this fat meat and corn bread,—the meat, and the meal of which the bread was made, having been bought at a high price at a store in town, notwithstanding the fact that the land all about the cabin homes could easily have been made to produce nearly every kind of garden vegetable that is raised anywhere in the country. Their one object seemed to be to plant nothing but cotton; and in many cases cotton was planted up to the very door of the cabin.

In these cabin homes I often found sewing-machines which had been bought, or were being bought, on instalments, frequently at a cost of as much as sixty dollars, or showy clocks for which the occupants of the cabins had paid twelve or fourteen dollars. I remember that on one occasion when I went into one of these cabins for dinner, when I sat down to the table for a meal with the four members of the family, I noticed that, while there were five of us at the table, there was but one fork for the five of us to use. Naturally there was an awkward pause on my part. In the opposite corner of that same cabin was an organ for which the people told me they were paying sixty dollars in monthly instalments. One fork, and a sixty-dollar organ!

In most cases the sewing-machine was not used, the clocks were so worthless that they did not keep correct time—and if they had, in nine cases out of ten there would have been no one in the family who could have told the time of day—while the organ, of course, was rarely used for want of a person who could play upon it.

ill be directed to a Negro who learned a trade during the days of ry.

n the morning that the school opened, thirty students reported for ission. I was the only teacher. The students were about equally ded between the sexes. Most of them lived in Macon County, the nty in which Tuskegee is situated, and of which it is the county-seat. eat many more students wanted to enter the school, but it had been ded to receive only those who were above fifteen years of age, and had previously received some education. The greater part of the were public-school teachers, and some of them were nearly forty f age. With the teachers came some of their former pupils, and hey were examined it was amusing to note that in several cases il entered a higher class than did his former teacher. It was also ng to note how many big books some of them had studied, and ny high-sounding subjects some of them claimed to have mas- e bigger the book and the longer the name of the subject, the ey felt of their accomplishment. Some had studied Latin, and Greek. This they thought entitled them to special distinction.

one of the saddest things I saw during the month of travel e described was a young man, who had attended some high g down in a one-room cabin, with grease on his clothing, d him, and weeds in the yard and garden, engaged in ch grammar.

who came first seemed to be fond of memorizing long "rules" in grammar and mathematics, but had little
h dge of applying these rules to the everyday affairs of
the ect which they liked to talk about, and tell me that
one or n arithmetic, was "banking and discount," but I
name of ither they nor almost any one in the neighbour-
"entitles." ed had ever had a bank account. In registering
thought it wo s, I found that almost every one of them had
Notwithstand s. When I asked what the "J" stood for, in the
never seen a mo as explained to me that this was a part of his
women than these st ts wanted to get an education because they
thing as soon as it was to earn more money as school-teachers.
start them off on a solid said about them in these respects, I have
were concerned. I soon lea willing company of young men and
tering of the high-sounding They were all willing to learn the right
could locate the Desert of Saha what was right. I was determined to
globe, I found out that the girls c gh foundation, so far as their books
most of them had the merest smat- at they had studied. While they capital of China on an artificial ot locate the proper places for

In the case to which I have referred, where the family sat down to the table for the meal at which I was their guest, I could see plainly that this was an awkward and unusual proceeding, and was done in my honour. In most cases, when the family got up in the morning, for example, the wife would put a piece of meat in a frying-pan and put a lump of dough in a "skillet," as they called it. These utensils would be placed on the fire, and in ten or fifteen minutes breakfast would be ready. Frequently the husband would take his bread and meat in his hand and start for the field, eating as he walked. The mother would sit down in a corner and eat her breakfast, perhaps from a plate and perhaps directly from the "skillet" or frying-pan, while the children would eat their portion of the bread and meat while running about the yard. At certain seasons of the year, when meat was scarce, it was rarely that the children who were not old enough or strong enough to work in the fields would have the luxury of meat.

The breakfast over, and with practically no attention given to the house, the whole family would, as a general thing, proceed to the cotton-field. Every child that was large enough to carry a hoe was put to work, and the baby—for usually there was at least one baby—would be laid down at the end of the cotton row, so that its mother could give it a certain amount of attention when she had finished chopping her row. The noon meal and the supper were taken in much the same way as the breakfast.

All the days of the family would be spent after much this same routine, except Saturday and Sunday. On Saturday the whole family would spend at least half a day, and often a whole day, in town. The idea in going to town was, I suppose, to do shopping, but all the shopping that the whole family had money for could have been attended to in ten minutes by one person. Still, the whole family remained in town for most of the day, spending the greater part of the time in standing on the streets, the women, too often, sitting about somewhere smoking or dipping snuff. Sunday was usually spent in going to some big meeting. With few exceptions, I found that the crops were mortgaged in the counties where I went, and that the most of the coloured farmers were in debt. The state had not been able to build schoolhouses in the country districts, and, as a rule, the schools were taught in churches or in log cabins. More than once, while on my journeys, I found that there was no provision made in the house used for school purposes for heating the building during the winter, and consequently a fire had to be built in the yard, and teacher and pupils passed in and out of the house as they got cold or warm. With few exceptions, I found the teachers in these country schools to be miserably poor in preparation for their work, and poor in moral character. The schools were in session from three to five months. There was practically no apparatus in the schoolhouses, except that occasionally there was a rough blackboard. I recall that one day I went into a schoolhouse—or rather into an abandoned log cabin that was being used as a schoolhouse—and found five pupils who were studying a lesson from one book. Two of these, on the front seat, were using the book between them; behind these were two others peeping over the shoulders of the first two, and behind the four was a fifth little fellow who was peeping over the shoulders of all four.

What I have said concerning the character of the schoolhouses and teachers will also apply quite accurately as a description of the church buildings and the ministers.

I met some very interesting characters during my travels. As illustrating the peculiar mental processes of the country people, I remember that I asked one coloured man, who was about sixty years old, to tell me something of his history. He said that he had been born in Virginia, and sold into Alabama in 1845. I asked him how many were sold at the same time. He said, "There were five of us; myself and brother and three mules."

In giving all these descriptions of what I saw during my month of travel in the country around Tuskegee, I wish my readers to keep in mind the fact that there were many encouraging exceptions to the conditions which I have described. I have stated in such plain words what I saw, mainly for the reason that later I want to emphasize the encouraging changes that have taken place in the community, not wholly by the work of the Tuskegee school, but by that of other institutions as well.

Chapter VIII

Teaching School in a Stable and a Hen-House

I confess that what I saw during my month of travel and investigation left me with a very heavy heart. The work to be done in order to lift these people up seemed almost beyond accomplishing. I was only one person, and it seemed to me that the little effort which I could put forth could go such a short distance toward bringing about results. I wondered if I could accomplish anything, and if it were worth while for me to try.

Of one thing I felt more strongly convinced than ever, after spending this month in seeing the actual life of the coloured people, and that was that, in order to lift them up, something must be done more than merely to imitate New England education as it then existed. I saw more clearly than ever the wisdom of the system which General Armstrong had inaugurated at Hampton. To take the children of such people as I had been among for a month, and each day give them a few hours of mere book education, I felt would be almost a waste of time.

After consultation with the citizens of Tuskegee, I set July 4, 1881, as the day for the opening of the school in the little shanty and church

which had been secured for its accommodation. The whi
well as the coloured, were greatly interested in the startin
school, and the opening day was looked forward to with
discussion. There were not a few white people in th
Tuskegee who looked with some disfavour upon the proje
tioned its value to the coloured people, and had a fear
result in bringing about trouble between the races. Some
that in proportion as the Negro received education, in the
tion would his value decrease as an economic factor in th
people feared the result of education would be that the
leave the farms, and that it would be difficult to secure th
tic service.

The white people who questioned the wisdom of st
school had in their minds pictures of what was cal
Negro, with a high hat, imitation gold eye-glasses,
stick, kid gloves, fancy boots, and what not—in a wo
determined to live by his wits. It was difficult for the
education would produce any other kind of a colo

In the midst of all the difficulties which I enco
little school started, and since then through a pe
there are two men among all the many friends of
upon whom I have depended constantly for a
the success of the undertaking is largely due t
I have never sought anything in vain. I men
One is a white man and an ex-slaveholder,
the other is a black man and an ex-slave, M
the men who wrote to General Armstrong

Mr. Campbell is a merchant and ban
ence in dealing with matters pertaining
mechanic, and had learned the trades
and tinsmithing during the days of slav
a day in his life, but in some way he h
a slave. From the first, these two
education was, sympathized with m
In the days which were darkest fina
was never appealed to when he w
his power. I do not know two me
slave, whose advice and judgme
everything which concerns the
Tuskegee than those of these tw

I have always felt that Mr
unusual power of mind from
of mastering well three trade
day into any Southern town
coloured man in the comm

the knives and forks on an actual dinner-table, or the places on which the bread and meat should be set.

I had to summon a good deal of courage to take a student who had been studying cube root and "banking and discount," and explain to him that the wisest thing for him to do first was thoroughly to master the multiplication table.

The number of pupils increased each week, until by the end of the first month there were nearly fifty. Many of them, however, said that, as they could remain only for two or three months, they wanted to enter a high class and get a diploma the first year if possible.

At the end of the first six weeks a new and rare face entered the school as a co-teacher. This was Miss Olivia A. Davidson, who later became my wife. Miss Davidson was born in Ohio, and received her preparatory education in the public schools of that state. When little more than a girl, she heard of the need of teachers in the South. She went to the state of Mississippi and began teaching there. Later she taught in the city of Memphis. While teaching in Mississippi, one of her pupils became ill with smallpox. Every one in the community was so frightened that no one would nurse the boy. Miss Davidson closed her school and remained by the bedside of the boy night and day until he recovered. While she was at her Ohio home on her vacation, the worst epidemic of yellow fever broke out in Memphis, Tenn., that perhaps has ever occurred in the South. When she heard of this, she at once telegraphed the Mayor of Memphis, offering her services as a yellow-fever nurse, although she had never had the disease.

Miss Davidson's experience in the South showed her that the people needed something more than mere book-learning. She heard of the Hampton system of education, and decided that this was what she wanted in order to prepare herself for better work in the South. The attention of Mrs. Mary Hemenway, of Boston, was attracted to her rare ability. Through Mrs. Hemenway's kindness and generosity, Miss Davidson, after graduating at Hampton, received an opportunity to complete a two years' course of training at the Massachusetts State Normal School at Framingham.

Before she went to Framingham, some one suggested to Miss Davidson that, since she was so very light in colour, she might find it more comfortable not to be known as a coloured woman in this school in Massachusetts. She at once replied that under no circumstances and for no considerations would she consent to deceive any one in regard to her racial identity.

Soon after her graduation from the Framingham institution, Miss Davidson came to Tuskegee, bringing into the school many valuable and fresh ideas as to the best methods of teaching, as well as a rare moral character and a life of unselfishness that I think has seldom been equalled. No single individual did more toward laying the foundations of the Tuskegee Institute so as to insure the successful work that has been done there than Olivia A. Davidson.

Miss Davidson and I began consulting as to the future of the school from the first. The students were making progress in learning books and in developing their minds; but it became apparent at once that, if we were to make any permanent impression upon those who had come to us for training, we must do something besides teach them mere books. The students had come from homes where they had had no opportunities for lessons which would teach them how to care for their bodies. With few exceptions, the homes in Tuskegee in which the students boarded were but little improvement upon those from which they had come. We wanted to teach the students how to bathe; how to care for their teeth and clothing. We wanted to teach them what to eat, and how to eat it properly, and how to care for their rooms. Aside from this, we wanted to give them such a practical knowledge of some one industry, together with the spirit of industry, thrift, and economy, that they would be sure of knowing how to make a living after they had left us. We wanted to teach them to study actual things instead of mere books alone.

We found that the most of our students came from the country districts, where agriculture in some form or other was the main dependence of the people. We learned that about eighty-five per cent of the coloured people in the Gulf states depended upon agriculture for their living. Since this was true, we wanted to be careful not to educate our students out of sympathy with agricultural life, so that they would be attracted from the country to the cities, and yield to the temptation of trying to live by their wits. We wanted to give them such an education as would fit a large proportion of them to be teachers, and at the same time cause them to return to the plantation districts and show the people there how to put new energy and new ideas into farming, as well as into the intellectual and moral and religious life of the people.

All these ideas and needs crowded themselves upon us with a seriousness that seemed well-nigh overwhelming. What were we to do? We had only the little old shanty and the abandoned church which the good coloured people of the town of Tuskegee had kindly loaned us for the accommodation of the classes. The number of students was increasing daily. The more we saw of them, and the more we travelled through the country districts, the more we saw that our efforts were reaching, to only a partial degree, the actual needs of the people whom we wanted to lift up through the medium of the students whom we should educate and send out as leaders.

The more we talked with the students, who were then coming to us from several parts of the state, the more we found that the chief ambition among a large proportion of them was to get an education so that they would not have to work any longer with their hands.

This is illustrated by a story told of a coloured man in Alabama, who, one hot day in July, while he was at work in a cotton-field, suddenly stopped, and, looking toward the skies, said: "O Lawd, de cotton am so grassy, de work am so hard, and the sun am so hot dat I b'lieve dis darky am called to preach!"

About three months after the opening of the school, and at the time when we were in the greatest anxiety about our work, there came into the market for sale an old and abandoned plantation which was situated about a mile from the town of Tuskegee. The mansion house—or "big house," as it would have been called—which had been occupied by the owners during slavery, had been burned. After making a careful examination of this place, it seemed to be just the location that we wanted in order to make our work effective and permanent.

But how were we to get it? The price asked for it was very little—only five hundred dollars—but we had no money, and we were strangers in the town and had no credit. The owner of the land agreed to let us occupy the place if we could make a payment of two hundred and fifty dollars down, with the understanding that the remaining two hundred and fifty dollars must be paid within a year. Although five hundred dollars was cheap for the land, it was a large sum when one did not have any part of it.

In the midst of the difficulty I summoned a great deal of courage and wrote to my friend General J. F. B. Marshall, the Treasurer of the Hampton Institute, putting the situation before him and beseeching him to lend me the two hundred and fifty dollars on my own personal responsibility. Within a few days a reply came to the effect that he had no authority to lend me money belonging to the Hampton Institute, but that he would gladly lend me the amount needed from his own personal funds.

I confess that the securing of this money in this way was a great surprise to me, as well as a source of gratification. Up to that time I never had had in my possession so much money as one hundred dollars at a time, and the loan which I had asked General Marshall for seemed a tremendously large sum to me. The fact of my being responsible for the repaying of such a large amount of money weighed very heavily upon me.

I lost no time in getting ready to move the school on to the new farm. At the time we occupied the place there were standing upon it a cabin, formerly used as the dining room, an old kitchen, a stable, and an old hen-house. Within a few weeks we had all of these structures in use. The stable was repaired and used as a recitation-room, and very presently the hen-house was utilized for the same purpose.

I recall that one morning, when I told an old coloured man who lived near, and who sometimes helped me, that our school had grown so large that it would be necessary for us to use the hen-house for school purposes, and that I wanted him to help me give it a thorough cleaning out the next day, he replied, in the most earnest manner: "What you mean, boss? You sholy ain't gwine clean out de hen-house in de *day*-time?"

Nearly all the work of getting the new location ready for school purposes was done by the students after school was over in the afternoon. As soon as we got the cabins in condition to be used, I determined to clear up some land so that we could plant a crop. When I explained my plan to the young men, I noticed that they did not seem to take to it very kindly. It was hard for them to see the connection between clearing land and an education. Besides, many of them had been school-teachers, and they questioned whether or not clearing land would be in keeping with their dignity. In order to relieve them from any embarrassment, each afternoon after school I took my axe and led the way to the woods. When they saw that I was not afraid or ashamed to work, they began to assist with more enthusiasm. We kept at the work each afternoon, until we had cleared about twenty acres and had planted a crop.

In the meantime Miss Davidson was devising plans to repay the loan. Her first effort was made by holding festivals, or "suppers." She made a personal canvass among the white and coloured families in the town of Tuskegee, and got them to agree to give something, like a cake, a chicken, bread, or pies, that could be sold at the festival. Of course the coloured people were glad to give anything that they could spare, but I want to add that Miss Davidson did not apply to a single white family, so far as I now remember, that failed to donate something; and in many ways the white families showed their interest in the school.

Several of these festivals were held, and quite a little sum of money was raised. A canvass was also made among the people of both races for direct gifts of money, and most of those applied to gave small sums. It was often pathetic to note the gifts of the older coloured people, most of whom had spent their best days in slavery. Sometimes they would give five cents, sometimes twenty-five cents. Sometimes the contribution was a quilt, or a quantity of sugarcane. I recall one old coloured woman, who was about seventy years of age, who came to see me when we were raising money to pay for the farm. She hobbled into the room where I was, leaning on a cane. She was clad in rags; but they were clean. She said: "Mr. Washin'ton, God knows I spent de bes' days of my life in slavery. God knows I's ignorant an' poor; but," she added, "I knows what you an' Miss Davidson is tryin' to do. I knows you is tryin' to make better men an' better women for de coloured race. I ain't got no money, but I wants you to take dese six eggs, what I's been savin' up, an' I wants you to put dese six eggs into de eddication of dese boys an' gals."

Since the work at Tuskegee started, it has been my privilege to receive many gifts for the benefit of the institution, but never any, I think, that touched me so deeply as this one.

Chapter IX

Anxious Days and Sleepless Nights

The coming of Christmas, that first year of our residence in Alabama, gave us an opportunity to get a farther insight into the real life of the people. The first thing that reminded us that Christmas had arrived was the "foreday" visits of scores of children rapping at our doors, asking for "Chris'mus gifts! Chris'mus gifts!" Between the hours of two o'clock and five o'clock in the morning I presume that we must have had a half-hundred such calls. This custom prevails throughout this portion of the South to-day.

During the days of slavery it was a custom quite generally observed throughout all the Southern states to give the coloured people a week of holiday at Christmas, or to allow the holiday to continue as long as the "yule log" lasted. The male members of the race, and often the female members, were expected to get drunk. We found that for a whole week the coloured people in and around Tuskegee dropped work the day before Christmas, and that it was difficult to get any one to perform any service from the time they stopped work until after the New Year. Persons who at other times did not use strong drink thought it quite the proper thing to indulge in it rather freely during the Christmas week. There was a widespread hilarity, and a free use of guns, pistols, and gunpowder generally. The sacredness of the season seemed to have been almost wholly lost sight of.

During this first Christmas vacation I went some distance from the town to visit the people on one of the large plantations. In their poverty and ignorance it was pathetic to see their attempts to get joy out of the season that in most parts of the country is so sacred and so dear to the heart. In one cabin I noticed that all that the five children had to remind them of the coming of Christ was a single bunch of firecrackers, which they had divided among them. In another cabin, where there were at least a half-dozen persons, they had only ten cents' worth of ginger-cakes, which had been bought in the store the day before. In another family they had only a few pieces of sugarcane. In still another cabin I found nothing but a new jug of cheap, mean whiskey, which the husband and wife were making free use of, notwithstanding the fact that the husband was one of the local ministers. In a few instances I found that the people had gotten hold of some bright-coloured cards that had been designed for advertising purposes, and were making the most of those. In other homes some member of the family had bought a new pistol. In the majority of cases there was nothing to be seen in the cabin to remind one of the coming of the Saviour, except that the people had ceased work in the fields and were lounging about their homes. At night, during Christmas week, they usually had what they called a "frolic," in some cabin on the plantation. This meant a kind of rough dance, where there was likely to be a good deal of whiskey used, and where there might be some shooting or cutting with razors.

While I was making this Christmas visit I met an old coloured man who was one of the numerous local preachers, who tried to convince me, from the experience Adam had in the Garden of Eden, that God had cursed all labour, and that, therefore, it was a sin for any man to work. For that reason this man sought to do as little work as possible. He seemed at that time to be supremely happy, because he was living, as he expressed it, through one week that was free from sin.

In the school we made a special effort to teach our students the meaning of Christmas, and to give them lessons in its proper observance. In this we have been successful to a degree that makes me feel safe in saying that the season now has a new meaning, not only through all that immediate region, but, in a measure, wherever our graduates have gone.

At the present time one of the most satisfactory features of the Christmas and Thanksgiving seasons at Tuskegee is the unselfish and beautiful way in which our graduates and students spend their time in administering to the comfort and happiness of others, especially the unfortunate. Not long ago some of our young men spent a holiday in rebuilding a cabin for a helpless coloured woman who is about seventy-five years old. At another time I remember that I made it known in chapel, one night, that a very poor student was suffering from cold, because he needed a coat. The next morning two coats were sent to my office for him.

I have referred to the disposition on the part of the white people in the town of Tuskegee and vicinity to help the school. From the first, I resolved to make the school a real part of the community in which it was located. I was determined that no one should have the feeling that it was a foreign institution, dropped down in the midst of the people, for which they had no responsibility and in which they had no interest. I noticed that the very fact that they had been asked to contribute toward the purchase of the land made them begin to feel as if it was going to be their school, to a large degree. I noted that just in proportion as we made the white people feel that the institution was a part of the life of the community, and that, while we wanted to make friends in Boston, for example, we also wanted to make white friends in Tuskegee, and that we wanted to make the school of real service to all the people, their attitude toward the school became favourable.

Perhaps I might add right here, what I hope to demonstrate later, that, so far as I know, the Tuskegee school at the present time has no warmer and more enthusiastic friends anywhere than it has among the white citizens of Tuskegee and throughout the state of Alabama and the entire South. From the first, I have advised our people in the South to make friends in every straightforward, manly way with their next-door neighbour, whether he be a black man or a white man. I have also advised them, where no principle is at stake, to consult the interests of their local communities, and to advise with their friends in regard to their voting.

For several months the work of securing the money with which to pay for the farm went on without ceasing. At the end of three months enough was secured to repay the loan of two hundred and fifty dollars to General Marshall, and within two months more we had secured the entire five hundred dollars and had received a deed of the one hundred acres of land. This gave us a great deal of satisfaction. It was not only a source of satisfaction to secure a permanent location for the school, but it was equally satisfactory to know that the greater part of the money with which it was paid for had been gotten from the white and coloured people in the town of Tuskegee. The most of this money was obtained by holding festivals and concerts, and from small individual donations.

Our next effort was in the direction of increasing the cultivation of the land, so as to secure some return from it, and at the same time give the students training in agriculture. All the industries at Tuskegee have been started in natural and logical order, growing out of the needs of a community settlement. We began with farming, because we wanted something to eat.

Many of the students, also, were able to remain in school but a few weeks at a time, because they had so little money with which to pay their board. Thus another object which made it desirable to get an industrial system started was in order to make it available as a means of helping the students to earn money enough so that they might be able to remain in school during the nine months' session of the school year.

The first animal that the school came into possession of was an old blind horse given us by one of the white citizens of Tuskegee. Perhaps I may add here that at the present time the school owns over two hundred horses, colts, mules, cows, calves, and oxen, and about seven hundred hogs and pigs, as well as a large number of sheep and goats.

The school was constantly growing in numbers, so much so that, after we had got the farm paid for, the cultivation of the land begun, and the old cabins which we had found on the place somewhat repaired, we turned our attention toward providing a large, substantial building. After having given a good deal of thought to the subject, we finally had the plans drawn for a building that was estimated to cost about six thousand dollars. This seemed to us a tremendous sum, but we knew that the school must go backward or forward, and that our work would mean little unless we could get hold of the students in their home life.

One incident which occurred about this time gave me a great deal of satisfaction as well as surprise. When it became known in the town that we were discussing the plans for a new, large building, a Southern white man who was operating a sawmill not far from Tuskegee came to me and said that he would gladly put all the lumber necessary to erect the building on the grounds, with no other guarantee for payment than my word that it would be paid for when we secured some money. I told the man frankly that at the time we did not have in our hands one dollar of the money needed. Notwithstanding this, he insisted on being allowed to put the lumber on the grounds. After we had secured some portion of the money we permitted him to do this.

Miss Davidson again began the work of securing in various ways small contributions for the new building from the white and coloured people in and near Tuskegee. I think I never saw a community of people so happy over anything as were the coloured people over the prospect of this new building. One day, when we were holding a meeting to secure funds for its erection, an old, ante-bellum coloured man came a distance of twelve miles and brought in his ox-cart a large hog. When the meeting was in progress, he rose in the midst of the company and said that he had no money which he could give, but that he had raised two fine hogs, and that he had brought one of them as a contribution toward the expenses of the building. He closed his announcement by saying: "Any nigger that's got any love for his race, or any respect for himself, will bring a hog to the next meeting." Quite a number of men in the community also volunteered to give several days' work, each, toward the erection of the building.

After we had secured all the help that we could in Tuskegee, Miss Davidson decided to go North for the purpose of securing additional funds. For weeks she visited individuals and spoke in churches and before Sunday schools and other organizations. She found this work quite trying, and often embarrassing. The school was not known, but she was not long in winning her way into the confidence of the best people in the North.

The first gift from any Northern person was received from a New York lady whom Miss Davidson met on the boat that was bringing her North. They fell into a conversation, and the Northern lady became so much interested in the effort being made at Tuskegee that before they parted Miss Davidson was handed a check for fifty dollars. For some time before our marriage, and also after it, Miss Davidson kept up the work of securing money in the North and in the South by interesting people by personal visits and through correspondence. At the same time she kept in close touch with the work at Tuskegee, as lady principal and classroom teacher. In addition to this, she worked among the older people in and near Tuskegee, and taught a Sunday school class in the town. She was never very strong, but never seemed happy unless she was giving all of her strength to the cause which she loved. Often, at night, after spending the day in going from door to door trying to interest persons in the work at Tuskegee, she would be so exhausted that she could not undress herself. A lady upon whom she called, in Boston, afterward told me that at one time when Miss Davidson called to see her and sent up her card the lady was detained a little before she could see Miss Davidson, and when she entered the parlour she found Miss Davidson so exhausted that she had fallen asleep.

While putting up our first building, which was named Porter Hall, after Mr. A. H. Porter, of Brooklyn, N.Y., who gave a generous sum toward its erection, the need for money became acute. I had given one of our creditors a promise that upon a certain day he should be paid four hundred dollars. On the morning of that day we did not have a dollar. The mail arrived at the school at ten o'clock, and in this mail there was a check sent by Miss Davidson for exactly four hundred dollars. I could relate many instances of almost the same character. This four hundred dollars was given by two ladies in Boston. Two years later, when the work at Tuskegee had grown considerably, and when we were in the midst of a season when we were so much in need of money that the future looked doubtful and gloomy, the same two Boston ladies sent us six thousand dollars. Words cannot describe our surprise, or the encouragement that the gift brought to us. Perhaps I might add here that for fourteen years these same friends have sent us six thousand dollars each year.

As soon as the plans were drawn for the new building, the students began digging out the earth where the foundations were to be laid, working after the regular classes were over. They had not fully outgrown the idea that it was hardly the proper thing for them to use their hands, since they had come there, as one of them expressed it, "to be educated, and not to work." Gradually, though, I noted with satisfaction that a sentiment in favour of work was gaining ground. After a few weeks of hard work the foundations were ready, and a day was appointed for the laying of the corner-stone.

When it is considered that the laying of this corner-stone took place in the heart of the South, in the "Black Belt," in the centre of that part of our country that was most devoted to slavery; that at that time slavery had been abolished only about sixteen years; that only sixteen years before that no Negro could be taught from books without the teacher receiving the condemnation of the law or of public sentiment—when all this is considered, the scene that was witnessed on that spring day at Tuskegee was a remarkable one. I believe there are few places in the world where it could have taken place.

The principal address was delivered by the Hon. Waddy Thompson, the Superintendent of Education for the county. About the corner-stone were gathered the teachers, the students, their parents and friends, the county officials—who were white—and all the leading white men in that vicinity, together with many of the black men and women whom these same white people but a few years before had held a title to as property. The members of both races were anxious to exercise the privilege of placing under the corner-stone some memento.

Before the building was completed we passed through some very trying seasons. More than once our hearts were made to bleed, as it were, because bills were falling due that we did not have the money to meet. Perhaps no one who has not gone through the experience, month after month, of trying to erect buildings and provide equipment for a school when no one knew where the money was to come from, can properly appreciate the difficulties under which we laboured. During the first years at Tuskegee I recall that night after night I would roll and toss on my bed, without sleep, because of the anxiety and uncertainty which we were in regarding money. I knew that, in a large degree, we were trying an experiment—that of testing whether or not it was possible for Negroes to build up and control the affairs of a large educational institution. I knew that if we failed it would injure the whole race. I knew that the presumption was against us. I knew that in the case of white people beginning such an enterprise it would be taken for granted that they were going to succeed, but in our case I felt that people would be surprised if we succeeded. All this made a burden which pressed down on us, sometimes, it seemed, at the rate of a thousand pounds to the square inch.

In all our difficulties and anxieties, however, I never went to a white or a black person in the town of Tuskegee for any assistance that was in their power to render, without being helped according to their means. More than a dozen times, when bills figuring up into the hundreds of dollars were falling due, I applied to the white men of Tuskegee for small loans, often borrowing small amounts from as many as a half-dozen persons, to meet our obligations. One thing I was determined to do from the first, and that was to keep the credit of the school high; and this, I think I can say without boasting, we have done all through these years.

I shall always remember a bit of advice given me by Mr. George W. Campbell, the white man to whom I have referred as the one who induced General Armstrong to send me to Tuskegee. Soon after I entered upon the work Mr. Campbell said to me, in his fatherly way: "Washington, always remember that credit is capital."

At one time when we were in the greatest distress for money that we ever experienced, I placed the situation frankly before General Armstrong. Without hesitation he gave me his personal check for all the money which he had saved for his own use. This was not the only time that General Armstrong helped Tuskegee in this way. I do not think I have ever made this fact public before.

During the summer of 1882, at the end of the first year's work of the school, I was married to Miss Fannie N. Smith, of Malden, W. Va. We began keeping house in Tuskegee early in the fall. This made a home for our teachers, who now had been increased to four in number. My wife was also a graduate of the Hampton Institute. After earnest and constant work in the interests of the school, together with her housekeeping duties, my wife passed away in May, 1884. One child, Portia M. Washington, was born during our marriage.

From the first, my wife most earnestly devoted her thoughts and time to the work of the school, and was completely one with me in every interest and ambition. She passed away, however, before she had an opportunity of seeing what the school was designed to be.

Chapter X

A Harder Task than making Bricks without Straw

From the very beginning, at Tuskegee, I was determined to have the students do not only the agricultural and domestic work, but to have them erect their own buildings. My plan was to have them, while performing this service, taught the latest and best methods of labour, so that the school would not only get the benefit of their efforts, but the students themselves would be taught to see not only utility in labour, but beauty and dignity; would be taught, in fact, how to lift labour up from mere drudgery and toil, and would learn to love work for its own sake. My plan was not to teach them to work in the old way, but to show them how to make the forces of nature—air, water, steam, electricity, horse-power—assist them in their labour.

At first many advised against the experiment of having the buildings erected by the labour of the students, but I was determined to stick to it. I told those who doubted the wisdom of the plan that I knew that our first buildings would not be so comfortable or so complete in their finish as buildings erected by the experienced hands of outside workmen, but that in the teaching of civilization, self-help, and self-reliance, the erection of the buildings by the students themselves would more than compensate for any lack of comfort or fine finish.

I further told those who doubted the wisdom of this plan, that the majority of our students came to us in poverty, from the cabins of the cotton, sugar, and rice plantations of the South, and that while I knew it would please the students very much to place them at once in finely constructed buildings, I felt that it would be following out a more natural process of development to teach them how to construct their own buildings. Mistakes I knew would be made, but these mistakes would teach us valuable lessons for the future.

During the now nineteen years' existence of the Tuskegee school, the plan of having the buildings erected by student labour has been adhered to. In this time forty buildings, counting small and large, have been built, and all except four are almost wholly the product of student labour. As an additional result, hundreds of men are now scattered throughout the South who received their knowledge of mechanics while being taught how to erect these buildings. Skill and knowledge are now handed down from one set of students to another in this way, until at the present time a building of any description or size can be constructed wholly by our instructors and students, from the drawing of the plans to the putting in of the electric fixtures, without going off the grounds for a single workman.

Not a few times, when a new student has been led into the temptation of marring the looks of some building by leadpencil marks or by the cuts of a jack-knife, I have heard an old student remind him: "Don't do that. That is our building. I helped put it up."

In the early days of the school I think my most trying experience was in the matter of brickmaking. As soon as we got the farm work reasonably well started, we directed our next efforts toward the industry of making bricks. We needed these for use in connection with the erection of our own buildings; but there was also another reason for establishing this industry. There was no brickyard in the town, and in addition to our own needs there was a demand for bricks in the general market.

I had always sympathized with the "Children of Israel," in their task of "making bricks without straw,"[1] but ours was the task of making bricks with no money and no experience.

In the first place, the work was hard and dirty, and it was difficult to get the students to help. When it came to brickmaking, their distaste for manual labour in connection with book education became especially manifest. It was not a pleasant task for one to stand in the mud-pit for hours, with the mud up to his knees. More than one man became disgusted and left the school.

We tried several locations before we opened up a pit that furnished brick clay. I had always supposed that brickmaking was very simple, but I soon found out by bitter experience that it required special skill and knowledge, particularly in the burning of the bricks. After a good deal of effort we moulded about twenty-five thousand bricks, and put them into a kiln to be burned. This kiln turned out to be a failure, because it was not properly constructed or properly burned. We began at once, however, on a second kiln. This, for some reason, also proved a failure. The failure of this kiln made it still more difficult to get the students to take any part in the work. Several of the teachers, however, who had been trained in the industries at Hampton, volunteered their services, and in some way we succeeded in getting a third kiln ready for burning. The burning of a kiln required about a week. Toward the latter part of the week, when it seemed as if we were going to have a good many

1. See Exodus 5.4–19.

thousand bricks in a few hours, in the middle of the night the kiln fell. For the third time we had failed.

The failure of this last kiln left me without a single dollar with which to make another experiment. Most of the teachers advised the abandoning of the effort to make bricks. In the midst of my troubles I thought of a watch which had come into my possession years before. I took this watch to the city of Montgomery, which was not far distant, and placed it in a pawn-shop. I secured cash upon it to the amount of fifteen dollars, with which to renew the brickmaking experiment. I returned to Tuskegee, and, with the help of the fifteen dollars, rallied our rather demoralized and discouraged forces and began a fourth attempt to make bricks. This time, I am glad to say, we were successful. Before I got hold of any money, the time-limit on my watch had expired, and I have never seen it since; but I have never regretted the loss of it.

Brickmaking has now become such an important industry at the school that last season our students manufactured twelve hundred thousand of first-class bricks, of a quality suitable to be sold in any market. Aside from this, scores of young men have mastered the brickmaking trade—both the making of bricks by hand and by machinery—and are now engaged in this industry in many parts of the South.

The making of these bricks taught me an important lesson in regard to the relations of the two races in the South. Many white people who had had no contact with the school, and perhaps no sympathy with it, came to us to buy bricks because they found out that ours were good bricks. They discovered that we were supplying a real want in the community. The making of these bricks caused many of the white residents of the neighbourhood to begin to feel that the education of the Negro was not making him worthless, but that in educating our students we were adding something to the wealth and comfort of the community. As the people of the neighbourhood came to us to buy bricks, we got acquainted with them; they traded with us and we with them. Our business interests became intermingled. We had something which they wanted; they had something which we wanted. This, in a large measure, helped to lay the foundation for the pleasant relations that have continued to exist between us and the white people in that section, and which now extend throughout the South.

Wherever one of our brickmakers has gone in the South, we find that he has something to contribute to the well-being of the community into which he has gone; something that has made the community feel that, in a degree, it is indebted to him, and perhaps, to a certain extent, dependent upon him. In this way pleasant relations between the races have been stimulated.

My experience is that there is something in human nature which always makes an individual recognize and reward merit, no matter under what colour of skin merit is found. I have found, too, that it is the visible, the tangible, that goes a long ways in softening prejudices. The actual sight of a first-class house that a Negro has built is ten times more potent than pages of discussion about a house that he ought to build, or perhaps could build.

The same principle of industrial education has been carried out in the building of our own wagons, carts, and buggies, from the first. We now own and use on our farm and about the school dozens of these vehicles, and every one of them has been built by the hands of the students. Aside from this, we help supply the local market with these vehicles. The supplying of them to the people in the community has had the same effect as the supplying of bricks, and the man who learns at Tuskegee to build and repair wagons and carts is regarded as a benefactor by both races in the community where he goes. The people with whom he lives and works are going to think twice before they part with such a man.

The individual who can do something that the world wants done will, in the end, make his way regardless of his race. One man may go into a community prepared to supply the people there with an analysis of Greek sentences. The community may not at that time be prepared for, or feel the need of, Greek analysis, but it may feel its need of bricks and houses and wagons. If the man can supply the need for those, then, it will lead eventually to a demand for the first product, and with the demand will come the ability to appreciate it and to profit by it.

About the time that we succeeded in burning our first kiln of bricks we began facing in an emphasized form the objection of the students to being taught to work. By this time it had gotten to be pretty well advertised throughout the state that every student who came to Tuskegee, no matter what his financial ability might be, must learn some industry. Quite a number of letters came from parents protesting against their children engaging in labour while they were in the school. Other parents came to the school to protest in person. Most of the new students brought a written or a verbal request from their parents to the effect that they wanted their children taught nothing but books. The more books, the larger they were, and the longer the titles printed upon them, the better pleased the students and their parents seemed to be.

I gave little heed to these protests, except that I lost no opportunity to go into as many parts of the state as I could, for the purpose of speaking to the parents, and showing them the value of industrial education. Besides, I talked to the students constantly on the subject. Notwithstanding the unpopularity of industrial work, the school continued to increase in numbers to such an extent that by the middle of the second year there was an attendance of about one hundred and fifty, representing almost all parts of the state of Alabama, and including a few from other states.

In the summer of 1882 Miss Davidson and I both went North and engaged in the work of raising funds for the completion of our new building. On my way North I stopped in New York to try to get a letter of recommendation from an officer of a missionary organization who had become somewhat acquainted with me a few years previous. This man not only refused to give me the letter, but advised me most earnestly to go back home at once, and not make an attempt to get money, for he was quite sure that I would never get more than enough to pay my travelling expenses. I thanked him for his advice, and proceeded on my journey.

The first place I went to in the North, was Northampton, Mass., where I spent nearly a half-day in looking for a coloured family with whom I could board, never dreaming that any hotel would admit me. I was greatly surprised when I found that I would have no trouble in being accommodated at a hotel.

We were successful in getting money enough so that on Thanksgiving Day of that year we held our first service in the chapel of Porter Hall, although the building was not completed.

In looking about for some one to preach the Thanksgiving sermon, I found one of the rarest men that it has ever been my privilege to know. This was the Rev. Robert C. Bedford, a white man from Wisconsin, who was then pastor of a little coloured Congregational church in Montgomery, Ala. Before going to Montgomery to look for some one to preach this sermon I had never heard of Mr. Bedford. He had never heard of me. He gladly consented to come to Tuskegee and hold the Thanksgiving service. It was the first service of the kind that the coloured people there had ever observed, and what a deep interest they manifested in it! The sight of the new building made it a day of Thanksgiving for them never to be forgotten.

Mr. Bedford consented to become one of the trustees of the school, and in that capacity, and as a worker for it, he has been connected with it for eighteen years. During this time he has borne the school upon his heart night and day, and is never so happy as when he is performing some service, no matter how humble, for it. He completely obliterates himself in everything, and looks only for permission to serve where service is most disagreeable, and where others would not be attracted. In all my relations with him he has seemed to me to approach as nearly to the spirit of the Master as almost any man I ever met.

A little later there came into the service of the school another man, quite young at the time, and fresh from Hampton, without whose service the school never could have become what it is. This was Mr. Warren Logan, who now for seventeen years has been the treasurer of the Institute, and the acting principal during my absence. He has always shown a degree of unselfishness and an amount of business tact, coupled with a clear judgment, that has kept the school in good condition no matter how long I have been absent from it. During all the financial stress through which the school has passed, his patience and faith in our ultimate success have not left him.

As soon as our first building was near enough to completion so that we could occupy a portion of it—which was near the middle of the second year of the school—we opened a boarding department. Students had begun coming from quite a distance, and in such increasing numbers that we felt more and more that we were merely skimming over the surface, in that we were not getting hold of the students in their home life.

We had nothing but the students and their appetites with which to begin a boarding department. No provision had been made in the new building for a kitchen and dining room; but we discovered that by digging out a large amount of earth from under the building we could make a partially lighted basement room that could be used for a kitchen and dining room. Again I called on the students to volunteer for work, this time to assist in digging out the basement. This they did, and in a few weeks we had a place to cook and eat in, although it was very rough and uncomfortable. Any one seeing the place now would never believe that it was once used for a dining room.

The most serious problem, though, was to get the boarding department started off in running order, with nothing to do with in the way of furniture, and with no money with which to buy anything. The merchants in the town would let us have what food we wanted on credit. In fact, in those earlier years I was constantly embarrassed because people seemed to have more faith in me than I had in myself. It was pretty hard to cook, however, without stoves, and awkward to eat without dishes. At first the cooking was done out-of-doors, in the old-fashioned, primitive style, in pots and skillets placed over a fire. Some of the carpenters' benches that had been used in the construction of the building were utilized for tables. As for dishes, there were too few to make it worth while to spend time in describing them.

No one connected with the boarding department seemed to have any idea that meals must be served at certain fixed and regular hours, and this was a source of great worry. Everything was so out of joint and so inconvenient that I feel safe in saying that for the first two weeks something was wrong at every meal. Either the meat was not done or had been burnt, or the salt had been left out of the bread, or the tea had been forgotten.

Early one morning I was standing near the dining-room door listening to the complaints of the students. The complaints that morning were especially emphatic and numerous, because the whole breakfast had been a failure. One of the girls who had failed to get any breakfast came out and went to the well to draw some water to drink to take the place of the breakfast which she had not been able to get. When she reached the well, she found that the rope was broken and that she could get no water. She turned from the well and said, in the most discouraged tone, not knowing that I was where I could hear her, "We can't even get water to drink at this school." I think no one remark ever came so near discouraging me as that one.

At another time, when Mr. Bedford—whom I have already spoken of as one of our trustees, and a devoted friend of the institution—was visiting the school, he was given a bedroom immediately over the dining room. Early in the morning he was awakened by a rather animated discussion between two boys in the dining room below. The discussion was over the question as to whose turn it was to use the coffee-cup that morning. One boy won the case by proving that for three mornings he had not had an opportunity to use the cup at all.

But gradually, by patience and hard work, we brought order out of chaos, just as will be true of any problem if we stick to it with patience and wisdom and earnest effort.

As I look back now over that part of our struggle, I am glad that we had it. I am glad that we endured all those discomforts and inconveniences. I am glad that our students had to dig out the place for their kitchen and dining room. I am glad that our first boarding-place was in that dismal, ill-lighted, and damp basement. Had we started in a fine, attractive, convenient room, I fear we would have "lost our heads" and become "stuck up." It means a great deal, I think, to start off on a foundation which one has made for one's self.

When our old students return to Tuskegee now, as they often do, and go into our large, beautiful, well-ventilated, and well-lighted dining room, and see tempting, well cooked food—largely grown by the students themselves—and see tables, neat tablecloths and napkins, and vases of flowers upon the tables, and hear singing birds, and note that each meal is served exactly upon the minute, with no disorder, and with almost no complaint coming from the hundreds that now fill our dining room, they, too, often say to me that they are glad that we started as we did, and built ourselves up year by year, by a slow and natural process of growth.

Chapter XI

Making their Beds before they could lie on them

A little later in the history of the school we had a visit from General J. F. B. Marshall, the Treasurer of the Hampton Institute, who had had faith enough to lend us the first two hundred and fifty dollars with which to make a payment down on the farm. He remained with us a week, and made a careful inspection of everything. He seemed well pleased with our progress, and wrote back interesting and encouraging reports to Hampton. A little later Miss Mary F. Mackie, the teacher who had given me the "sweeping" examination when I entered Hampton, came to see us, and still later General Armstrong himself came.

At the time of the visits of these Hampton friends the number of teachers at Tuskegee had increased considerably, and the most of the new teachers were graduates of the Hampton Institute. We gave our Hampton friends, especially General Armstrong, a cordial welcome. They were all surprised and pleased at the rapid progress that the school had made within so short a time. The coloured people from miles around came to the school to get a look at General Armstrong, about whom they had heard so much. The General was not only welcomed by the members of my own race, but by the Southern white people as well.

This first visit which General Armstrong made to Tuskegee gave me an opportunity to get an insight into his character such as I had not before had. I refer to his interest in the Southern white people. Before this I had had the thought that General Armstrong, having fought the Southern white man, rather cherished a feeling of bitterness toward the white South, and was interested in helping only the coloured man there. But this visit convinced me that I did not know the greatness and the generosity of the man. I soon learned, by his visits to the Southern white people, and from his conversations with them, that he was as anxious about the prosperity and the happiness of the white race as the black. He cherished no bitterness against the South, and was happy when an opportunity offered for manifesting his sympathy. In all my acquaintance with General Armstrong I never heard him speak, in public or in private, a single bitter word against the white man in the South. From his example in this respect I learned the lesson that great men cultivate love, and that only little men cherish a spirit of hatred. I learned that assistance given to the weak makes the one who gives it strong; and that oppression of the unfortunate makes one weak.

It is now long ago that I learned this lesson from General Armstrong, and resolved that I would permit no man, no matter what his colour might be, to narrow and degrade my soul by making me hate him. With God's help, I believe that I have completely rid myself of any ill feeling toward the Southern white man for any wrong that he may have inflicted upon my race. I am made to feel just as happy now when I am rendering service to Southern white men as when the service is rendered to a member of my own race. I pity from the bottom of my heart any individual who is so unfortunate as to get into the habit of holding race prejudice.

The more I consider the subject, the more strongly I am convinced that the most harmful effect of the practice to which the people in certain sections of the South have felt themselves compelled to resort, in order to get rid of the force of the Negroes' ballot, is not wholly in the wrong done to the Negro, but in the permanent injury to the morals of the white man. The wrong to the Negro is temporary, but to the morals of the white man the injury is permanent. I have noted time and time again that when an individual perjures himself in order to break the force of the black man's ballot, he soon learns to practise dishonesty in other relations of life, not only where the Negro is concerned, but equally so where a white man is concerned. The white man who begins by cheating a Negro usually ends by cheating a white man. The white man who begins to break the law by lynching a Negro soon yields to the temptation to lynch a white man. All this, it seems to me, makes it important that the whole Nation lend a hand in trying to lift the burden of ignorance from the South.

Another thing that is becoming more apparent each year in the development of education in the South is the influence of General Armstrong's idea of education; and this not upon the blacks alone, but upon the whites also. At the present time there is almost no Southern state that is not putting forth efforts in the direction of securing industrial education for its white boys and girls, and in most cases it is easy to trace the history of these efforts back to General Armstrong.

Soon after the opening of our humble boarding department students began coming to us in still larger numbers. For weeks we not only had to contend with the difficulty of providing board, with no money, but also with that of providing sleeping accommodations. For this purpose we rented a number of cabins near the school. These cabins were in a dilapidated condition, and during the winter months the students who occupied them necessarily suffered from the cold. We charged the students eight dollars a month—all they were able to pay—for their board. This included, besides board, room, fuel, and washing. We also gave the students credit on their board bills for all the work which they did for the school which was of any value to the institution. The cost of tuition, which was fifty dollars a year for each student, we had to secure then, as now, wherever we could.

This small charge in cash gave us no capital with which to start a boarding department. The weather during the second winter of our work was very cold. We were not able to provide enough bed-clothes to keep the students warm. In fact, for some time we were not able to provide, except in a few cases, bedsteads and mattresses of any kind. During the coldest nights I was so troubled about the discomfort of the students that I could not sleep myself. I recall that on several occasions I went in the middle of the night to the shanties occupied by the young men, for the purpose of comforting them. Often I found some of them sitting huddled around a fire, with the one blanket which we had been able to provide wrapped around them, trying in this way to keep warm. During the whole night some of them did not attempt to lie down. One morning, when the night previous had been unusually cold, I asked those of the students in the chapel who thought that they had been frostbitten during the night to raise their hands. Three hands went up. Notwithstanding these experiences, there was almost no complaining on the part of the students. They knew that we were doing the best that we could for them. They were happy in the privilege of being permitted to enjoy any kind of opportunity that would enable them to improve their condition. They were constantly asking what they might do to lighten the burdens of the teachers.

I have heard it stated more than once, both in the North and in the South, that coloured people would not obey and respect each other when one member of the race is placed in a position of authority over others. In regard to this general belief and these statements, I can say that during the nineteen years of my experience at Tuskegee I never, either by word or act, have been treated with disrespect by any student or officer connected with the institution. On the other hand, I am constantly embarrassed by the many acts of thoughtful kindness. The students do not seem to want to see me carry a large book or a satchel or any kind of a burden through the grounds. In such cases more than one always offers to relieve me. I almost never go out of my office when the rain is falling that some student does not come to my side with an umbrella and ask to be allowed to hold it over me.

While writing upon this subject, it is a pleasure for me to add that in all my contact with the white people of the South I have never received a single personal insult. The white people in and near Tuskegee, to an especial degree, seem to count it a privilege to show me all the respect within their power, and often go out of their way to do this.

Not very long ago I was making a journey between Dallas (Texas) and Houston. In some way it became known in advance that I was on the train. At nearly every station at which the train stopped, numbers of white people, including in most cases the officials of the town, came aboard and introduced themselves and thanked me heartily for the work that I was trying to do for the South.

On another occasion, when I was making a trip from Augusta, Georgia, to Atlanta, being rather tired from much travel, I rode in a Pullman sleeper. When I went into the car, I found there two ladies from Boston whom I knew well. These good ladies were perfectly ignorant, it seems, of the customs of the South, and in the goodness of their hearts insisted that I take a seat with them in their section. After some hesitation I consented. I had been there but a few minutes when one of them, without my knowledge, ordered supper to be served to the three of us. This embarrassed me still further. The car was full of Southern white men, most of whom had their eyes on our party. When I found that supper had been ordered, I tried to contrive some excuse that would permit me to leave the section, but the ladies insisted that I must eat with them. I finally settled back in my seat with a sigh, and said to myself, "I am in for it now, sure."

To add further to the embarrassment of the situation, soon after the supper was placed on the table one of the ladies remembered that she had in her satchel a special kind of tea which she wished served, and as she said she felt quite sure the porter did not know how to brew it properly, she insisted upon getting up and preparing and serving it herself. At last the meal was over; and it seemed the longest one that I had ever eaten. When we were through, I decided to get myself out of the embarrassing situation and go into the smoking-room, where most of the men were by that time, to see how the land lay. In the meantime, however, it had become known in some way throughout the car who I was. When I went into the smoking-room I was never more surprised in my life than when each man, nearly every one of them a citizen of Georgia, came up and introduced himself to me and thanked me earnestly for the work that I was trying to do for the whole South. This was not flattery, because each one of these individuals knew that he had nothing to gain by trying to flatter me.

From the first I have sought to impress the students with the idea that Tuskegee is not my institution, or that of the officers, but that it is their institution, and that they have as much interest in it as any of the trustees or instructors. I have further sought to have them feel that I am at the institution as their friend and adviser, and not as their overseer. It has been my aim to have them speak with directness and frankness about anything that concerns the life of the school. Two or three times a year I ask the students to write me a letter criticising or making complaints or suggestions about anything connected with the institution. When this is not done, I have them meet me in the chapel for a heart-to-heart talk about the conduct of the school. There are no meetings with our students that I enjoy more than these, and none are more helpful to me in planning for the future. These meetings, it seems to me, enable me to get at the very heart of all that concerns the school. Few things help an individual more than to place responsibility upon him, and to let him know that you trust him. When I have read of labour troubles between employers and employees, I have often thought that many strikes and similar disturbances might be avoided if the employers would cultivate the habit of getting nearer to their employees, of consulting and advising with them, and letting them feel that the interests of the two are the same. Every individual responds to confidence, and this is not more true of any race than of the Negroes. Let them once understand that you are unselfishly interested in them, and you can lead them to any extent.

It was my aim from the first at Tuskegee to not only have the buildings erected by the students themselves, but to have them make their own furniture as far as was possible. I now marvel at the patience of the students while sleeping upon the floor while waiting for some kind of a bedstead to be constructed, or at their sleeping without any kind of a mattress while waiting for something that looked like a mattress to be made.

In the early days we had very few students who had been used to handling carpenters' tools, and the bedsteads made by the students then were very rough and very weak. Not unfrequently when I went into the students' rooms in the morning I would find at least two bedsteads lying about on the floor. The problem of providing mattresses was a difficult one to solve. We finally mastered this, however, by getting some cheap cloth and sewing pieces of this together so as to make large bags. These bags we filled with the pine straw—or, as it is sometimes called, pine needles—which we secured from the forests near by. I am glad to say that the industry of mattress-making has grown steadily since then, and has been improved to such an extent that at the present time it is an important branch of the work which is taught systematically to a number of our girls, and that the mattresses that now come out of the mattress-shop at Tuskegee are about as good as those bought in the average store. For some time after the opening of the boarding department we had no chairs in the students' bedrooms or in the dining rooms. Instead of chairs we used stools which the students constructed by nailing together three pieces of rough board. As a rule, the furniture in the students' rooms during the early days of the school consisted of a bed, some stools, and sometimes a rough table made by the students. The plan of having the students make the furniture is still followed, but the number of pieces in a room has been increased, and the workmanship has so improved that little fault can be found with the articles now. One thing that I have always insisted upon at Tuskegee is that everywhere there should be absolute cleanliness. Over and over again the students were reminded in those first years—and are reminded now—that people would excuse us for our poverty, for our lack of comforts and conveniences, but that they would not excuse us for dirt.

Another thing that has been insisted upon at the school is the use of the tooth-brush. "The gospel of the tooth-brush," as General Armstrong used to call it, is a part of our creed at Tuskegee. No student is permitted to remain who does not keep and use a tooth-brush. Several times, in recent years, students have come to us who brought with them almost no other article except a tooth-brush. They had heard from the lips of older students about our insisting upon the use of this, and so, to make a good impression, they brought at least a tooth-brush with them. I remember that one morning, not long ago, I went with the lady principal on her usual morning tour of inspection of the girls' rooms. We found one room that contained three girls who had recently arrived at the school. When I asked them if they had tooth-brushes, one of the girls replied, pointing to a brush: "Yes, sir. That is our brush. We bought it together, yesterday." It did not take them long to learn a different lesson.

It has been interesting to note the effect that the use of the tooth-brush has had in bringing about a higher degree of civilization among the students. With few exceptions, I have noticed that, if we can get a student to the point where, when the first or second tooth-brush disappears, he of his own motion buys another, I have not been disappointed in the future of that individual. Absolute cleanliness of the body has been insisted upon from the first. The students have been taught to bathe as regularly as to take their meals. This lesson we began teaching before we had anything in the shape of a bath-house. Most of the students came from plantation districts, and often we had to teach them how to sleep at night; that is, whether between the two sheets—after we got to the point where we could provide them two sheets—or under both of them. Naturally I found it difficult to teach them to sleep between two sheets when we were able to supply but one. The importance of the use of the nightgown received the same attention.

For a long time one of the most difficult tasks was to teach the students that all the buttons were to be kept on their clothes, and that there must be no torn places and no grease-spots. This lesson, I am pleased to be able to say, has been so thoroughly learned and so faithfully handed down from year to year by one set of students to another that often at the present time, when the students march out of chapel in the evening and their dress is inspected, as it is every night, not one button is to be found missing.

Chapter XII

Raising Money

When we opened our boarding department, we provided rooms in the attic of Porter Hall, our first building, for a number of girls. But the number of students, of both sexes, continued to increase. We could find rooms outside the school grounds for many of the young men, but the girls we did not care to expose in this way. Very soon the problem of providing more rooms for the girls, as well as a larger boarding department for all the students, grew serious. As a result, we finally decided to undertake the construction of a still larger building—a building that would contain rooms for the girls and boarding accommodations for all.

After having had a preliminary sketch of the needed building made, we found that it would cost about ten thousand dollars. We had no money whatever with which to begin; still we decided to give the needed building a name. We knew we could name it, even though we were in doubt about our ability to secure the means for its construction. We decided to call the proposed building Alabama Hall, in honour of the state in which we were labouring. Again Miss Davidson began making efforts to enlist the interest and help of the coloured and white people in and near Tuskegee. They responded willingly, in proportion to their means. The students, as in the case of our first building, Porter Hall, began digging out the dirt in order to allow of the laying of the foundations.

When we seemed at the end of our resources, so far as securing money was concerned, something occurred which showed the greatness of General Armstrong—something which proved how far he was above the ordinary individual. When we were in the midst of great anxiety as to where and how we were to get funds for the new building, I received a telegram from General Armstrong asking me if I could spend a month travelling with him through the North, and asking me, if I could do so, to come to Hampton at once. Of course I accepted General Armstrong's invitation, and went to Hampton immediately. On arriving there I found that the General had decided to take a quartette of singers through the North, and hold meetings for a month in important cities, at which meetings he and I were to speak. Imagine my surprise when the General told me, further, that these meetings were to be held, not in the interests of Hampton, but in the interests of Tuskegee, and that the Hampton Institute was to be responsible for all the expenses.

Although he never told me so in so many words, I found out that General Armstrong took this method of introducing me to the people of the North, as well as for the sake of securing some immediate funds to be used in the erection of Alabama Hall. A weak and narrow man would have reasoned that all the money which came to Tuskegee in this way would be just so much taken from the Hampton Institute; but none of these selfish or short-sighted feelings ever entered the breast of General Armstrong. He was too big to be little, too good to be mean. He knew that the people in the North who gave money gave it for the purpose of helping the whole cause of Negro civilization, and not merely for the advancement of any one school. The General knew, too, that the way to strengthen Hampton was to make it a centre of unselfish power in the working out of the whole Southern problem.

In regard to the addresses which I was to make in the North, I recall just one piece of advice which the General gave me. He said: "Give them an idea for every word." I think it would be hard to improve upon this advice; and it might be made to apply to all public speaking. From that time to the present I have always tried to keep his advice in mind.

Meetings were held in New York, Brooklyn, Boston, Philadelphia, and other large cities, and at all of these meetings General Armstrong pleaded, together with myself, for help, not for Hampton, but for Tuskegee. At these meetings an especial effort was made to secure help for the building of Alabama Hall, as well as to introduce the school to the attention of the general public. In both these respects the meetings proved successful.

After that kindly introduction I began going North alone to secure funds. During the last fifteen years I have been compelled to spend a large proportion of my time away from the school, in an effort to secure money to provide for the growing needs of the institution. In my efforts to get funds I have had some experiences that may be of interest to my readers. Time and time again I have been asked, by people who are trying to secure money for philanthropic purposes, what rule or rules I followed to secure the interest and help of people who were able to contribute money to worthy objects. As far as the science of what is called begging can be reduced to rules, I would say that I have had but two rules. First, always to do my whole duty regarding making our work known to individuals and organizations; and, second, not to worry about the results. This second rule has been the hardest for me to live up to. When bills are on the eve of falling due, with not a dollar in hand with which to meet them, it is pretty difficult to learn not to worry, although I think I am learning more and more each year that all worry simply consumes, and to no purpose, just so much physical and mental strength that might otherwise be given to effective work. After considerable experience in coming into contact with wealthy and noted men, I have observed that those who have accomplished the greatest results are those who "keep under the body";[1] are those who never grow excited or lose self-control, but are always calm, self-possessed, patient, and polite. I think that President William McKinley[2] is the best example of a man of this class that I have ever seen.

In order to be successful in any kind of undertaking, I think the main thing is for one to grow to the point where he completely forgets himself; that is, to lose himself in a great cause. In proportion as one loses himself in this way, in the same degree does he get the highest happiness out of his work.

My experience in getting money for Tuskegee has taught me to have no patience with those people who are always condemning the rich because they are rich, and because they do not give more to objects of charity. In the first place, those who are guilty of such sweeping criticisms do not know how many people would be made poor, and how much suffering would result, if wealthy people were to part all at once with any large proportion of their wealth in a way to disorganize and cripple great business enterprises. Then very few persons have any idea of the large number of applications for help that rich people are constantly being flooded with. I know wealthy people who receive as many

1. See I Corinthians 9.27.
2. President of the United States from 1897 to 1901.

as twenty calls a day for help. More than once, when I have gone into the offices of rich men, I have found half a dozen persons waiting to see them, and all come for the same purpose, that of securing money. And all these calls in person, to say nothing of the applications received through the mails. Very few people have any idea of the amount of money given away by persons who never permit their names to be known. I have often heard persons condemned for not giving away money, who, to my own knowledge, were giving away thousands of dollars every year so quietly that the world knew nothing about it.

As an example of this, there are two ladies in New York, whose names rarely appear in print, but who, in a quiet way, have given us the means with which to erect three large and important buildings during the last eight years. Besides the gift of these buildings, they have made other generous donations to the school. And they not only help Tuskegee, but they are constantly seeking opportunities to help other worthy causes.

Although it has been my privilege to be the medium through which a good many hundred thousand dollars have been received for the work at Tuskegee, I have always avoided what the world calls "begging." I often tell people that I have never "begged" any money, and that I am not a "beggar." My experience and observation have convinced me that persistent asking outright for money from the rich does not, as a rule, secure help. I have usually proceeded on the principle that persons who possess sense enough to earn money have sense enough to know how to give it away, and that the mere making known of the facts regarding Tuskegee, and especially the facts regarding the work of the graduates, has been more effective than outright begging. I think that the presentation of facts, on a high, dignified plane, is all the begging that most rich people care for.

While the work of going from door to door and from office to office is hard, disagreeable, and costly in bodily strength, yet it has some compensations. Such work gives one a rare opportunity to study human nature. It also has its compensations in giving one an opportunity to meet some of the best people in the world—to be more correct, I think I should say *the best* people in the world. When one takes a broad survey of the country, he will find that the most useful and influential people in it are those who take the deepest interest in institutions that exist for the purpose of making the world better.

At one time, when I was in Boston, I called at the door of a rather wealthy lady, and was admitted to the vestibule and sent up my card. While I was waiting for an answer, her husband came in, and asked me in the most abrupt manner what I wanted. When I tried to explain the object of my call, he became still more ungentlemanly in his words and manner, and finally grew so excited that I left the house without waiting for a reply from the lady. A few blocks from that house I called to see a gentleman who received me in the most cordial manner. He wrote me his check for a generous sum, and then, before I had had an opportunity to thank him, said: "I am so grateful to you, Mr. Washington, for giving me the opportunity to help a good cause. It is a privilege to have a share in it. We in Boston are constantly indebted to you for doing *our* work." My experience in securing money convinces me that the first type of man is growing more rare all the time, and that the latter type is increasing; that is, that, more and more, rich people are coming to regard men and women who apply to them for help for worthy objects, not as beggars, but as agents for doing their work.

In the city of Boston I have rarely called upon an individual for funds that I have not been thanked for calling, usually before I could get an opportunity to thank the donor for the money. In that city the donors seem to feel, in a large degree, that an honour is being conferred upon them in their being permitted to give. Nowhere else have I met with, in so large a measure, this fine and Christlike spirit as in the city of Boston, although there are many notable instances of it outside that city. I repeat my belief that the world is growing in the direction of giving. I repeat that the main rule by which I have been guided in collecting money is to do my full duty in regard to giving people who have money an opportunity to help.

In the early years of the Tuskegee school I walked the streets or travelled country roads in the North for days and days without receiving a dollar. Often it has happened, when during the week I had been disappointed in not getting a cent from the very individuals from whom I most expected help, and when I was almost broken down and discouraged, that generous help has come from some one who I had had little idea would give at all.

I recall that on one occasion I obtained information that led me to believe that a gentleman who lived about two miles out in the country from Stamford, Conn., might become interested in our efforts at Tuskegee if our conditions and needs were presented to him. On an unusually cold and stormy day I walked the two miles to see him. After some difficulty I succeeded in securing an interview with him. He listened with some degree of interest to what I had to say, but did not give me anything. I could not help having the feeling that, in a measure, the three hours that I had spent in seeing him had been thrown away. Still, I had followed my usual rule of doing my duty. If I had not seen him, I should have felt unhappy over neglect of duty.

Two years after this visit a letter came to Tuskegee from this man, which read like this: "Enclosed I send you a New York draft for ten thousand dollars, to be used in furtherance of your work. I had placed this sum in my will for your school, but deem it wiser to give it to you while I live. I recall with pleasure your visit to me two years ago."

I can hardly imagine any occurrence which could have given me more genuine satisfaction than the receipt of this draft. It was by far the largest single donation which up to that time the school had ever received. It came at a time when an unusually long period had passed since we had received any money. We were in great distress because of lack of funds, and the nervous strain was tremendous. It is difficult for me to think of any situation that is more trying on the nerves than that of conducting a large institution, with heavy financial obligations to meet, without knowing where the money is to come from to meet these obligations from month to month.

In our case I felt a double responsibility, and this made the anxiety all the more intense. If the institution had been officered by white persons, and had failed, it would have injured the cause of Negro education; but I knew that the failure of our institution, officered by Negroes, would not only mean the loss of a school, but would cause people, in a large degree, to lose faith in the ability of the entire race. The receipt of this draft for ten thousand dollars, under all these circumstances, partially lifted a burden that had been pressing down upon me for days.

From the beginning of our work to the present I have always had the feeling, and lose no opportunity to impress our teachers with the same idea, that the school will always be supported in proportion as the inside of the institution is kept clean and pure and wholesome.

The first time I ever saw the late Collis P. Huntington, the great railroad man, he gave me two dollars for our school. The last time I saw him, which was a few months before he died, he gave me fifty thousand dollars toward our endowment fund. Between these two gifts there were others of generous proportions which came every year from both Mr. and Mrs. Huntington.

Some people may say that it was Tuskegee's good luck that brought to us this gift of fifty thousand dollars. No, it was not luck. It was hard work. Nothing ever comes to one, that is worth having, except as a result of hard work. When Mr. Huntington gave me the first two dollars, I did not blame him for not giving me more, but made up my mind that I was going to convince him by tangible results that we were worthy of larger gifts. For a dozen years I made a strong effort to convince Mr. Huntington of the value of our work. I noted that just in proportion as the usefulness of the school grew, his donations increased. Never did I meet an individual who took a more kindly and sympathetic interest in our school than did Mr. Huntington. He not only gave money to us, but took time in which to advise me, as a father would a son, about the general conduct of the school.

More than once I have found myself in some pretty tight places while collecting money in the North. The following incident I have never related but once before, for the reason that I feared that people would not believe it. One morning I found myself in Providence, Rhode Island, without a cent of money with which to buy breakfast. In crossing the street to see a lady from whom I hoped to get some money, I found a bright new twenty-five-cent piece in the middle of the streetcar track. I not only had this twenty-five cents for my breakfast, but within a few minutes I had a donation from the lady on whom I had started to call.

At one of our Commencements I was bold enough to invite the Rev. E. Winchester Donald, D. D., rector of Trinity Church, Boston, to preach the Commencement sermon. As we then had no room large enough to accommodate all who would be present, the place of meeting was under a large, improvised arbour, built partly of brush and partly of rough boards. Soon after Dr. Donald had begun speaking, the rain came down in torrents, and he had to stop, while some one held an umbrella over him.

The boldness of what I had done never dawned upon me until I saw the picture made by the rector of Trinity Church standing before that large audience under an old umbrella, waiting for the rain to cease so that he could go on with his address.

It was not very long before the rain ceased and Dr. Donald finished his sermon; and an excellent sermon it was, too, in spite of the weather. After he had gone to his room, and had gotten the wet threads of his clothes dry, Dr. Donald ventured the remark that a large chapel at Tuskegee would not be out of place. The next day a letter came from two ladies who were then travelling in Italy, saying that they had decided to give us the money for such a chapel as we needed.

A short time ago we received twenty thousand dollars from Mr. Andrew Carnegie,[3] to be used for the purpose of erecting a new library building. Our first library and reading-room were in a corner of a shanty, and the whole thing occupied a space about five by twelve feet. It required ten years of work before I was able to secure Mr. Carnegie's interest and help. The first time I saw him, ten years ago, he seemed to take but little interest in our school, but I was determined to show him that we were worthy of his help. After ten years of hard work I wrote him a letter reading as follows:

December 15, 1900.

MR. ANDREW CARNEGIE, 5 W. FIFTY-FIRST ST., NEW YORK.

DEAR SIR: Complying with the request which you made of me when I saw you at your residence a few days ago, I now submit in writing an appeal for a library building for our institution.

We have 1100 students, 86 officers and instructors, together with their families, and about 200 coloured people living near the school, all of whom would make use of the library building.

We have over 12,000 books, periodicals, etc., gifts from our friends, but we have no suitable place for them, and we have no suitable reading-room.

Our graduates go to work in every section of the South, and

3. Andrew Carnegie (1835–1919), millionaire industrialist and philanthropist.

whatever knowledge might be obtained in the library would serve to assist in the elevation of the whole Negro race.

Such a building as we need could be erected for about $20,000. All of the work for the building, such as brickmaking, brick-masonry, carpentry, blacksmithing, etc., would be done by the students. The money which you would give would not only supply the building, but the erection of the building would give a large number of students an opportunity to learn the building trades, and the students would use the money paid to them to keep themselves in school. I do not believe that a similar amount of money often could be made go so far in uplifting a whole race.

If you wish further information, I shall be glad to furnish it.

Yours truly,
BOOKER T. WASHINGTON, Principal.

The next mail brought back the following reply: "I will be very glad to pay the bills for the library building as they are incurred, to the extent of twenty thousand dollars, and I am glad of this opportunity to show the interest I have in your noble work."

I have found that strict business methods go a long way in securing the interest of rich people. It has been my constant aim at Tuskegee to carry out, in our financial and other operations, such business methods as would be approved of by any New York banking house.

I have spoken of several large gifts to the school; but by far the greater proportion of the money that has built up the institution has come in the form of small donations from persons of moderate means. It is upon these small gifts, which carry with them the interest of hundreds of donors, that any philanthropic work must depend largely for its support. In my efforts to get money I have often been surprised at the patience and deep interest of the ministers, who are besieged on every hand and at all hours of the day for help. If no other consideration had convinced me of the value of the Christian life, the Christlike work which the Church of all denominations in America has done during the last thirty-five years for the elevation of the black man would have made me a Christian. In a large degree it has been the pennies, the nickels, and the dimes which have come from the Sunday-schools, the Christian Endeavour societies, and the missionary societies, as well as from the church proper, that have helped to elevate the Negro at so rapid a rate.

This speaking of small gifts reminds me to say that very few Tuskegee graduates fail to send us an annual contribution. These contributions range from twenty-five cents up to ten dollars.

Soon after beginning our third year's work we were surprised to receive money from three special sources, and up to the present time we have continued to receive help from them. First, the State Legislature of Alabama increased its annual appropriation from two thousand dollars to three thousand dollars; I might add that still later it increased this sum to four thousand five hundred dollars a year. The effort to secure this increase was led by the Hon. M. F. Foster, the member of the Legislature from Tuskegee. Second, we received one thousand dollars from the John F. Slater Fund. Our work seemed to please the trustees of this fund, as they soon began increasing their annual grant. This has been added to from time to time until at present we receive eleven thousand dollars annually from this Fund. The other help to which I have referred came in the shape of an allowance from the Peabody Fund. This was at first five hundred dollars, but it has since been increased to fifteen hundred dollars.

The effort to secure help from the Slater and Peabody Funds brought me into contact with two rare men—men who have had much to do in shaping the policy for the education of the Negro. I refer to the Hon. J. L. M. Curry, of Washington, who is the general agent for these two funds, and Mr. Morris K. Jesup, of New York. Dr. Curry is a native of the South, an ex-Confederate soldier, yet I do not believe there is any man in the country who is more deeply interested in the highest welfare of the Negro than Dr. Curry, or one who is more free from race prejudice. He enjoys the unique distinction of possessing to an equal degree the confidence of the black man and the Southern white man. I shall never forget the first time I met him. It was in Richmond, Va., where he was then living. I had heard much about him. When I first went into his presence, trembling because of my youth and inexperience, he took me by the hand so cordially, and spoke such encouraging words, and gave me such helpful advice regarding the proper course to pursue, that I came to know him then, as I have known him ever since, as a high example of one who is constantly and unselfishly at work for the betterment of humanity.

Mr. Morris K. Jesup, the treasurer of the Slater Fund, I refer to because I know of no man of wealth and large and complicated business responsibilities who gives not only money but his time and thought to the subject of the proper method of elevating the Negro to the extent that is true of Mr. Jesup. It is very largely through his effort and influence that during the last few years the subject of industrial education has assumed the importance that it has, and been placed on its present footing.

Chapter XIII

Two Thousand Miles for a Five-Minute Speech

Soon after the opening of our boarding department, quite a number of students who evidently were worthy, but who were so poor that they did not have any money to pay even the small charges at the school, began applying for admission. This class was composed of both men and women. It was a great trial to refuse admission to these applicants, and in 1884 we established a night-school to accommodate a few of them.

The night-school was organized on a plan similar to the one which I had helped to establish at Hampton. At first it was composed of about a dozen students. They were admitted to the night-school only when they had no money with which to pay any part of their board in the regular day-school. It was further required that they must work for ten hours during the day at some trade or industry, and study academic branches for two hours during the evening. This was the requirement for the first one or two years of their stay. They were to be paid something above the cost of their board, with the understanding that all of their earnings, except a very small part, were to be reserved in the school's treasury, to be used for paying their board in the regular day-school after they had entered that department. The night-school, started in this manner, has grown until there are at present four hundred and fifty-seven students enrolled in it alone.

There could hardly be a more severe test of a student's worth than this branch of the Institute's work. It is largely because it furnishes such a good opportunity to test the backbone of a student that I place such high value upon our night-school. Any one who is willing to work ten hours a day at the brick-yard, or in the laundry, through one or two years, in order that he or she may have the privilege of studying academic branches for two hours in the evening, has enough bottom to warrant being further educated.

After the student has left the night-school he enters the day-school, where he takes academic branches four days in a week, and works at his trade two days. Besides this he usually works at his trade during the three summer months. As a rule, after a student has succeeded in going through the night-school test, he finds a way to finish the regular course in industrial and academic training. No student, no matter how much money he may be able to command, is permitted to go through school without doing manual labour. In fact, the industrial work is now as popular as the academic branches. Some of the most successful men and women who have graduated from the institution obtained their start in the night-school.

While a great deal of stress is laid upon the industrial side of the work at Tuskegee, we do not neglect or overlook in any degree the religious and spiritual side. The school is strictly undenominational, but it is thoroughly Christian, and the spiritual training of the students is not neglected. Our preaching service, prayer-meetings, Sunday-school, Christian Endeavour Society, Young Men's Christian Association, and various missionary organizations, testify to this.

In 1885, Miss Olivia Davidson, to whom I have already referred as being largely responsible for the success of the school during its early history, and I were married. During our married life she continued to divide her time and strength between our home and the work for the school. She not only continued to work in the school at Tuskegee, but also kept up her habit of going North to secure funds. In 1889 she died, after four years of happy married life and eight years of hard and happy work for the school. She literally wore herself out in her never ceasing efforts in behalf of the work that she so dearly loved. During our married life there were born to us two bright, beautiful boys, Booker Taliaferro and Ernest Davidson. The older of these, Booker, has already mastered the brickmaker's trade at Tuskegee.

I have often been asked how I began the practice of public speaking. In answer I would say that I never planned to give any large part of my life to speaking in public. I have always had more of an ambition to *do* things than merely to talk *about* doing them. It seems that when I went North with General Armstrong to speak at the series of public meetings to which I have referred, the President of the National Educational Association, the Hon. Thomas W. Bicknell, was present at one of those meetings and heard me speak. A few days afterward he sent me an invitation to deliver an address at the next meeting of the Educational Association. This meeting was to be held in Madison, Wis. I accepted the invitation. This was, in a sense, the beginning of my public-speaking career.

On the evening that I spoke before the Association there must have been not far from four thousand persons present. Without my knowing it, there were a large number of people present from Alabama, and some from the town of Tuskegee. These white people afterward frankly told me that they went to this meeting expecting to hear the South roundly abused, but were pleasantly surprised to find that there was no word of abuse in my address. On the contrary, the South was given credit for all the praiseworthy things that it had done. A white lady who was teacher in a college in Tuskegee wrote back to the local paper that she was gratified, as well as surprised, to note the credit which I gave the white people of Tuskegee for their help in getting the school started. This address at Madison was the first that I had delivered that in any large measure dealt with the general problem of the races. Those who heard it seemed to be pleased with what I said and with the general position that I took.

When I first came to Tuskegee, I determined that I would make it my home, that I would take as much pride in the right actions of the people of the town as any white man could do, and that I would, at the same time, deplore the wrong-doing of the people as much as any white man. I determined never to say anything in a public address in the North that I would not be willing to say in the South. I early learned that it is a hard matter to convert an individual by abusing him, and that this is more often accomplished by giving credit for all the praiseworthy actions performed than by calling attention alone to all the evil done.

While pursuing this policy I have not failed, at the proper time and in the proper manner, to call attention, in no uncertain terms, to the wrongs which any part of the South has been guilty of. I have found that there is a large element in the South that is quick to respond to straightforward, honest criticism of any wrong policy. As a rule, the place to criticise the South, when criticism is necessary, is in the South—not in Boston. A Boston man who came to Alabama to criticise Boston would not effect so much good, I think, as one who had his word of criticism to say in Boston.

In this address at Madison I took the ground that the policy to be pursued with reference to the races was, by every honourable means, to bring them together and to encourage the cultivation of friendly relations, instead of doing that which would embitter. I further contended that, in relation to his vote, the Negro should more and more consider the interests of the community in which he lived, rather than seek alone to please some one who lived a thousand miles away from him and from his interests.

In this address I said that the whole future of the Negro rested largely upon the question as to whether or not he should make himself, through his skill, intelligence, and character, of such undeniable value to the community in which he lived that the community could not dispense with his presence. I said that any individual who learned to do something better than anybody else—learned to do a common thing in an uncommon manner—had solved his problem, regardless of the colour of his skin, and that in proportion as the Negro learned to produce what other people wanted and must have, in the same proportion would he be respected.

I spoke of an instance where one of our graduates had produced two hundred and sixty-six bushels of sweet potatoes from an acre of ground, in a community where the average production had been only forty-nine bushels to the acre. He had been able to do this by reason of his knowledge of the chemistry of the soil and by his knowledge of improved methods of agriculture. The white farmers in the neighborhood respected him, and came to him for ideas regarding the raising of sweet potatoes. These white farmers honoured and respected him because he, by his skill and knowledge, had added something to the wealth and the comfort of the community in which he lived. I explained that my theory of education for the Negro would not, for example, confine him for all time to farm life—to the production of the best and the most sweet potatoes—but that, if he succeeded in this line of industry, he could lay the foundations upon which his children and grandchildren could grow to higher and more important things in life.

Such, in brief, were some of the views I advocated in this first address dealing with the broad question of the relations of the two races, and since that time I have not found any reason for changing my views on any important point.

In my early life I used to cherish a feeling of ill will toward any one who spoke in bitter terms against the Negro, or who advocated measures that tended to oppress the black man or take from him opportunities for growth in the most complete manner. Now, whenever I hear any one advocating measures that are meant to curtail the development of another, I pity the individual who would do this. I know that the one who makes this mistake does so because of his own lack of opportunity for the highest kind of growth. I pity him because I know that he is trying to stop the progress of the world, and because I know that in time the development and the ceaseless advance of humanity will make him ashamed of his weak and narrow position. One might as well try to stop the progress of a mighty railroad train by throwing his body across the track, as to try to stop the growth of the world in the direction of giving mankind more intelligence, more culture, more skill, more liberty, and in the direction of extending more sympathy and more brotherly kindness.

The address which I delivered at Madison, before the National Educational Association, gave me a rather wide introduction in the North, and soon after that opportunities began offering themselves for me to address audiences there.

I was anxious, however, that the way might also be opened for me to speak directly to a representative Southern white audience. A partial opportunity of this kind, one that seemed to me might serve as an entering wedge, presented itself in 1893, when the international meeting of Christian Workers was held at Atlanta, Ga. When this invitation came to me, I had engagements in Boston that seemed to make it impossible for me to speak in Atlanta. Still, after looking over my list of dates and places carefully, I found that I could take a train from Boston that would get me into Atlanta about thirty minutes before my address was to be delivered, and that I could remain in that city about sixty minutes before taking another train for Boston. My invitation to speak in Atlanta stipulated that I was to confine my address to five minutes. The question, then, was whether or not I could put enough into a five-minute address to make it worth while for me to make such a trip.

I knew that the audience would be largely composed of the most influential class of white men and women, and that it would be a rare opportunity for me to let them know what we were trying to do at Tuskegee, as well as to speak to them about the relations of the races. So I decided to make the trip. I spoke for five minutes to an audience of two thousand people, composed mostly of Southern and Northern whites. What I said seemed to be received with favour and enthusiasm.

The Atlanta papers of the next day commented in friendly terms on my address, and a good deal was said about it in different parts of the country. I felt that I had in some degree accomplished my object—that of getting a hearing from the dominant class of the South.

The demands made upon me for public addresses continued to increase, coming in about equal numbers from my own people and from Northern whites. I gave as much time to these addresses as I could spare from the immediate work at Tuskegee. Most of the addresses in the North were made for the direct purpose of getting funds with which to support the school. Those delivered before the coloured people had for their main object the impressing upon them of the importance of industrial and technical education in addition to academic and religious training.

I now come to that one of the incidents in my life which seems to have excited the greatest amount of interest, and which perhaps went further than anything else in giving me a reputation that in a sense might be called National. I refer to the address which I delivered at the opening of the Atlanta Cotton states and International Exposition, at Atlanta, Ga., September 18, 1895.

So much has been said and written about this incident, and so many questions have been asked me concerning the address, that perhaps I may be excused for taking up the matter with some detail. The five-minute address in Atlanta, which I came from Boston to deliver, was possibly the prime cause for an opportunity being given me to make the second address there. In the spring of 1895 I received a telegram from prominent citizens in Atlanta asking me to accompany a committee from that city to Washington for the purpose of appearing before a committee of Congress in the interest of securing Government help for the Exposition. The committee was composed of about twenty-five of the most prominent and most influential white men of Georgia. All the members of this committee were white men except Bishop Grant, Bishop Gaines,[1] and myself. The Mayor and several other city and state officials spoke before the committee. They were followed by the two coloured bishops. My name was the last on the list of speakers. I had never before appeared before such a committee, nor had I ever delivered any address in the capital of the Nation. I had many misgivings as to what I ought to say, and as to the impression that my address would make. While I cannot recall in detail what I said, I remember that I tried to impress upon the committee, with all the earnestness and plainness of any language that I could command, that if Congress wanted to do something which would assist in ridding the South of the race question and making friends between the two races, it should, in every proper way, encourage the material and intellectual growth of both races. I said

1. Abraham L. Grant (1847–1911), bishop of the African Methodist Episcopal Church; Wesley John Gaines (1840–1912), bishop of the African Methodist Episcopal Church.

that the Atlanta Exposition would present an opportunity for both races to show what advance they had made since freedom, and would at the same time afford encouragement to them to make still greater progress.

I tried to emphasize the fact that while the Negro should not be deprived by unfair means of the franchise, political agitation alone would not save him, and that back of the ballot he must have property, industry, skill, economy, intelligence, and character, and that no race without these elements could permanently succeed. I said that in granting the appropriation Congress could do something that would prove to be of real and lasting value to both races, and that it was the first great opportunity of the kind that had been presented since the close of the Civil War.

I spoke for fifteen or twenty minutes, and was surprised at the close of my address to receive the hearty congratulations of the Georgia committee and of the members of Congress who were present. The Committee was unanimous in making a favourable report, and in a few days the bill passed Congress. With the passing of this bill the success of the Atlanta Exposition was assured.

Soon after this trip to Washington the directors of the Exposition decided that it would be a fitting recognition of the coloured race to erect a large and attractive building which should be devoted wholly to showing the progress of the Negro since freedom. It was further decided to have the building designed and erected wholly by Negro mechanics. This plan was carried out. In design, beauty, and general finish the Negro Building was equal to the others on the grounds.

After it was decided to have a separate Negro exhibit, the question arose as to who should take charge of it. The officials of the Exposition were anxious that I should assume this responsibility, but I declined to do so, on the plea that the work at Tuskegee at that time demanded my time and strength. Largely at my suggestion, Mr. I. Garland Penn,[2] of Lynchburg, Va., was selected to be at the head of the Negro department. I gave him all the aid that I could. The Negro exhibit, as a whole, was large and creditable. The two exhibits in this department which attracted the greatest amount of attention were those from the Hampton Institute and the Tuskegee Institute. The people who seemed to be the most surprised, as well as pleased, at what they saw in the Negro Building were the Southern white people.

As the day for the opening of the Exposition drew near, the Board of Directors began preparing the programme for the opening exercises. In the discussion from day to day of the various features of this programme, the question came up as to the advisability of putting a member of the Negro race on for one of the opening addresses, since the Negroes had been asked to take such a prominent part in the Exposition. It was

2. Irvine Garland Penn (1867–1930), teacher, journalist, and author of an early history of the African American press.

argued, further, that such recognition would mark the good feeling prevailing between the two races. Of course there were those who were opposed to any such recognition of the rights of the Negro, but the Board of Directors, composed of men who represented the best and most progressive element in the South, had their way, and voted to invite a black man to speak on the opening day. The next thing was to decide upon the person who was thus to represent the Negro race. After the question had been canvassed for several days, the directors voted unanimously to ask me to deliver one of the opening-day addresses, and in a few days after that I received the official invitation.

The receiving of this invitation brought to me a sense of responsibility that it would be hard for any one not placed in my position to appreciate. What were my feelings when this invitation came to me? I remembered that I had been a slave; that my early years had been spent in the lowest depths of poverty and ignorance, and that I had had little opportunity to prepare me for such a responsibility as this. It was only a few years before that time that any white man in the audience might have claimed me as his slave; and it was easily possible that some of my former owners might be present to hear me speak.

I knew, too, that this was the first time in the entire history of the Negro that a member of my race had been asked to speak from the same platform with white Southern men and women on any important National occasion. I was asked now to speak to an audience composed of the wealth and culture of the white South, the representatives of my former masters. I knew, too, that while the greater part of my audience would be composed of Southern people, yet there would be present a large number of Northern whites, as well as a great many men and women of my own race.

I was determined to say nothing that I did not feel from the bottom of my heart to be true and right. When the invitation came to me, there was not one word of intimation as to what I should say or as to what I should omit. In this I felt that the Board of Directors had paid a tribute to me. They knew that by one sentence I could have blasted, in a large degree, the success of the Exposition. I was also painfully conscious of the fact that, while I must be true to my own race in my utterances, I had it in my power to make such an ill-timed address as would result in preventing any similar invitation being extended to a black man again for years to come. I was equally determined to be true to the North, as well as to the best element of the white South, in what I had to say.

The papers, North and South, had taken up the discussion of my coming speech, and as the time for it drew near this discussion became more and more widespread. Not a few of the Southern white papers were unfriendly to the idea of my speaking. From my own race I received many suggestions as to what I ought to say. I prepared myself as best I could for the address, but as the eighteenth of September drew nearer, the heavier my heart became, and the more I feared that my effort would prove a failure and a disappointment.

The invitation had come at a time when I was very busy with my school work, as it was the beginning of our school year. After preparing my address, I went through it, as I usually do with all those utterances which I consider particularly important, with Mrs. Washington, and she approved of what I intended to say. On the sixteenth of September, the day before I was to start for Atlanta, so many of the Tuskegee teachers expressed a desire to hear my address that I consented to read it to them in a body. When I had done so, and had heard their criticisms and comments, I felt somewhat relieved, since they seemed to think well of what I had to say.

On the morning of September 17, together with Mrs. Washington and my three children, I started for Atlanta. I felt a good deal as I suppose a man feels when he is on his way to the gallows. In passing through the town of Tuskegee I met a white farmer who lived some distance out in the country. In a jesting manner this man said: "Washington, you have spoken before the Northern white people, the Negroes in the South, and to us country white people in the South; but in Atlanta, to-morrow, you will have before you the Northern whites, the Southern whites, and the Negroes all together. I am afraid that you have got yourself into a tight place." This farmer diagnosed the situation correctly, but his frank words did not add anything to my comfort.

In the course of the journey from Tuskegee to Atlanta both coloured and white people came to the train to point me out, and discussed with perfect freedom, in my hearing, what was going to take place the next day. We were met by a committee in Atlanta. Almost the first thing that I heard when I got off the train in that city was an expression something like this, from an old coloured man near by: "Dat's de man of my race what's gwine to make a speech at de Exposition to-morrow. I'se sho' gwine to hear him."

Atlanta was literally packed, at the time, with people from all parts of this country, and with representatives of foreign governments, as well as with military and civic organizations. The afternoon papers had forecasts of the next day's proceedings in flaring headlines. All this tended to add to my burden. I did not sleep much that night. The next morning, before day, I went carefully over what I intended to say. I also kneeled down and asked God's blessing upon my effort. Right here, perhaps, I ought to add that I make it a rule never to go before an audience, on any occasion, without asking the blessing of God upon what I want to say.

I always make it a rule to make especial preparation for each separate address. No two audiences are exactly alike. It is my aim to reach and talk to the heart of each individual audience, taking it into my confidence very much as I would a person. When I am speaking to an audience, I care little for how what I am saying is going to sound in the newspapers, or to another audience, or to an individual. At the time, the audience before me absorbs all my sympathy, thought, and energy.

Early in the morning a committee called to escort me to my place in the procession which was to march to the Exposition grounds. In this procession were prominent coloured citizens in carriages, as well as several Negro military organizations. I noted that the Exposition officials seemed to go out of their way to see that all of the coloured people in the procession were properly placed and properly treated. The procession was about three hours in reaching the Exposition grounds, and during all of this time the sun was shining down upon us disagreeably hot. When we reached the grounds, the heat, together with my nervous anxiety, made me feel as if I were about ready to collapse, and to feel that my address was not going to be a success. When I entered the audience-room, I found it packed with humanity from bottom to top, and there were thousands outside who could not get in.

The room was very large, and well suited to public speaking. When I entered the room, there were vigorous cheers from the coloured portion of the audience, and faint cheers from some of the white people. I had been told, while I had been in Atlanta, that while many white people were going to be present to hear me speak, simply out of curiosity, and that others who would be present would be in full sympathy with me, there was a still larger element of the audience which would consist of those who were going to be present for the purpose of hearing me make a fool of myself, or, at least, of hearing me say some foolish thing, so that they could say to the officials who had invited me to speak, "I told you so!"

One of the trustees of the Tuskegee Institute, as well as my personal friend, Mr. William H. Baldwin, Jr., was at the time General Manager of the Southern Railroad, and happened to be in Atlanta on that day. He was so nervous about the kind of reception that I would have, and the effect that my speech would produce, that he could not persuade himself to go into the building, but walked back and forth in the grounds outside until the opening exercises were over.

Chapter XIV

The Atlanta Exposition Address

The Atlanta Exposition, at which I had been asked to make an address as a representative of the Negro race, as stated in the last chapter, was opened with a short address from Governor Bullock. After other interesting exercises, including an invocation from Bishop Nelson, of Georgia, a dedicatory ode by Albert Howell, Jr., and addresses by the President of the Exposition and Mrs. Joseph Thompson, the President of the Woman's Board, Governor Bullock introduced me with the words, "We have with us to-day a representative of Negro enterprise and Negro civilization."

When I arose to speak, there was considerable cheering, especially from the coloured people. As I remember it now, the thing that was uppermost in my mind was the desire to say something that would cement the friendship of the races and bring about hearty coöperation between them. So far as my outward surroundings were concerned, the only thing that I recall distinctly now is that when I got up, I saw thousands of eyes looking intently into my face. The following is the address which I delivered:—

MR. PRESIDENT AND GENTLEMEN OF THE BOARD OF DIRECTORS AND CITIZENS.

One-third of the population of the South is of the Negro race. No enterprise seeking the material, civil, or moral welfare of this section can disregard this element of our population and reach the highest success. I but convey to you, Mr. President and Directors, the sentiment of the masses of my race when I say that in no way have the value and manhood of the American Negro been more fittingly and generously recognized than by the managers of this magnificent Exposition at every stage of its progress. It is a recognition that will do more to cement the friendship of the two races than any occurrence since the dawn of our freedom.

Not only this, but the opportunity here afforded will awaken among us a new era of industrial progress. Ignorant and inexperienced, it is not strange that in the first years of our new life we began at the top instead of at the bottom; that a seat in Congress or the state legislature was more sought than real estate or industrial skill; that the political convention or stump speaking had more attractions than starting a dairy farm or truck garden.

A ship lost at sea for many days suddenly sighted a friendly vessel. From the mast of the unfortunate vessel was seen a signal, "Water, water; we die of thirst!" The answer from the friendly vessel at once came back, "Cast down your bucket where you are." A second time the signal, "Water, water; send us water!" ran up from the distressed vessel, and was answered, "Cast down your bucket where you are." And a third and fourth signal for water was answered, "Cast down your bucket where you are." The captain of the distressed vessel, at last heeding the injunction, cast down his bucket, and it came up full of fresh, sparkling water from the mouth of the Amazon River. To those of my race who depend on bettering their condition in a foreign land or who underestimate the importance of cultivating friendly relations with the Southern white man, who is their next-door neighbour, I would say: "Cast down your bucket where you are"—cast it down in making friends in every manly way of the people of all races by whom we are surrounded.

Cast it down in agriculture, mechanics, in commerce, in domestic service, and in the professions. And in this connection it is well to bear in mind that whatever other sins the South may be called to bear, when it comes to business, pure and simple, it is in the South that the Negro is given a man's chance in the commercial world, and in nothing is this Exposition more eloquent than in emphasizing this chance. Our greatest danger is that in the great leap from slavery to freedom we may overlook the fact that the masses of us are to live by the productions of our hands, and fail to keep in mind that we shall prosper in proportion as we learn to dignify and glorify common labour and put brains and skill into the common occupations of life; shall prosper in proportion as we learn to draw the line between the superficial and the substantial, the ornamental gewgaws of life and the useful. No race can prosper till it learns that there is as much dignity in tilling a field as in writing a poem. It is at the bottom of life we must begin, and not at the top. Nor should we permit our grievances to overshadow our opportunities.

To those of the white race who look to the incoming of those of foreign birth and strange tongue and habits for the prosperity of the South, were I permitted I would repeat what I say to my own race, "Cast down your bucket where you are." Cast it down among the eight millions of Negroes whose habits you know, whose fidelity and love you have tested in days when to have proved treacherous meant the ruin of your firesides. Cast down your bucket among these people who have, without strikes and labour wars, tilled your fields, cleared your forests, builded your railroads and cities, and brought forth treasures from the bowels of the earth, and helped make possible this magnificent representation of the progress of the South. Casting down your bucket among my people, helping and encouraging them as you are doing on these grounds, and to education of head, hand, and heart, you will find that they will buy your surplus land, make blossom the waste places in your fields, and run your factories. While doing this, you can be sure in the future, as in the past, that you and your families will be surrounded by the most patient, faithful, law-abiding, and unresentful people that the world has seen. As we have proved our loyalty to you in the past, in nursing your children, watching by the sick-bed of your mothers and fathers, and often following them with tear-dimmed eyes to their graves, so in the future, in our humble way, we shall stand by you with a devotion that no foreigner can approach, ready to lay down our lives, if need be, in defence of yours, interlacing our industrial, commercial, civil, and religious life with yours in a way that shall make the interests of both races one. In all things that are purely social we can be as separate as the fingers, yet one as the hand in all things essential to mutual progress.

There is no defence or security for any of us except in the highest intelligence and development of all. If anywhere there are efforts tending to curtail the fullest growth of the Negro, let these efforts be turned into stimulating, encouraging, and making him the most useful and intelligent citizen. Effort or means so invested will pay a thousand per cent interest. These efforts will be twice blessed—"blessing him that gives and him that takes."[1]

There is no escape through law of man or God from the inevitable:—

The laws of changeless justice bind
  Oppressor with oppressed;
And close as sin and suffering joined
  We march to fate abreast.[2]

Nearly sixteen millions of hands will aid you in pulling the load upward, or they will pull against you the load downward. We shall constitute one-third and more of the ignorance and crime of the South, or one-third its intelligence and progress; we shall contribute one-third to the business and industrial prosperity of the South, or we shall prove a veritable body of death, stagnating, depressing, retarding every effort to advance the body politic.

Gentlemen of the Exposition, as we present to you our humble effort at an exhibition of our progress, you must not expect overmuch. Starting thirty years ago with ownership here and there in a few quilts and pumpkins and chickens (gathered from miscellaneous sources), remember the path that has led from these to the inventions and production of agricultural implements, buggies, steam-engines, newspapers, books, statuary, carving, paintings, the management of drug-stores and banks, has not been trodden without contact with thorns and thistles. While we take pride in what we exhibit as a result of our independent efforts, we do not for a moment forget that our part in this exhibition would fall far short of your expectations but for the constant help that has come to our educational life, not only from the Southern states, but especially from Northern philanthropists, who have made their gifts a constant stream of blessing and encouragement.

The wisest among my race understand that the agitation of questions of social equality is the extremest folly, and that progress in the enjoyment of all the privileges that will come to us must be the result of severe and constant struggle rather than of artificial forcing. No race that has anything to contribute to the markets of the world is long in any degree ostracized. It is important and right that all privileges of the law be ours, but it is vastly more important that we be prepared for the exercises of these privileges. The opportunity to earn a dollar in a factory just now

1. William Shakespeare, *The Merchant of Venice* 4.1.187.
2. See "The Song of the Negro Boatmen" in *At Port Royal* (1862) by the American antislavery poet John Greenleaf Whittier.

is worth infinitely more than the opportunity to spend a dollar in an opera-house.

In conclusion, may I repeat that nothing in thirty years has given us more hope and encouragement, and drawn us so near to you of the white race, as this opportunity offered by the Exposition; and here bending, as it were, over the altar that represents the results of the struggles of your race and mine, both starting practically empty-handed three decades ago, I pledge that in your effort to work out the great and intricate problem which God has laid at the doors of the South, you shall have at all times the patient, sympathetic help of my race; only let this be constantly in mind, that, while from representations in these buildings of the product of field, of forest, of mine, of factory, letters, and art, much good will come, yet far above and beyond material benefits will be that higher good, that, let us pray God, will come, in a blotting out of sectional differences and racial animosities and suspicions, in a determination to administer absolute justice, in a willing obedience among all classes to the mandates of law. This, this, coupled with our material prosperity, will bring into our beloved South a new heaven and a new earth.

The first thing that I remember, after I had finished speaking, was that Governor Bullock rushed across the platform and took me by the hand, and that others did the same. I received so many and such hearty congratulations that I found it difficult to get out of the building. I did not appreciate to any degree, however, the impression which my address seemed to have made, until the next morning, when I went into the business part of the city. As soon as I was recognized, I was surprised to find myself pointed out and surrounded by a crowd of men who wished to shake hands with me. This was kept up on every street on to which I went, to an extent which embarrassed me so much that I went back to my boarding-place. The next morning I returned to Tuskegee. At the station in Atlanta, and at almost all of the stations at which the train stopped between that city and Tuskegee, I found a crowd of people anxious to shake hands with me.

The papers in all parts of the United States published the address in full, and for months afterward there were complimentary editorial references to it. Mr. Clark Howell, the editor of the Atlanta *Constitution*, telegraphed to a New York paper, among other words, the following, "I do not exaggerate when I say that Professor Booker T. Washington's address yesterday was one of the most notable speeches, both as to character and as to the warmth of its reception, ever delivered to a Southern audience. The address was a revelation. The whole speech is a platform upon which blacks and whites can stand with full justice to each other."

The Boston *Transcript* said editorially: "The speech of Booker T.

Washington at the Atlanta Exposition, this week, seems to have dwarfed all the other proceedings and the Exposition itself. The sensation that it has caused in the press has never been equalled."

I very soon began receiving all kinds of propositions from lecture bureaus, and editors of magazines and papers, to take the lecture platform, and to write articles. One lecture bureau offered me fifty thousand dollars, or two hundred dollars a night and expenses, if I would place my services at its disposal for a given period. To all these communications I replied that my life-work was at Tuskegee; and that whenever I spoke it must be in the interests of the Tuskegee school and my race, and that I would enter into no arrangements that seemed to place a mere commercial value upon my services.

Some days after its delivery I sent a copy of my address to the President of the United States, the Hon. Grover Cleveland. I received from him the following autograph reply:—

Gray Gables, Buzzard's Bay, Mass.,
October 6, 1895.

BOOKER T. WASHINGTON, ESQ.:

MY DEAR SIR: I thank you for sending me a copy of your address delivered at the Atlanta Exposition.

I thank you with much enthusiasm for making the address. I have read it with intense interest, and I think the Exposition would be fully justified if it did not do more than furnish the opportunity for its delivery. Your words cannot fail to delight and encourage all who wish well for your race; and if our coloured fellow-citizens do not from your utterances gather new hope and form new determinations to gain every valuable advantage offered them by their citizenship, it will be strange indeed.

Yours very truly,
GROVER CLEVELAND.

Later I met Mr. Cleveland, for the first time, when, as President, he visited the Atlanta Exposition. At the request of myself and others he consented to spend an hour in the Negro Building, for the purpose of inspecting the Negro exhibit and of giving the coloured people in attendance an opportunity to shake hands with him. As soon as I met Mr. Cleveland I became impressed with his simplicity, greatness, and rugged honesty. I have met him many times since then, both at public functions and at his private residence in Princeton, and the more I see of him the more I admire him. When he visited the Negro Building in Atlanta he seemed to give himself up wholly, for that hour, to the coloured people. He seemed to be as careful to shake hands with some old coloured "auntie" clad partially in rags, and to take as much pleasure in doing so, as if he were greeting some millionnaire. Many of the coloured people took advantage of the occasion to get him to write his name in a book or on a slip of paper. He was as careful and patient in doing this as if he were putting his signature to some great state document.

Mr. Cleveland has not only shown his friendship for me in many personal ways, but has always consented to do anything I have asked of him for our school. This he has done, whether it was to make a personal donation or to use his influence in securing the donations of others. Judging from my personal acquaintance with Mr. Cleveland, I do not believe that he is conscious of possessing any colour prejudice. He is too great for that. In my contact with people I find that, as a rule, it is only the little, narrow people who live for themselves, who never read good books, who do not travel, who never open up their souls in a way to permit them to come into contact with other souls—with the great outside world. No man whose vision is bounded by colour can come into contact with what is highest and best in the world. In meeting men, in many places, I have found that the happiest people are those who do the most for others; the most miserable are those who do the least. I have also found that few things, if any, are capable of making one so blind and narrow as race prejudice. I often say to our students, in the course of my talks to them on Sunday evenings in the chapel, that the longer I live and the more experience I have of the world, the more I am convinced that, after all, the one thing that is most worth living for—and dying for, if need be—is the opportunity of making some one else more happy and more useful.

The coloured people and the coloured newspapers at first seemed to be greatly pleased with the character of my Atlanta address, as well as with its reception. But after the first burst of enthusiasm began to die away, and the coloured people began reading the speech in cold type, some of them seemed to feel that they had been hypnotized. They seemed to feel that I had been too liberal in my remarks toward the Southern whites, and that I had not spoken out strongly enough for what they termed the "rights" of the race. For a while there was a reaction, so far as a certain element of my own race was concerned, but later these reactionary ones seemed to have been won over to my way of believing and acting.

While speaking of changes in public sentiment, I recall that about ten years after the school at Tuskegee was established, I had an experience that I shall never forget. Dr. Lyman Abbott, then the pastor of Plymouth Church, and also editor of the *Outlook* (then the *Christian Union*), asked me to write a letter for his paper giving my opinion of the exact condition, mental and moral, of the coloured ministers in the South, as based upon my observations. I wrote the letter, giving the exact facts as I conceived them to be. The picture painted was a rather black one—or, since I am black, shall I say "white"? It could not be otherwise with a race but a few years out of slavery, a race which had not had time or opportunity to produce a competent ministry.

What I said soon reached every Negro minister in the country, I think, and the letters of condemnation which I received from them were not few. I think that for a year after the publication of this article every association and every conference or religious body of any kind, of my race, that met, did not fail before adjourning to pass a resolution condemning me, or calling upon me to retract or modify what I had said. Many of these organizations went so far in their resolutions as to advise parents to cease sending their children to Tuskegee. One association even appointed a "missionary" whose duty it was to warn the people against sending their children to Tuskegee. This missionary had a son in the school, and I noticed that, whatever the "missionary" might have said or done with regard to others, he was careful not to take his son away from the institution. Many of the coloured papers, especially those that were the organs of religious bodies, joined in the general chorus of condemnation or demands for retraction.

During the whole time of the excitement, and through all the criticism, I did not utter a word of explanation or retraction. I knew that I was right, and that time and the sober second thought of the people would vindicate me. It was not long before the bishops and other church leaders began to make a careful investigation of the conditions of the ministry, and they found out that I was right. In fact, the oldest and most influential bishop in one branch of the Methodist Church said that my words were far too mild. Very soon public sentiment began making itself felt, in demanding a purifying of the ministry. While this is not yet complete by any means, I think I may say, without egotism, and I have been told by many of our most influential ministers, that my words had much to do with starting a demand for the placing of a higher type of men in the pulpit. I have had the satisfaction of having many who once condemned me thank me heartily for my frank words.

The change of the attitude of the Negro ministry, so far as regards myself, is so complete that at the present time I have no warmer friends among any class than I have among the clergymen. The improvement in the character and life of the Negro ministers is one of the most gratifying evidences of the progress of the race. My experience with them, as well as other events in my life, convince me that the thing to do, when one feels sure that he has said or done the right thing, and is condemned, is to stand still and keep quiet. If he is right, time will show it.

In the midst of the discussion which was going on concerning my Atlanta speech, I received the letter which I give below, from Dr. Gilman, the President of Johns Hopkins University, who had been made chairman of the judges of award in connection with the Atlanta Exposition:—

Johns Hopkins University, Baltimore,
President's Office, September 30, 1895.

DEAR MR. WASHINGTON: Would it be agreeable to you to be one of the Judges of Award in the Department of Education at Atlanta? If so, I shall be glad to place your name upon the list. A line by telegraph will be welcomed.

Yours very truly,
D. C. GILMAN.

I think I was even more surprised to receive this invitation than I had been to receive the invitation to speak at the opening of the Exposition. It was to be a part of my duty, as one of the jurors, to pass not only upon the exhibits of the coloured schools, but also upon those of the white schools. I accepted the position, and spent a month in Atlanta in performance of the duties which it entailed. The board of jurors was a large one, consisting in all of sixty members. It was about equally divided between Southern white people and Northern white people. Among them were college presidents, leading scientists and men of letters, and specialists in many subjects. When the group of jurors to which I was assigned met for organization, Mr. Thomas Nelson Page,[3] who was one of the number, moved that I be made secretary of that division, and the motion was unanimously adopted. Nearly half of our division were Southern people. In performing my duties in the inspection of the exhibits of white schools I was in every case treated with respect, and at the close of our labours I parted from my associates with regret.

I am often asked to express myself more freely than I do upon the political condition and the political future of my race. These recollections of my experience in Atlanta give me the opportunity to do so briefly. My own belief is, although I have never before said so in so many words, that the time will come when the Negro in the South will be accorded all the political rights which his ability, character, and material possessions entitle him to. I think, though, that the opportunity to freely exercise such political rights will not come in any large degree through outside or artificial forcing, but will be accorded to the Negro by the Southern white people themselves, and that they will protect him in the exercise of those rights. Just as soon as the South gets over the old feeling that it is being forced by "foreigners," or "aliens," to do something which it does not want to do, I believe that the change in the direction that I have indicated is going to begin. In fact, there are indications that it is already beginning in a slight degree.

Let me illustrate my meaning. Suppose that some months before the opening of the Atlanta Exposition there had been a general demand from the press and public platform outside the South that a Negro be

3. Thomas Nelson Page (1853–1922), popular Virginia author of *In Ole Virginia* (1887) and other romances of the South.

given a place on the opening programme, and that a Negro be placed upon the board of jurors of award. Would any such recognition of the race have taken place? I do not think so. The Atlanta officials went as far as they did because they felt it to be a pleasure, as well as a duty, to reward what they considered merit in the Negro race. Say what we will, there is something in human nature which we cannot blot out, which makes one man, in the end, recognize and reward merit in another, regardless of colour or race.

I believe it is the duty of the Negro—as the greater part of the race is already doing—to deport himself modestly in regard to political claims, depending upon the slow but sure influences that proceed from the possession of property, intelligence, and high character for the full recognition of his political rights. I think that the according of the full exercise of political rights is going to be a matter of natural, slow growth, not an over-night, gourd-vine affair. I do not believe that the Negro should cease voting, for a man cannot learn the exercise of self-government by ceasing to vote, any more than a boy can learn to swim by keeping out of the water, but I do believe that in his voting he should more and more be influenced by those of intelligence and character who are his next-door neighbours.

I know coloured men who, through the encouragement, help, and advice of Southern white people, have accumulated thousands of dollars' worth of property, but who, at the same time, would never think of going to those same persons for advice concerning the casting of their ballots. This, it seems to me, is unwise and unreasonable, and should cease. In saying this I do not mean that the Negro should truckle, or not vote from principle, for the instant he ceases to vote from principle he loses the confidence and respect of the Southern white man even.

I do not believe that any state should make a law that permits an ignorant and poverty-stricken white man to vote, and prevents a black man in the same condition from voting. Such a law is not only unjust, but it will react, as all unjust laws do, in time; for the effect of such a law is to encourage the Negro to secure education and property, and at the same time it encourages the white man to remain in ignorance and poverty. I believe that in time, through the operation of intelligence and friendly race relations, all cheating at the ballot-box in the South will cease. It will become apparent that the white man who begins by cheating a Negro out of his ballot soon learns to cheat a white man out of his, and that the man who does this ends his career of dishonesty by the theft of property or by some equally serious crime. In my opinion, the time will come when the South will encourage all of its citizens to vote. It will see that it pays better, from every standpoint, to have healthy, vigorous life than to have that political stagnation which always results when one-half of the population has no share and no interest in the Government.

As a rule, I believe in universal, free suffrage, but I believe that in the South we are confronted with peculiar conditions that justify the protection of the ballot in many of the states, for a while at least, either by an educational test, a property test, or by both combined; but whatever tests are required, they should be made to apply with equal and exact justice to both races.

Chapter XV

The Secret of Success in Public Speaking

As to how my address at Atlanta was received by the audience in the Exposition building, I think I prefer to let Mr. James Creelman, the noted war correspondent, tell. Mr. Creelman was present, and telegraphed the following account to the New York *World*:—

> Atlanta, September 18.
>
> While President Cleveland was waiting at Gray Gables to-day, to send the electric spark that started the machinery of the Atlanta Exposition, a Negro Moses stood before a great audience of white people and delivered an oration that marks a new epoch in the history of the South; and a body of Negro troops marched in a procession with the citizen soldiery of Georgia and Louisiana. The whole city is thrilling to-night with a realization of the extraordinary significance of these two unprecedented events. Nothing has happened since Henry Grady's immortal speech[1] before the New England society in New York that indicates so profoundly the spirit of the New South, except, perhaps the opening of the Exposition itself.
>
> When Professor Booker T. Washington, Principal of an industrial school for coloured people in Tuskegee, Ala., stood on the platform of the Auditorium, with the sun shining over the heads of his auditors into his eyes, and with his whole face lit up with the fire of prophecy, Clark Howell, the successor of Henry Grady, said to me, "That man's speech is the beginning of a moral revolution in America."
>
> It is the first time that a Negro has made a speech in the South on any important occasion before an audience composed of white men and women. It electrified the audience, and the response was as if it had come from the throat of a whirlwind.
>
> Mrs. Thompson had hardly taken her seat when all eyes were turned on a tall tawny Negro sitting in the front row of the platform. It was Professor Booker T. Washington, President of the

1. Henry Woodfin Grady (1850–1889), Georgia journalist, whose oration "The New South," before the New England Club in December 1886, proclaimed the renewal of the South.

Tuskegee (Alabama) Normal and Industrial Institute, who must rank from this time forth as the foremost man of his race in America. Gilmore's Band played the "Star-Spangled Banner," and the audience cheered. The tune changed to "Dixie" and the audience roared with shrill "hi-yis." Again the music changed, this time to "Yankee Doodle," and the clamour lessened.

All this time the eyes of the thousands present looked straight at the Negro orator. A strange thing was to happen. A black man was to speak for his people, with none to interrupt him. As Professor Washington strode to the edge of the stage, the low, descending sun shot fiery rays through the windows into his face. A great shout greeted him. He turned his head to avoid the blinding light, and moved about the platform for relief. Then he turned his wonderful countenance to the sun without a blink of the eyelids, and began to talk.

There was a remarkable figure; tall, bony, straight as a Sioux chief, high forehead, straight nose, heavy jaws, and strong, determined mouth, with big white teeth, piercing eyes, and a commanding manner. The sinews stood out on his bronzed neck, and his muscular right arm swung high in the air, with a lead-pencil grasped in the clinched brown fist. His big feet were planted squarely, with the heels together and the toes turned out. His voice rang out clear and true, and he paused impressively as he made each point. Within ten minutes the multitude was in an uproar of enthusiasm—handkerchiefs were waved, canes were flourished, hats were tossed in the air. The fairest women of Georgia stood up and cheered. It was as if the orator had bewitched them.

And when he held his dusky hand high above his head, with the fingers stretched wide apart, and said to the white people of the South on behalf of his race, "In all things that are purely social we can be as separate as the fingers, yet one as the hand in all things essential to mutual progress," the great wave of sound dashed itself against the walls, and the whole audience was on its feet in a delirium of applause, and I thought at that moment of the night when Henry Grady stood among the curling wreaths of tobacco-smoke in Delmonico's banquet-hall and said, "I am a Cavalier among Roundheads."

I have heard the great orators of many countries, but not even Gladstone[2] himself could have pleaded a cause with more consummate power than did this angular Negro, standing in a nimbus of sunshine, surrounded by the men who once fought to keep his race in bondage. The roar might swell ever so high, but the expression of his earnest face never changed.

A ragged, ebony giant, squatted on the floor in one of the aisles,

2. William Ewart Gladstone (1809–1898), prime minister of England from 1868 to 1874, 1880 to 1885, in 1886, and from 1892 to 1894.

> watched the orator with burning eyes and tremulous face until the supreme burst of applause came, and then the tears ran down his face. Most of the Negroes in the audience were crying, perhaps without knowing just why.
>
> At the close of the speech Governor Bullock rushed across the stage and seized the orator's hand. Another shout greeted this demonstration, and for a few minutes the two men stood facing each other, hand in hand.

So far as I could spare the time from the immediate work at Tuskegee, after my Atlanta address, I accepted some of the invitations to speak in public which came to me, especially those that would take me into territory where I thought it would pay to plead the cause of my race, but I always did this with the understanding that I was to be free to talk about my life-work and the needs of my people. I also had it understood that I was not to speak in the capacity of a professional lecturer, or for mere commercial gain.

In my efforts on the public platform I never have been able to understand why people come to hear me speak. This question I never can rid myself of. Time and time again, as I have stood in the street in front of a building and have seen men and women passing in large numbers into the audience-room where I was to speak, I have felt ashamed that I should be the cause of people—as it seemed to me—wasting a valuable hour of time. Some years ago I was to deliver an address before a literary society in Madison, Wis. An hour before the time set for me to speak, a fierce snow-storm began, and continued for several hours. I made up my mind that there would be no audience, and that I should not have to speak, but, as a matter of duty, I went to the church, and found it packed with people. The surprise gave me a shock that I did not recover from during the whole evening.

People often ask me if I feel nervous before speaking, or else they suggest that, since I speak so often, they suppose that I get used to it. In answer to this question I have to say that I always suffer intensely from nervousness before speaking. More than once, just before I was to make an important address, this nervous strain has been so great that I have resolved never again to speak in public. I not only feel nervous before speaking, but after I have finished I usually feel a sense of regret, because it seems to me as if I had left out of my address the main thing and the best thing that I had meant to say.

There is a great compensation, though, for this preliminary nervous suffering, that comes to me after I have been speaking for about ten minutes, and have come to feel that I have really mastered my audience, and that we have gotten into full and complete sympathy with each other. It seems to me that there is rarely such a combination of mental and physical delight in any effort as that which comes to a public speaker when he feels that he has a great audience completely within his control. There is a thread of sympathy and oneness that connects a public speaker with his audience, that is just as strong as though it was something tangible and visible. If in an audience of a thousand people there is one person who is not in sympathy with my views, or is inclined to be doubtful, cold, or critical, I can pick him out. When I have found him I usually go straight at him, and it is a great satisfaction to watch the process of his thawing out. I find that the most effective medicine for such individuals is administered at first in the form of a story, although I never tell an anecdote simply for the sake of telling one. That kind of thing, I think, is empty and hollow, and an audience soon finds it out.

I believe that one always does himself and his audience an injustice when he speaks merely for the sake of speaking. I do not believe that one should speak unless, deep down in his heart, he feels convinced that he has a message to deliver. When one feels, from the bottom of his feet to the top of his head, that he has something to say that is going to help some individual or some cause, then let him say it; and in delivering his message I do not believe that many of the artificial rules of elocution can, under such circumstances, help him very much. Although there are certain things, such as pauses, breathing, and pitch of voice, that are very important, none of these can take the place of *soul* in an address. When I have an address to deliver, I like to forget all about the rules for the proper use of the English language, and all about rhetoric and that sort of thing, and I like to make the audience forget all about these things, too.

Nothing tends to throw me off my balance so quickly, when I am speaking, as to have some one leave the room. To prevent this, I make up my mind, as a rule, that I will try to make my address so interesting, will try to state so many interesting facts one after another, that no one can leave. The average audience, I have come to believe, wants facts rather than generalities or sermonizing. Most people, I think, are able to draw proper conclusions if they are given the facts in an interesting form on which to base them.

As to the kind of audience that I like best to talk to, I would put at the top of the list an organization of strong, wide-awake, business men, such, for example, as is found in Boston, New York, Chicago, and Buffalo. I have found no other audience so quick to see a point, and so responsive. Within the last few years I have had the privilege of speaking before most of the leading organizations of this kind in the large cities of the United States. The best time to get hold of an organization of business men is after a good dinner, although I think that one of the worst instruments of torture that was ever invented is the custom which makes it necessary for a speaker to sit through a fourteen-course dinner, every minute of the time feeling sure that his speech is going to prove a dismal failure and disappointment.

I rarely take part in one of these long dinners that I do not wish that I could put myself back in the little cabin where I was a slave boy, and again go through the experience there—one that I shall never forget—of getting molasses to eat once a week from the "big house." Our usual diet on the plantation was corn bread and pork, but on Sunday morning my mother was permitted to bring down a little molasses from the "big house" for her three children, and when it was received how I did wish that every day was Sunday! I would get my tin plate and hold it up for the sweet morsel, but I would always shut my eyes while the molasses was being poured out into the plate, with the hope that when I opened them I would be surprised to see how much I had got. When I opened my eyes I would tip the plate in one direction and another, so as to make the molasses spread all over it, in the full belief that there would be more of it and that it would last longer if spread out in this way. So strong are my childish impressions of those Sunday morning feasts that it would be pretty hard for any one to convince me that there is not more molasses on a plate when it is spread all over the plate than when it occupies a little corner—if there is a corner in a plate. At any rate, I have never believed in "cornering" syrup. My share of the syrup was usually about two tablespoonfuls, and those two spoonfuls of molasses were much more enjoyable to me than is a fourteen-course dinner after which I am to speak.

Next to a company of business men, I prefer to speak to an audience of Southern people, of either race, together or taken separately. Their enthusiasm and responsiveness are a constant delight. The "amens" and "dat's de truf" that come spontaneously from the coloured individuals are calculated to spur any speaker on to his best efforts. I think that next in order of preference I would place a college audience. It has been my privilege to deliver addresses at many of our leading colleges, including Harvard, Yale, Williams, Amherst, Fisk University, the University of Pennsylvania, Wellesley, the University of Michigan, Trinity College in North Carolina, and many others.

It has been a matter of deep interest to me to note the number of people who have come to shake hands with me after an address, who say that this is the first time they have ever called a Negro "Mister."

When speaking directly in the interests of the Tuskegee Institute, I usually arrange, some time in advance, a series of meetings in important centres. This takes me before churches, Sunday-schools, Christian Endeavour Societies, and men's and women's clubs. When doing this I sometimes speak before as many as four organizations in a single day.

Three years ago, at the suggestion of Mr. Morris K. Jesup, of New York, and Dr. J. L. M. Curry, the general agent of the fund, the trustees of the John F. Slater Fund[3] voted a sum of money to be used in paying

3. Established in 1881, the fund offered financial aid to African American industrial education.

the expenses of Mrs. Washington and myself while holding a series of meetings among the coloured people in the large centres of Negro population, especially in the large cities of the ex-slaveholding states. Each year during the last three years we have devoted some weeks to this work. The plan that we have followed has been for me to speak in the morning to the ministers, teachers, and professional men. In the afternoon Mrs. Washington would speak to the women alone, and in the evening I spoke to a large mass-meeting. In almost every case the meetings have been attended not only by the coloured people in large numbers, but by the white people. In Chattanooga, Tenn., for example, there was present at the mass-meeting an audience of not less than three thousand persons, and I was informed that eight hundred of these were white. I have done no work that I really enjoyed more than this, or that I think has accomplished more good.

These meetings have given Mrs. Washington and myself an opportunity to get first-hand, accurate information as to the real condition of the race, by seeing the people in their homes, their churches, their Sunday-schools, and their places of work, as well as in the prisons and dens of crime. These meetings also gave us an opportunity to see the relations that exist between the races. I never feel so hopeful about the race as I do after being engaged in a series of these meetings. I know that on such occasions there is much that comes to the surface that is superficial and deceptive, but I have had experience enough not to be deceived by mere signs and fleeting enthusiasms. I have taken pains to go to the bottom of things and get facts, in a cold, business-like manner.

I have seen the statement made lately, by one who claims to know what he is talking about,[4] that, taking the whole Negro race into account, ninety per cent of the Negro women are not virtuous. There never was a baser falsehood uttered concerning a race, or a statement made that was less capable of being proved by actual facts.

No one can come into contact with the race for twenty years, as I have done in the heart of the South, without being convinced that the race is constantly making slow but sure progress materially, educationally, and morally. One might take up the life of the worst element in New York City, for example, and prove almost anything he wanted to prove concerning the white man, but all will agree that this is not a fair test.

Early in the year 1897 I received a letter inviting me to deliver an address at the dedication of the Robert Gould Shaw[5] monument in Boston. I accepted the invitation. It is not necessary for me, I am sure, to explain who Robert Gould Shaw was, and what he did. The monument to his memory stands near the head of Boston Common, facing

4. William Hannibal Thomas, author of *The American Negro* (1901).
5. Robert Gould Shaw (1837–1863), white colonel in the black Fifty-Fourth Massachusetts Volunteers, killed in the assault on Fort Wagner in Charleston, South Carolina.

the State House. It is counted to be the most perfect piece of art of the kind to be found in the country.

The exercises connected with the dedication were held in Music Hall, in Boston, and the great hall was packed from top to bottom with one of the most distinguished audiences that ever assembled in the city. Among those present there were more persons representing the famous old anti-slavery element than it is likely will ever be brought together in the country again. The late Hon. Roger Wolcott, then Governor of Massachusetts, was the presiding officer, and on the platform with him were many other officials and hundreds of distinguished men. A report of the meeting which appeared in the Boston *Transcript* will describe it better than any words of mine could do:—

> The core and kernel of yesterday's great noon meeting in honour of the Brotherhood of Man, in Music Hall, was the superb address of the Negro President of Tuskegee. "Booker T. Washington received his Harvard A. M. last June, the first of his race," said Governor Wolcott, "to receive an honorary degree from the oldest university in the land, and this for the wise leadership of his people." When Mr. Washington rose in the flag-filled, enthusiasm-warmed, patriotic, and glowing atmosphere of Music Hall, people felt keenly that here was the civic justification of the old abolition spirit of Massachusetts; in his person the proof of her ancient and indomitable faith; in his strong thought and rich oratory, the crown and glory of the old war days of suffering and strife. The scene was full of historic beauty and deep significance. "Cold" Boston was alive with the fire that is always hot in her heart for righteousness and truth. Rows and rows of people who are seldom seen at any public function, whole families of those who are certain to be out of town on a holiday, crowded the place to overflowing. The city was at her birthright *fête* in the persons of hundreds of her best citizens, men and women whose names and lives stand for the virtues that make for honourable civic pride.
>
> Battle-music had filled the air. Ovation after ovation, applause warm and prolonged, had greeted the officers and friends of Colonel Shaw, the sculptor, St. Gaudens, the memorial Committee, the Governor and his staff, and the Negro soldiers of the Fifty-fourth Massachusetts as they came upon the platform or entered the hall. Colonel Henry Lee, of Governor Andrew's old staff, had made a noble, simple presentation speech for the committee, paying tribute to Mr. John M. Forbes, in whose stead he served. Governor Wolcott had made his short, memorable speech, saying, "Fort Wagner marked an epoch in the history of a race, and called it into manhood." Mayor Quincy had received the monument for the city of Boston. The story of Colonel Shaw and his black regiment had been told in gallant words, and then, after the singing of

> Mine eyes have seen the glory
> Of the coming of the Lord,[6]
>
> Booker Washington arose. It was, of course, just the moment for him. The multitude, shaken out of its usual symphony-concert calm, quivered with an excitement that was not suppressed. A dozen times it had sprung to its feet to cheer and wave and hurrah, as one person. When this man of culture and voice and power, as well as a dark skin, began, and uttered the names of Stearns and of Andrew, feeling began to mount. You could see tears glisten in the eyes of soldiers and civilians. When the orator turned to the coloured soldiers on the platform, to the colour-bearer of Fort Wagner, who smilingly bore still the flag he had never lowered even when wounded, and said, "To you, to the scarred and scattered remnants of the Fifty-fourth, who, with empty sleeve and wanting leg, have honoured this occasion with your presence, to you, your commander is not dead. Though Boston erected no monument and history recorded no story, in you and in the loyal race which you represent, Robert Gould Shaw would have a monument which time could not wear away," then came the climax of the emotion of the day and the hour. It was Roger Wolcott, as well as the Governor of Massachusetts, the individual representative of the people's sympathy as well as the chief magistrate, who had sprung first to his feet and cried, "Three cheers to Booker T. Washington!"

Among those on the platform was Sergeant William H. Carney, of New Bedford, Mass., the brave coloured officer who was the colour-bearer at Fort Wagner and held the American flag. In spite of the fact that a large part of his regiment was killed, he escaped, and exclaimed, after the battle was over, "The old flag never touched the ground."

This flag Sergeant Carney held in his hands as he sat on the platform, and when I turned to address the survivors of the coloured regiment who were present, and referred to Sergeant Carney, he rose, as if by instinct, and raised the flag. It has been my privilege to witness a good many satisfactory and rather sensational demonstrations in connection with some of my public addresses, but in dramatic effect I have never seen or experienced anything which equalled this. For a number of minutes the audience seemed to entirely lose control of itself.

In the general rejoicing throughout the country which followed the close of the Spanish-American war, peace celebrations were arranged in several of the large cities. I was asked by President William R. Harper, of the University of Chicago, who was chairman of the committee of invitations for the celebration to be held in the city of Chicago, to

6. Opening lines of Julia Ward Howe's "The Battle Hymn of the Republic" (1861).

deliver one of the addresses at the celebration there. I accepted the invitation, and delivered two addresses there during the Jubilee week. The first of these, and the principal one, was given in the Auditorium, on the evening of Sunday, October 16. This was the largest audience that I have ever addressed, in any part of the country; and besides speaking in the main Auditorium, I also addressed, that same evening, two overflow audiences in other parts of the city.

It was said that there were sixteen thousand persons in the Auditorium, and it seemed to me as if there were as many more on the outside trying to get in. It was impossible for any one to get near the entrance without the aid of a policeman. President William McKinley attended this meeting, as did also the members of his Cabinet, many foreign ministers, and a large number of army and navy officers, many of whom had distinguished themselves in the war which had just closed. The speakers, besides myself, on Sunday evening, were Rabbi Emil G. Hirsch, Father Thomas P. Hodnett, and Dr. John H. Barrows.

The Chicago *Times-Herald*, in describing the meeting, said of my address:—

> He pictured the Negro choosing slavery rather than extinction; recalled Crispus Attucks[7] shedding his blood at the beginning of the American Revolution, that white Americans might be free, while black Americans remained in slavery; rehearsed the conduct of the Negroes with Jackson at New Orleans;[8] drew a vivid and pathetic picture of the Southern slaves protecting and supporting the families of their masters while the latter were fighting to perpetuate black slavery; recounted the bravery of coloured troops at Port Hudson and Forts Wagner and Pillow, and praised the heroism of the black regiments that stormed El Caney and Santiago to give freedom to the enslaved people of Cuba,[9] forgetting, for the time being, the unjust discrimination that law and custom make against them in their own country.
>
> In all of these things, the speaker declared, his race had chosen the better part. And then he made his eloquent appeal to the consciences of the white Americans: "When you have gotten the full story of the heroic conduct of the Negro in the Spanish-American war, have heard it from the lips of Northern soldier and Southern soldier, from ex-abolitionist and ex-masters, then decide within yourselves whether a race that is thus willing to die for its country should not be given the highest opportunity to live for its country."

7. Crispus Attucks (1750?–1770), shot by British soldiers in the Boston Massacre, a prelude to the American Revolution.
8. General Andrew Jackson led the victorious American forces in the Battle of New Orleans, January 8, 1815.
9. Cuba became independent of Spain after United States intervention in the Spanish-American War (1898).

The part of the speech which seemed to arouse the wildest and most sensational enthusiasm was that in which I thanked the President for his recognition of the Negro in his appointments during the Spanish-American war. The President was sitting in a box at the right of the stage. When I addressed him I turned toward the box, and as I finished the sentence thanking him for his generosity, the whole audience rose and cheered again and again, waving handkerchiefs and hats and canes, until the President arose in the box and bowed his acknowledgments. At that the enthusiasm broke out again, and the demonstration was almost indescribable.

One portion of my address at Chicago seemed to have been misunderstood by the Southern press, and some of the Southern papers took occasion to criticise me rather strongly. These criticisms continued for several weeks, until I finally received a letter from the editor of the *Age-Herald*, published in Birmingham, Ala., asking me if I would say just what I meant by this part of my address. I replied to him in a letter which seemed to satisfy my critics. In this letter I said that I had made it a rule never to say before a Northern audience anything that I would not say before an audience in the South. I said that I did not think it was necessary for me to go into extended explanations; if my seventeen years of work in the heart of the South had not been explanation enough, I did not see how words could explain. I said that I made the same plea that I had made in my address at Atlanta, for the blotting out of race prejudice in "commercial and civil relations." I said that what is termed social recognition was a question which I never discussed, and then I quoted from my Atlanta address what I had said there in regard to that subject.

In meeting crowds of people at public gatherings, there is one type of individual that I dread. I mean the crank. I have become so accustomed to these people now that I can pick them out at a distance when I see them elbowing their way up to me. The average crank has a long beard, poorly cared for, a lean, narrow face, and wears a black coat. The front of his vest and coat are slick with grease, and his trousers bag at the knees.

In Chicago, after I had spoken at a meeting, I met one of these fellows. They usually have some process for curing all of the ills of the world at once. This Chicago specimen had a patent process by which he said Indian corn could be kept through a period of three or four years, and he felt sure that if the Negro race in the South would, as a whole, adopt his process, it would settle the whole race question. It mattered nothing that I tried to convince him that our present problem was to teach the Negroes how to produce enough corn to last them through one year. Another Chicago crank had a scheme by which he wanted me to join him in an effort to close up all the National banks in the country. If that was done, he felt sure it would put the Negro on his feet.

The number of people who stand ready to consume one's time, to no purpose, is almost countless. At one time I spoke before a large audience in Boston in the evening. The next morning I was awakened by having a card brought to my room, and with it a message that some one was anxious to see me. Thinking that it must be something very important, I dressed hastily and went down. When I reached the hotel office I found a blank and innocent-looking individual waiting for me, who coolly remarked: "I heard you talk at a meeting last night. I rather liked your talk, and so I came in this morning to hear you talk some more."

I am often asked how it is possible for me to superintend the work at Tuskegee and at the same time be so much away from the school. In partial answer to this I would say that I think I have learned, in some degree at least, to disregard the old maxim which says, "Do not get others to do that which you can do yourself." My motto, on the other hand, is, "Do not do that which others can do as well."

One of the most encouraging signs in connection with the Tuskegee school is found in the fact that the organization is so thorough that the daily work of the school is not dependent upon the presence of any one individual. The whole executive force, including instructors and clerks, now numbers eighty-six. This force is so organized and subdivided that the machinery of the school goes on day by day like clockwork. Most of our teachers have been connected with the institution for a number of years, and are as much interested in it as I am. In my absence, Mr. Warren Logan, the treasurer, who has been at the school seventeen years, is the executive. He is efficiently supported by Mrs. Washington, and by my faithful secretary, Mr. Emmett J. Scott, who handles the bulk of my correspondence and keeps me in daily touch with the life of the school, and who also keeps me informed of whatever takes place in the South that concerns the race. I owe more to his tact, wisdom, and hard work than I can describe.

The main executive work of the school, whether I am at Tuskegee or not, centres in what we call the executive council. This council meets twice a week, and is composed of the nine persons who are at the head of the nine departments of the school. For example: Mrs. B. K. Bruce, the Lady Principal, the widow of the late ex-senator Bruce, is a member of the council, and represents in it all that pertains to the life of the girls at the school. In addition to the executive council there is a financial committee of six, that meets every week and decides upon the expenditures for the week. Once a month, and sometimes oftener, there is a general meeting of all the instructors. Aside from these there are innumerable smaller meetings, such as that of the instructors in the Phelps Hall Bible Training School, or of the instructors in the agricultural department.

In order that I may keep in constant touch with the life of the institution, I have a system of reports so arranged that a record of the school's work reaches me every day in the year, no matter in what part of the country I am. I know by these reports even what students are excused from school, and why they are excused—whether for reasons of ill health or otherwise. Through the medium of these reports I know each day what the income of the school in money is; I know how many gallons of milk and how many pounds of butter come from the dairy; what the bill of fare for the teachers and students is; whether a certain kind of meat was boiled or baked, and whether certain vegetables served in the dining room were bought from a store or procured from our own farm. Human nature I find to be very much the same the world over, and it is sometimes not hard to yield to the temptation to go to a barrel of rice that has come from the store—with the grain all prepared to go into the pot—rather than to take the time and trouble to go to the field and dig and wash one's own sweet potatoes, which might be prepared in a manner to take the place of the rice.

I am often asked how, in the midst of so much work, a large part of which is before the public, I can find time for any rest or recreation, and what kind of recreation or sports I am fond of. This is rather a difficult question to answer. I have a strong feeling that every individual owes it to himself, and to the cause which he is serving, to keep a vigorous, healthy body, with the nerves steady and strong, prepared for great efforts and prepared for disappointments and trying positions. As far as I can, I make it a rule to plan for each day's work—not merely to go through with the same routine of daily duties, but to get rid of the routine work as early in the day as possible, and then to enter upon some new or advance work. I make it a rule to clear my desk every day, before leaving my office, of all correspondence and memoranda, so that on the morrow I can begin a *new* day of work. I make it a rule never to let my work drive me, but to so master it, and keep it in such complete control, and to keep so far ahead of it, that I will be the master instead of the servant. There is a physical and mental and spiritual enjoyment that comes from a consciousness of being the absolute master of one's work, in all its details, that is very satisfactory and inspiring. My experience teaches me that, if one learns to follow this plan, he gets a freshness of body and vigour of mind out of work that goes a long way toward keeping him strong and healthy. I believe that when one can grow to the point where he loves his work, this gives him a kind of strength that is most valuable.

When I begin my work in the morning, I expect to have a successful and pleasant day of it, but at the same time I prepare myself for unpleasant and unexpected hard places. I prepare myself to hear that one of our school buildings is on fire, or has burned, or that some disagreeable accident has occurred, or that some one has abused me in a public address or printed article, for something that I have done or omitted to do, or for something that he had heard that I had said—probably something that I had never thought of saying.

In nineteen years of continuous work I have taken but one vacation. That was two years ago, when some of my friends put the money into my hands and forced Mrs. Washington and myself to spend three months in Europe. I have said that I believe it is the duty of every one to keep his body in good condition. I try to look after the little ills, with the idea that if I take care of the little ills the big ones will not come. When I find myself unable to sleep well, I know that something is wrong. If I find any part of my system the least weak, and not performing its duty, I consult a good physician. The ability to sleep well, at any time and in any place, I find of great advantage. I have so trained myself that I can lie down for a nap of fifteen or twenty minutes, and get up refreshed in body and mind.

I have said that I make it a rule to finish up each day's work before leaving it. There is, perhaps, one exception to this. When I have an unusually difficult question to decide—one that appeals strongly to the emotions—I find it a safe rule to sleep over it for a night, or to wait until I have had an opportunity to talk it over with my wife and friends.

As to my reading; the most time I get for solid reading is when I am on the cars. Newspapers are to me a constant source of delight and recreation. The only trouble is that I read too many of them. Fiction I care little for. Frequently I have to almost force myself to read a novel that is on every one's lips. The kind of reading that I have the greatest fondness for is biography. I like to be sure that I am reading about a real man or a real thing. I think I do not go too far when I say that I have read nearly every book and magazine article that has been written about Abraham Lincoln. In literature he is my patron saint.

Out of the twelve months in a year I suppose that, on an average, I spend six months away from Tuskegee. While my being absent from the school so much unquestionably has its disadvantages, yet there are at the same time some compensations. The change of work brings a certain kind of rest. I enjoy a ride of a long distance on the cars, when I am permitted to ride where I can be comfortable. I get rest on the cars, except when the inevitable individual who seems to be on every train approaches me with the now familiar phrase: "Isn't this Booker Washington? I want to introduce myself to you." Absence from the school enables me to lose sight of the unimportant details of the work, and study it in a broader and more comprehensive manner than I could do on the grounds. This absence also brings me into contact with the best work being done in educational lines, and into contact with the best educators in the land.

But, after all this is said, the time when I get the most solid rest and recreation is when I can be at Tuskegee, and, after our evening meal is over, can sit down, as is our custom, with my wife and Portia and Baker and Davidson, my three children, and read a story, or each take turns in telling a story. To me there is nothing on earth equal to that, although what is nearly equal to it is to go with them for an hour or more, as we like to do on Sunday afternoons, into the woods, where we can live for a while near the heart of nature, where no one can disturb or vex us, surrounded by pure air, the trees, the shrubbery, the flowers, and the sweet fragrance that springs from a hundred plants, enjoying the chirp of the crickets and the songs of the birds. This is solid rest.

My garden, also, what little time I can be at Tuskegee, is another source of rest and enjoyment. Somehow I like, as often as possible, to touch nature, not something that is artificial or an imitation, but the real thing. When I can leave my office in time so that I can spend thirty or forty minutes in spading the ground, in planting seeds, in digging about the plants, I feel that I am coming into contact with something that is giving me strength for the many duties and hard places that await me out in the big world. I pity the man or woman who has never learned to enjoy nature and to get strength and inspiration out of it.

Aside from the large number of fowls and animals kept by the school, I keep individually a number of pigs and fowls of the best grades, and in raising these I take a great deal of pleasure. I think the pig is my favourite animal. Few things are more satisfactory to me than a high-grade Berkshire or Poland China pig.

Games I care little for. I have never seen a game of football. In cards I do not know one card from another. A game of old-fashioned marbles with my two boys, once in a while, is all I care for in this direction. I suppose I would care for games now if I had had any time in my youth to give to them, but that was not possible.

Chapter XVI

Europe

In 1893 I was married to Miss Margaret James Murray, a native of Mississippi, and a graduate of Fisk University, in Nashville, Tenn., who had come to Tuskegee as a teacher several years before, and at the time we were married was filling the position of Lady Principal. Not only is Mrs. Washington completely one with me in the work directly connected with the school, relieving me of many burdens and perplexities, but aside from her work on the school grounds, she carries on a mothers' meeting in the town of Tuskegee, and a plantation work among the women, children, and men who live in a settlement connected with a large plantation about eight miles from Tuskegee. Both the mothers' meeting and the plantation work are carried on, not only with a view to helping those who are directly reached, but also for the purpose of furnishing object-lessons in these two kinds of work that may be followed by our students when they go out into the world for their own life-work.

Aside from these two enterprises, Mrs. Washington is also largely responsible for a woman's club at the school which brings together, twice a month, the women who live on the school grounds and those who live near, for the discussion of some important topic. She is also the President of what is known as the Federation of Southern Coloured Women's Clubs, and is Chairman of the Executive Committee of the National Federation of Coloured Women's Clubs.

Portia, the oldest of my three children, has learned dressmaking. She has unusual ability in instrumental music. Aside from her studies at Tuskegee, she has already begun to teach there.

Booker Taliaferro is my next oldest child. Young as he is, he has already nearly mastered the brickmason's trade. He began working at this trade when he was quite small, dividing his time between this and class work; and he has developed great skill in the trade and a fondness for it. He says that he is going to be an architect and brickmason. One of the most satisfactory letters that I have ever received from any one came to me from Booker last summer. When I left home for the summer, I told him that he must work at his trade half of each day, and that the other half of the day he could spend as he pleased. When I had been away from home two weeks, I received the following letter from him:

> Tuskegee, Alabama.
>
> My dear Papa: Before you left home you told me to work at my trade half of each day. I like my work so much that I want to work at my trade all day. Besides, I want to earn all the money I can, so that when I go to another school I shall have money to pay my expenses.
>
> Your son,
> Booker.

My youngest child, Ernest Davidson Washington, says that he is going to be a physician. In addition to going to school, where he studies books and has manual training, he regularly spends a portion of his time in the office of our resident physician, and has already learned to do many of the duties which pertain to a doctor's office.

The thing in my life which brings me the keenest regret is that my work in connection with public affairs keeps me for so much of the time away from my family, where, of all places in the world, I delight to be. I always envy the individual whose life-work is so laid that he can spend his evenings at home. I have sometimes thought that people who have this rare privilege do not appreciate it as they should. It is such a rest and relief to get away from crowds of people, and handshaking, and travelling, and get home, even if it be for but a very brief while.

Another thing at Tuskegee out of which I get a great deal of pleasure and satisfaction is in the meeting with our students, and teachers, and their families, in the chapel for devotional exercises every evening at half-past eight, the last thing before retiring for the night. It is an inspiring sight when one stands on the platform there and sees before him eleven or twelve hundred earnest young men and women; and one cannot but feel that it is a privilege to help to guide them to a higher and more useful life.

In the spring of 1899 there came to me what I might describe as almost the greatest surprise of my life. Some good ladies in Boston arranged a public meeting in the interests of Tuskegee, to be held in the Hollis Street Theatre. This meeting was attended by large numbers of the best people of Boston, of both races. Bishop Lawrence presided. In addition to an address made by myself, Mr. Paul Lawrence Dunbar read from his poems, and Dr. W. E. B. Du Bois[1] read an original sketch.

Some of those who attended this meeting noticed that I seemed unusually tired, and some little time after the close of the meeting, one of the ladies who had been interested in it asked me in a casual way if I had ever been to Europe. I replied that I never had. She asked me if I had ever thought of going, and I told her no; that it was something entirely beyond me. This conversation soon passed out of my mind, but a few days afterward I was informed that some friends in Boston, including Mr. Francis J. Garrison, had raised a sum of money sufficient to pay all the expenses of Mrs. Washington and myself during a three or four months' trip to Europe. It was added with emphasis that we *must* go. A year previous to this Mr. Garrison had attempted to get me to promise to go to Europe for a summer's rest, with the understanding that he would be responsible for raising the money among his friends for the expenses of the trip. At that time such a journey seemed so entirely foreign to anything that I should ever be able to undertake that I confess I did not give the matter very serious attention; but later Mr. Garrison joined his efforts to those of the ladies whom I have mentioned, and when their plans were made known to me Mr. Garrison not only had the route mapped out, but had, I believe, selected the steamer upon which we were to sail.

The whole thing was so sudden and so unexpected that I was completely taken off my feet. I had been at work steadily for eighteen years in connection with Tuskegee, and I had never thought of anything else but ending my life in that way. Each day the school seemed to depend upon me more largely for its daily expenses, and I told these Boston

1. William Edward Burghardt Du Bois (1868–1963), widely respected African American man of letters, soon to become a public critic of many Washington policies; William Lawrence (1850–1941), Protestant Episcopal bishop of Massachusetts; Paul Laurence Dunbar (1872–1906), the most popular African American poet of the time.

friends that, while I thanked them sincerely for their thoughtfulness and generosity, I could not go to Europe, for the reason that the school could not live financially while I was absent. They then informed me that Mr. Henry L. Higginson, and some other good friends who I know do not want their names made public, were then raising a sum of money which would be sufficient to keep the school in operation while I was away. At this point I was compelled to surrender. Every avenue of escape had been closed.

Deep down in my heart the whole thing seemed more like a dream than like reality, and for a long time it was difficult for me to make myself believe that I was actually going to Europe. I had been born and largely reared in the lowest depths of slavery, ignorance, and poverty. In my childhood I had suffered for want of a place to sleep, for lack of food, clothing, and shelter. I had not had the privilege of sitting down to a dining-table until I was quite well grown. Luxuries had always seemed to me to be something meant for white people, not for my race. I had always regarded Europe, and London, and Paris, much as I regard heaven. And now could it be that I was actually going to Europe? Such thoughts as these were constantly with me.

Two other thoughts troubled me a good deal. I feared that people who heard that Mrs. Washington and I were going to Europe might not know all the circumstances, and might get the idea that we had become, as some might say, "stuck up," and were trying to "show off." I recalled that from my youth I had heard it said that too often, when people of my race reached any degree of success, they were inclined to unduly exalt themselves; to try and ape the wealthy, and in so doing to lose their heads. The fear that people might think this of us haunted me a good deal. Then, too, I could not see how my conscience would permit me to spare the time from my work and be happy. It seemed mean and selfish in me to be taking a vacation while others were at work, and while there was so much that needed to be done. From the time I could remember, I had always been at work, and I did not see how I could spend three or four months in doing nothing. The fact was that I did not know how to take a vacation.

Mrs. Washington had much the same difficulty in getting away, but she was anxious to go because she thought that I needed the rest. There were many important National questions bearing upon the life of the race which were being agitated at that time, and this made it all the harder for us to decide to go. We finally gave our Boston friends our promise that we would go, and then they insisted that the date of our departure be set as soon as possible. So we decided upon May 10. My good friend Mr. Garrison kindly took charge of all the details necessary for the success of the trip, and he, as well as other friends, gave us a great number of letters of introduction to people in France and England, and made other arrangements for our comfort and convenience abroad.

Good-bys were said at Tuskegee, and we were in New York May 9, ready to sail the next day. Our daughter Portia, who was then studying in South Framingham, Mass., came to New York to see us off. Mr. Scott, my secretary, came with me to New York, in order that I might clear up the last bit of business before I left. Other friends also came to New York to see us off. Just before we went on board the steamer another pleasant surprise came to us in the form of a letter from two generous ladies, stating that they had decided to give us the money with which to erect a new building to be used in properly housing all our industries for girls at Tuskegee.

We were to sail on the *Friesland*, of the Red Star Line, and a beautiful vessel she was. We went on board just before noon, the hour of sailing. I had never before been on board a large ocean steamer, and the feeling which took possession of me when I found myself there is rather hard to describe. It was a feeling, I think, of awe mingled with delight. We were agreeably surprised to find that the captain, as well as several of the other officers, not only knew who we were, but was expecting us and gave us a pleasant greeting. There were several passengers whom we knew, including Senator Sewell, of New Jersey, and Edward Marshall, the newspaper correspondent. I had just a little fear that we would not be treated civilly by some of the passengers. This fear was based upon what I had heard other people of my race, who had crossed the ocean, say about unpleasant experiences in crossing the ocean in American vessels. But in our case, from the captain down to the most humble servant, we were treated with the greatest kindness. Nor was this kindness confined to those who were connected with the steamer; it was shown by all the passengers also. There were not a few Southern men and women on board, and they were as cordial as those from other parts of the country.

As soon as the last good-bys were said, and the steamer had cut loose from the wharf, the load of care, anxiety, and responsibility which I had carried for eighteen years began to lift itself from my shoulders at the rate, it seemed to me, of a pound a minute. It was the first time in all those years that I had felt, even in a measure, free from care; and my feeling of relief it is hard to describe on paper. Added to this was the delightful anticipation of being in Europe soon. It all seemed more like a dream than like a reality.

Mr. Garrison had thoughtfully arranged to have us have one of the most comfortable rooms on the ship. The second or third day out I began to sleep, and I think that I slept at the rate of fifteen hours a day during the remainder of the ten days' passage. Then it was that I began to understand how tired I really was. These long sleeps I kept up for a month after we landed on the other side. It was such an unusual feeling to wake up in the morning and realize that I had no engagements; did not have to take a train at a certain hour; did not have an appointment to meet some one, or to make an address, at a certain hour. How different all this was from some of the experiences that I have been through when travelling, when I have sometimes slept in three different beds in a single night!

When Sunday came, the captain invited me to conduct the religious services, but, not being a minister, I declined. The passengers, however, began making requests that I deliver an address to them in the dining-saloon some time during the voyage, and this I consented to do. Senator Sewell presided at this meeting. After ten days of delightful weather, during which I was not seasick for a day, we landed at the interesting old city of Antwerp, in Belgium.

The next day after we landed happened to be one of those numberless holidays which the people of those countries are in the habit of observing. It was a bright, beautiful day. Our room in the hotel faced the main public square, and the sights there—the people coming in from the country with all kinds of beautiful flowers to sell, the women coming in with their dogs drawing large, brightly polished cans filled with milk, the people streaming into the cathedral—filled me with a sense of newness that I had never before experienced.

After spending some time in Antwerp, we were invited to go with a party of a half-dozen persons on a trip through Holland. This party included Edward Marshall and some American artists who had come over on the same steamer with us. We accepted the invitation, and enjoyed the trip greatly. I think it was all the more interesting and instructive because we went for most of the way on one of the slow, old-fashioned canal-boats. This gave us an opportunity of seeing and studying the real life of the people in the country districts. We went in this way as far as Rotterdam, and later went to The Hague, where the Peace Conference was then in session, and where we were kindly received by the American representatives.

The thing that impressed itself most on me in Holland was the thoroughness of the agriculture and the excellence of the Holstein cattle. I never knew, before visiting Holland, how much it was possible for people to get out of a small plot of ground. It seemed to me that absolutely no land was wasted. It was worth a trip to Holland, too, just to get a sight of three or four hundred fine Holstein cows grazing in one of those intensely green fields.

From Holland we went to Belgium, and made a hasty trip through that country, stopping at Brussels, where we visited the battlefield of Waterloo. From Belgium we went direct to Paris, where we found that Mr. Theodore Stanton, the son of Mrs. Elizabeth Cady Stanton,[2] had kindly provided accommodations for us. We had barely got settled in

2. Elizabeth Cady Stanton (1815–1902), antislavery activist and pioneering women's rights advocate.

Paris before an invitation came to me from the University Club of Paris to be its guest at a banquet which was soon to be given. The other guests were ex-President Benjamin Harrison[3] and Archbishop Ireland, who were in Paris at the time. The American Ambassador, General Horace Porter, presided at the banquet. My address on this occasion seemed to give satisfaction to those who heard it. General Harrison kindly devoted a large portion of his remarks at dinner to myself and to the influence of the work at Tuskegee on the American race question. After my address at this banquet other invitations came to me, but I declined the most of them, knowing that if I accepted them all, the object of my visit would be defeated. I did, however, consent to deliver an address in the American chapel the following Sunday morning, and at this meeting General Harrison, General Porter, and other distinguished Americans were present.

Later we received a formal call from the American Ambassador, and were invited to attend a reception at his residence. At this reception we met many Americans, among them Justices Fuller and Harlan, of the United States Supreme Court. During our entire stay of a month in Paris, both the American Ambassador and his wife, as well as several other Americans, were very kind to us.

While in Paris we saw a good deal of the now famous American Negro painter, Mr. Henry O. Tanner,[4] whom we had formerly known in America. It was very satisfactory to find how well known Mr. Tanner was in the field of art, and to note the high standing which all classes accorded to him. When we told some Americans that we were going to the Luxembourg Palace to see a painting by an American Negro, it was hard to convince them that a Negro had been thus honoured. I do not believe that they were really convinced of the fact until they saw the picture for themselves. My acquaintance with Mr. Tanner reënforced in my mind the truth which I am constantly trying to impress upon our students at Tuskegee—and on our people throughout the country, as far as I can reach them with my voice—that any man, regardless of colour, will be recognized and rewarded just in proportion as he learns to do something well—learns to do it better than some one else—however humble the thing may be. As I have said, I believe that my race will succeed in proportion as it learns to do a common thing in an uncommon manner; learns to do a thing so thoroughly that no one can improve upon what it has done; learns to make its services of indispensable value. This was the spirit that inspired me in my first effort at Hampton, when I was given the opportunity to sweep and dust that schoolroom. In a degree I felt that my whole future life depended upon the thoroughness with which I cleaned that room, and I was determined

3. Benjamin Harrison, president of the United States from 1889 to 1893.
4. Henry Ossawa Tanner (1859–1937), African American expatriate painter.

to do it so well that no one could find any fault with the job. Few people ever stopped, I found, when looking at his pictures, to inquire whether Mr. Tanner was a Negro painter, a French painter, or a German painter. They simply knew that he was able to produce something which the world wanted—a great painting—and the matter of his colour did not enter into their minds. When a Negro girl learns to cook, to wash dishes, to sew, to write a book, or a Negro boy learns to groom horses, or to grow sweet potatoes, or to produce butter, or to build a house, or to be able to practise medicine, as well or better than some one else, they will be rewarded regardless of race or colour. In the long run, the world is going to have the best, and any difference in race, religion, or previous history will not long keep the world from what it wants.

I think that the whole future of my race hinges on the question as to whether or not it can make itself of such indispensable value that the people in the town and the state where we reside will feel that our presence is necessary to the happiness and well-being of the community. No man who continues to add something to the material, intellectual, and moral well-being of the place in which he lives is long left without proper reward. This is a great human law which cannot be permanently nullified.

The love of pleasure and excitement which seems in a large measure to possess the French people impressed itself upon me. I think they are more noted in this respect than is true of the people of my own race. In point of morality and moral earnestness I do not believe that the French are ahead of my own race in America. Severe competition and the great stress of life have led them to learn to do things more thoroughly and to exercise greater economy; but time, I think, will bring my race to the same point. In the matter of truth and high honour I do not believe that the average Frenchman is ahead of the American Negro; while so far as mercy and kindness to dumb animals go, I believe that my race is far ahead. In fact, when I left France, I had more faith in the future of the black man in America than I had ever possessed.

From Paris we went to London, and reached there early in July, just about the height of the London social season. Parliament was in session, and there was a great deal of gaiety. Mr. Garrison and other friends had provided us with a large number of letters of introduction, and they had also sent letters to other persons in different parts of the United Kingdom, apprising these people of our coming. Very soon after reaching London we were flooded with invitations to attend all manner of social functions, and a great many invitations came to me asking that I deliver public addresses. The most of these invitations I declined, for the reason that I wanted to rest. Neither were we able to accept more than a small proportion of the other invitations. The Rev. Dr. Brooke Herford and Mrs. Herford, whom I had known in Boston, consulted with the American Ambassador, the Hon. Joseph Choate, and arranged for me to speak at a public meeting to be held in Essex Hall. Mr. Choate kindly consented to preside. The meeting was largely attended. There were many distinguished persons present, among them several members of Parliament, including Mr. James Bryce, who spoke at the meeting. What the American Ambassador said in introducing me, as well as a synopsis of what I said, was widely published in England and in the American papers at the time. Dr. and Mrs. Herford gave Mrs. Washington and myself a reception, at which we had the privilege of meeting some of the best people in England. Throughout our stay in London Ambassador Choate was most kind and attentive to us. At the Ambassador's reception I met, for the first time, Mark Twain.

We were the guests several times of Mrs. T. Fisher Unwin, the daughter of the English statesman, Richard Cobden. It seemed as if both Mr. and Mrs. Unwin could not do enough for our comfort and happiness. Later, for nearly a week, we were the guests of the daughter of John Bright, now Mrs. Clark, of Street, England. Both Mr. and Mrs. Clark, with their daughter, visited us at Tuskegee the next year. In Birmingham, England, we were the guests for several days of Mr. Joseph Sturge, whose father was a great abolitionist and friend of Whittier[5] and Garrison. It was a great privilege to meet throughout England those who had known and honoured the late William Lloyd Garrison, the Hon. Frederick Douglass, and other abolitionists. The English abolitionists with whom we came in contact never seemed to tire of talking about these two Americans. Before going to England I had had no proper conception of the deep interest displayed by the abolitionists of England in the cause of freedom, nor did I realize the amount of substantial help given by them.

In Bristol, England, both Mrs. Washington and I spoke at the Women's Liberal Club. I was also the principal speaker at the Commencement exercises of the Royal College for the Blind. These exercises were held in the Crystal Palace, and the presiding officer was the late Duke of Westminster, who was said to be, I believe, the richest man in England, if not in the world. The Duke, as well as his wife and their daughter, seemed to be pleased with what I said, and thanked me heartily. Through the kindness of Lady Aberdeen, my wife and I were enabled to go with a party of those who were attending the International Congress of Women, then in session in London, to see Queen Victoria, at Windsor Castle, where, afterward, we were all the guests of her Majesty at tea. In our party was Miss Susan B. Anthony,[6] and I was deeply impressed with the fact that one did not often get an opportunity to see, during the same hour, two women so remarkable in different ways as Susan B. Anthony and Queen Victoria.

5. John Greenleaf Whittier (1807–1892), American poet and antislavery editor.
6. Susan Brownell Anthony (1820–1906), American antislavery and women's rights activist.

In the House of Commons, which we visited several times, we met Sir Henry M. Stanley.[7] I talked with him about Africa and its relation to the American Negro, and after my interview with him I became more convinced than ever that there was no hope of the American Negro's improving his condition by emigrating to Africa.

On various occasions Mrs. Washington and I were the guests of Englishmen in their country homes, where, I think, one sees the Englishman at his best. In one thing, at least, I feel sure that the English are ahead of Americans, and that is, that they have learned how to get more out of life. The home life of the English seems to me to be about as perfect as anything can be. Everything moves like clockwork. I was impressed, too, with the deference that the servants show to their "masters" and "mistresses,"—terms which I suppose would not be tolerated in America. The English servant expects, as a rule, to be nothing but a servant, and so he perfects himself in the art to a degree that no class of servants in America has yet reached. In our country the servant expects to become, in a few years, a "master" himself. Which system is preferable? I will not venture an answer.

Another thing that impressed itself upon me throughout England was the high regard that all classes have for law and order, and the ease and thoroughness with which everything is done. The Englishmen, I found, took plenty of time for eating, as for everything else. I am not sure if, in the long run, they do not accomplish as much or more than rushing, nervous Americans do.

My visit to England gave me a higher regard for the nobility than I had had. I had no idea that they were so generally loved and respected by the masses, nor had I any correct conception of how much time and money they spent in works of philanthropy, and how much real heart they put into this work. My impression had been that they merely spent money freely and had a "good time."

It was hard for me to get accustomed to speaking to English audiences. The average Englishman is so serious, and is so tremendously in earnest about everything, that when I told a story that would have made an American audience roar with laughter, the Englishmen simply looked me straight in the face without even cracking a smile.

When the Englishman takes you into his heart and friendship, he binds you there as with cords of steel, and I do not believe that there are many other friendships that are so lasting or so satisfactory. Perhaps I can illustrate this point in no better way than by relating the following incident. Mrs. Washington and I were invited to attend a reception given by the Duke and Duchess of Sutherland, at Stafford House—said to be the finest house in London; I may add that I believe the Duchess

7. Henry Morton Stanley (1841–1904), Anglo-American reporter, explorer, and promoter of European imperialism in Africa.

of Sutherland is said to be the most beautiful woman in England. There must have been at least three hundred persons at this reception. Twice during the evening the Duchess sought us out for a conversation, and she asked me to write her when we got home, and tell her more about the work at Tuskegee. This I did. When Christmas came we were surprised and delighted to receive her photograph with her autograph on it. The correspondence has continued, and we now feel that in the Duchess of Sutherland we have one of our warmest friends.

After three months in Europe we sailed from Southampton in the steamship *St. Louis*. On this steamer there was a fine library that had been presented to the ship by the citizens of St. Louis, Mo. In this library I found a life of Frederick Douglass,[8] which I began reading. I became especially interested in Mr. Douglass's description of the way he was treated on shipboard during his first or second visit to England. In this description he told how he was not permitted to enter the cabin, but had to confine himself to the deck of the ship. A few minutes after I had finished reading this description I was waited on by a committee of ladies and gentlemen with the request that I deliver an address at a concert which was to be given the following evening. And yet there are people who are bold enough to say that race feeling in America is not growing less intense! At this concert the Hon. Benjamin B. Odell, Jr., the present governor of New York, presided. I was never given a more cordial hearing anywhere. A large proportion of the passengers were Southern people. After the concert some of the passengers proposed that a subscription be raised to help the work at Tuskegee, and the money to support several scholarships was the result.

While we were in Paris I was very pleasantly surprised to receive the following invitation from the citizens of West Virginia and of the city near which I had spent my boyhood days:—

Charleston, W. Va., May 16, 1899.

PROFESSOR BOOKER T. WASHINGTON, PARIS, FRANCE:

DEAR SIR: Many of the best citizens of West Virginia have united in liberal expressions of admiration and praise of your worth and work, and desire that on your return from Europe you should favour them with your presence and with the inspiration of your words. We most sincerely indorse this move, and on behalf of the citizens of Charleston extend to you our most cordial invitation to have you come to us, that we may honour you who have done so much by your life and work to honour us.

We are, Very truly yours,

THE COMMON COUNCIL OF THE CITY OF CHARLESTON,
By W. HERMAN SMITH, Mayor.

8. Probably the *Life and Times of Frederick Douglass* (1881, 1892).

This invitation from the City Council of Charleston was accompanied by the following:—

> PROFESSOR BOOKER T. WASHINGTON, PARIS, FRANCE:
>
> DEAR SIR: We, the citizens of Charleston and West Virginia, desire to express our pride in you and the splendid career that you have thus far accomplished, and ask that we be permitted to show our pride and interest in a substantial way.
>
> Your recent visit to your old home in our midst awoke within us the keenest regret that we were not permitted to hear you and render some substantial aid to your work, before you left for Europe.
>
> In view of the foregoing, we earnestly invite you to share the hospitality of our city upon your return from Europe, and give us the opportunity to hear you and put ourselves in touch with your work in a way that will be most gratifying to yourself, and that we may receive the inspiration of your words and presence.
>
> An early reply to this invitation, with an indication of the time you may reach our city, will greatly oblige,
>
> Yours very respectfully,
>
> The Charleston *Daily Gazette*, The *Daily Mail-Tribune*; G. W. Atkinson, Governor; E. L. Boggs, Secretary to Governor; Wm. M. O. Dawson, Secretary of State; L. M. La Follette, Auditor; J. R. Trotter, Superintendent of Schools; E. W. Wilson, ex-Governor; W. A. MacCorkle, ex-Governor; John Q. Dickinson, President Kanawha Valley Bank; L. Prichard, President Charleston National Bank; Geo. S. Couch, President Kanawha National Bank; Ed. Reid, Cashier Kanawha National Bank; Geo. S. Laidley, Superintendent City Schools; L. E. McWhorter, President Board of Education; Chas. K. Payne, wholesale merchant; and many others.

This invitation, coming as it did from the City Council, the state officers, and all the substantial citizens of both races of the community where I had spent my boyhood, and from which I had gone a few years before, unknown, in poverty and ignorance, in quest of an education, not only surprised me, but almost unmanned me. I could not understand what I had done to deserve it all.

I accepted the invitation, and at the appointed day was met at the railway station at Charleston by a committee headed by ex-Governor W. A. MacCorkle, and composed of men of both races. The public reception was held in the Opera-House at Charleston. The Governor of the state, the Hon. George W. Atkinson, presided, and an address of welcome was made by ex-Governor MacCorkle. A prominent part in the reception was taken by the coloured citizens. The Opera-House was filled with citizens of both races, and among the white people were many for whom I had worked when a boy. The next day Governor and Mrs. Atkinson gave me a public reception at the State House, which was attended by all classes.

Not long after this the coloured people in Atlanta, Georgia, gave me a reception at which the Governor of the state presided, and a similar reception was given me in New Orleans, which was presided over by the Mayor of the city. Invitations came from many other places which I was not able to accept.

Chapter XVII

Last Words

Before going to Europe some events came into my life which were great surprises to me. In fact, my whole life has largely been one of surprises. I believe that any man's life will be filled with constant, unexpected encouragements of this kind if he makes up his mind to do his level best each day of his life—that is, tries to make each day reach as nearly as possible the high-water mark of pure, unselfish, useful living. I pity the man, black or white, who has never experienced the joy and satisfaction that come to one by reason of an effort to assist in making some one else more useful and more happy.

Six months before he died, and nearly a year after he had been stricken with paralysis, General Armstrong expressed a wish to visit Tuskegee again before he passed away. Notwithstanding the fact that he had lost the use of his limbs to such an extent that he was practically helpless, his wish was gratified, and he was brought to Tuskegee. The owners of the Tuskegee Railroad, white men living in the town, offered to run a special train, without cost, out to the main station—Chehaw, five miles away—to meet him. He arrived on the school grounds about nine o'clock in the evening. Some one had suggested that we give the General a "pine-knot torchlight reception." This plan was carried out, and the moment that his carriage entered the school grounds he began passing between two lines of lighted and waving "fat pine" wood knots held by over a thousand students and teachers. The whole thing was so novel and surprising that the General was completely overcome with happiness. He remained a guest in my home for nearly two months, and, although almost wholly without the use of voice or limb, he spent nearly every hour in devising ways and means to help the South. Time and time again he said to me, during this visit, that it was not only the duty of the country to assist in elevating the Negro of the South, but the poor white man as well. At the end of his visit I resolved anew to devote myself more earnestly than ever to the cause which was so near his heart. I said that if a man in his condition was willing to think, work, and act, I should not be wanting in furthering in every possible way the wish of his heart.

The death of General Armstrong, a few weeks later, gave me the privilege of getting acquainted with one of the finest, most unselfish, and most attractive men that I have ever come in contact with. I refer to the Rev. Dr. Hollis B. Frissell, now the Principal of the Hampton Institute, and General Armstrong's successor. Under the clear, strong, and almost perfect leadership of Dr. Frissell, Hampton has had a career of prosperity and usefulness that is all that the General could have wished for. It seems to be the constant effort of Dr. Frissell to hide his own great personality behind that of General Armstrong—to make himself of "no reputation"[1] for the sake of the cause.

More than once I have been asked what was the greatest surprise that ever came to me. I have little hesitation in answering that question. It was the following letter, which came to me one Sunday morning when I was sitting on the veranda of my home at Tuskegee, surrounded by my wife and three children:—

Harvard University, Cambridge, May 28, 1896.

PRESIDENT BOOKER T. WASHINGTON,

MY DEAR SIR: Harvard University desires to confer on you at the approaching Commencement an honorary degree; but it is our custom to confer degrees only on gentlemen who are present. Our Commencement occurs this year on June 24, and your presence would be desirable from about noon till about five o'clock in the afternoon. Would it be possible for you to be in Cambridge on that day?

Believe me, with great regard,

Very truly yours,
CHARLES W. ELIOT.[2]

This was a recognition that had never in the slightest manner entered into my mind, and it was hard for me to realize that I was to be honoured by a degree from the oldest and most renowned university in America. As I sat upon my veranda, with this letter in my hand, tears came into my eyes. My whole former life—my life as a slave on the plantation, my work in the coal-mine, the times when I was without food and clothing, when I made my bed under a sidewalk, my struggles for an education, the trying days I had had at Tuskegee, days when I did not know where to turn for a dollar to continue the work there, the ostracism and sometimes oppression of my race,—all this passed before me and nearly overcame me.

I had never sought or cared for what the world calls fame. I have always looked upon fame as something to be used in accomplishing good. I have often said to my friends that if I can use whatever promi-

1. See Philippians 2.7.
2. Charles William Eliot (1834–1926), president of Harvard University from 1869 to 1909.

nence may have come to me as an instrument with which to do good, I am content to have it. I care for it only as a means to be used for doing good, just as wealth may be used. The more I come into contact with wealthy people, the more I believe that they are growing in the direction of looking upon their money simply as an instrument which God has placed in their hand for doing good with. I never go to the office of Mr. John D. Rockefeller,[3] who more than once has been generous to Tuskegee, without being reminded of this. The close, careful, and minute investigation that he always makes in order to be sure that every dollar that he gives will do the most good—an investigation that is just as searching as if he were investing money in a business enterprise—convinces me that the growth in this direction is most encouraging.

At nine o'clock, on the morning of June 24, I met President Eliot, the Board of Overseers of Harvard University, and the other guests, at the designated place on the university grounds, for the purpose of being escorted to Sanders Theatre, where the Commencement exercises were to be held and degrees conferred. Among others invited to be present for the purpose of receiving a degree at this time were General Nelson A. Miles, Dr. Bell, the inventor of the Bell telephone, Bishop Vincent, and the Rev. Minot J. Savage. We were placed in line immediately behind the President and the Board of Overseers, and directly afterward the Governor of Massachusetts, escorted by the Lancers, arrived and took his place in the line of march by the side of President Eliot. In the line there were also various other officers and professors, clad in cap and gown. In this order we marched to Sanders Theatre, where, after the usual Commencement exercises, came the conferring of the honorary degrees. This, it seems, is always considered the most interesting feature at Harvard. It is not known, until the individuals appear, upon whom the honorary degrees are to be conferred, and those receiving these honours are cheered by the students and others in proportion to their popularity. During the conferring of the degrees excitement and enthusiasm are at the highest pitch.

When my name was called, I rose, and President Eliot, in beautiful and strong English, conferred upon me the degree of Master of Arts. After these exercises were over, those who had received honorary degrees were invited to lunch with the President. After the lunch we were formed in line again, and were escorted by the Marshal of the day, who that year happened to be Bishop William Lawrence, through the grounds, where, at different points, those who had been honoured were called by name and received the Harvard yell. This march ended at Memorial Hall, where the alumni dinner was served. To see over a thousand strong men, representing all that is best in State, Church,

3. John Davison Rockefeller (1839–1937), founder of the Standard Oil Company.

business, and education, with the glow and enthusiasm of college loyalty and college pride,—which has, I think, a peculiar Harvard flavour,—is a sight that does not easily fade from memory.

Among the speakers after dinner were President Eliot, Governor Roger Wolcott, General Miles, Dr. Minot J. Savage, the Hon. Henry Cabot Lodge, and myself. When I was called upon, I said, among other things:—

> It would in some measure relieve my embarrassment if I could, even in a slight degree, feel myself worthy of the great honour which you do me to-day. Why you have called me from the Black Belt of the South, from among my humble people, to share in the honours of this occasion, is not for me to explain; and yet it may not be inappropriate for me to suggest that it seems to me that one of the most vital questions that touch our American life is how to bring the strong, wealthy, and learned into helpful touch with the poorest, most ignorant, and humblest, and at the same time make one appreciate the vitalizing, strengthening influence of the other. How shall we make the mansions on yon Beacon Street feel and see the need of the spirits in the lowliest cabin in Alabama cottonfields or Louisiana sugar-bottoms? This problem Harvard University is solving, not by bringing itself down, but by bringing the masses up.
>
> * * * * * * *
>
> If my life in the past has meant anything in the lifting up of my people and the bringing about of better relations between your race and mine, I assure you from this day it will mean doubly more. In the economy of God there is but one standard by which an individual can succeed—there is but one for a race. This country demands that every race shall measure itself by the American standard. By it a race must rise or fall, succeed or fail, and in the last analysis mere sentiment counts for little. During the next half-century and more, my race must continue passing through the severe American crucible. We are to be tested in our patience, our forbearance, our perseverance, our power to endure wrong, to withstand temptations, to economize, to acquire and use skill; in our ability to compete, to succeed in commerce, to disregard the superficial for the real, the appearance for the substance, to be great and yet small, learned and yet simple, high and yet the servant of all.

As this was the first time that a New England university had conferred an honorary degree upon a Negro, it was the occasion of much newspaper comment throughout the country. A correspondent of a New York paper said:—

> When the name of Booker T. Washington was called, and he arose to acknowledge and accept, there was such an outburst of

applause as greeted no other name except that of the popular soldier patriot, General Miles. The applause was not studied and stiff, sympathetic and condoling; it was enthusiasm and admiration. Every part of the audience from pit to gallery joined in, and a glow covered the cheeks of those around me, proving sincere appreciation of the rising struggle of an ex-slave and the work he has accomplished for his race.

A Boston paper said, editorially:—

> In conferring the honorary degree of Master of Arts upon the Principal of Tuskegee Institute, Harvard University has honoured itself as well as the object of this distinction. The work which Professor Booker T. Washington has accomplished for the education, good citizenship, and popular enlightenment in his chosen field of labour in the South entitles him to rank with our national benefactors. The university which can claim him on its list of sons, whether in regular course or *honoris causa*, may be proud.
>
> It has been mentioned that Mr. Washington is the first of his race to receive an honorary degree from a New England university. This, in itself, is a distinction. But the degree was not conferred because Mr. Washington is a coloured man, or because he was born in slavery, but because he has shown, by his work for the elevation of the people of the Black Belt of the South, a genius and a broad humanity which count for greatness in any man, whether his skin be white or black.

Another Boston paper said:—

> It is Harvard which, first among New England colleges, confers an honorary degree upon a black man. No one who has followed the history of Tuskegee and its work can fail to admire the courage, persistence, and splendid common sense of Booker T. Washington. Well may Harvard honour the ex-slave, the value of whose services, alike to his race and country, only the future can estimate.

The correspondent of the New York *Times* wrote:—

> All the speeches were enthusiastically received, but the coloured man carried off the oratorical honours, and the applause which broke out when he had finished was vociferous and long-continued.

Soon after I began work at Tuskegee I formed a resolution, in the secret of my heart, that I would try to build up a school that would be of so much service to the country that the President of the United States would one day come to see it. This was, I confess, rather a bold resolution, and for a number of years I kept it hidden in my own thoughts, not daring to share it with any one.

In November, 1897, I made the first move in this direction, and that was in securing a visit from a member of President McKinley's Cabinet, the Hon. James Wilson, Secretary of Agriculture. He came to deliver an address at the formal opening of the Slater-Armstrong Agricultural Building, our first large building to be used for the purpose of giving training to our students in agriculture and kindred branches.

In the fall of 1898 I heard that President McKinley was likely to visit Atlanta, Georgia, for the purpose of taking part in the Peace Jubilee exercises to be held there to commemorate the successful close of the Spanish-American war. At this time I had been hard at work, together with our teachers, for eighteen years, trying to build up a school that we thought would be of service to the Nation, and I determined to make a direct effort to secure a visit from the President and his Cabinet. I went to Washington, and I was not long in the city before I found my way to the White House. When I got there I found the waiting rooms full of people, and my heart began to sink, for I feared there would not be much chance of my seeing the President that day, if at all. But, at any rate, I got an opportunity to see Mr. J. Addison Porter, the secretary to the President, and explained to him my mission. Mr. Porter kindly sent my card directly to the President, and in a few minutes word came from Mr. McKinley that he would see me.

How any man can see so many people of all kinds, with all kinds of errands, and do so much hard work, and still keep himself calm, patient, and fresh for each visitor in the way that President McKinley does, I cannot understand. When I saw the President he kindly thanked me for the work which we were doing at Tuskegee for the interests of the country. I then told him, briefly, the object of my visit. I impressed upon him the fact that a visit from the Chief Executive of the Nation would not only encourage our students and teachers, but would help the entire race. He seemed interested, but did not make a promise to go to Tuskegee, for the reason that his plans about going to Atlanta were not then fully made; but he asked me to call the matter to his attention a few weeks later.

By the middle of the following month the President had definitely decided to attend the Peace Jubilee at Atlanta. I went to Washington again and saw him, with a view of getting him to extend his trip to Tuskegee. On this second visit Mr. Charles W. Hare, a prominent white citizen of Tuskegee, kindly volunteered to accompany me, to reënforce my invitation with one from the white people of Tuskegee and the vicinity.

Just previous to my going to Washington the second time, the country had been excited, and the coloured people greatly depressed, because of several severe race riots which had occurred at different points in the South. As soon as I saw the President, I perceived that his heart was greatly burdened by reason of these race disturbances. Although there were many people waiting to see him, he detained me for some time, discussing the condition and prospects of the race. He remarked several times that he was determined to show his interest and faith in the race, not merely in words, but by acts. When I told him that I thought that at that time scarcely anything would go farther in giving hope and encouragement to the race than the fact that the President of the Nation would be willing to travel one hundred and forty miles out of his way to spend a day at a Negro institution, he seemed deeply impressed.

While I was with the President, a white citizen of Atlanta, a Democrat and an ex-slaveholder, came into the room, and the President asked his opinion as to the wisdom of his going to Tuskegee. Without hesitation the Atlanta man replied that it was the proper thing for him to do. This opinion was reënforced by that friend of the race, Dr. J. L. M. Curry. The President promised that he would visit our school on the 16th of December.

When it became known that the President was going to visit our school, the white citizens of the town of Tuskegee—a mile distant from the school—were as much pleased as were our students and teachers. The white people of the town, including both men and women, began arranging to decorate the town, and to form themselves into committees for the purpose of coöperating with the officers of our school in order that the distinguished visitor might have a fitting reception. I think I never realized before this how much the white people of Tuskegee and vicinity thought of our institution. During the days when we were preparing for the President's reception, dozens of these people came to me and said that, while they did not want to push themselves into prominence, if there was anything they could do to help, or to relieve me personally, I had but to intimate it and they would be only too glad to assist. In fact, the thing that touched me almost as deeply as the visit of the President itself was the deep pride which all classes of citizens in Alabama seemed to take in our work.

The morning of December 16th brought to the little city of Tuskegee such a crowd as it had never seen before. With the President came Mrs. McKinley and all of the Cabinet officers but one; and most of them brought their wives or some members of their families. Several prominent generals came, including General Shafter and General Joseph Wheeler, who were recently returned from the Spanish-American war. There was also a host of newspaper correspondents. The Alabama Legislature was in session at Montgomery at this time. This body passed a resolution to adjourn for the purpose of visiting Tuskegee. Just before the arrival of the President's party the Legislature arrived, headed by the governor and other state officials.

The citizens of Tuskegee had decorated the town from the station to the school in a generous manner. In order to economize in the matter of time, we arranged to have the whole school pass in review before the President. Each student carried a stalk of sugar-cane with some open bolls of cotton fastened to the end of it. Following the students the work of all departments of the school passed in review, displayed on "floats" drawn by horses, mules, and oxen. On these floats we tried to exhibit not only the present work of the school, but to show the contrasts between the old methods of doing things and the new. As an example, we showed the old method of dairying in contrast with the improved methods, the old methods of tilling the soil in contrast with the new, the old methods of cooking and housekeeping in contrast with the new. These floats consumed an hour and a half of time in passing.

In his address in our large, new chapel, which the students had recently completed, the President said, among other things:—

> To meet you under such pleasant auspices and to have the opportunity of a personal observation of your work is indeed most gratifying. The Tuskegee Normal and Industrial Institute is ideal in its conception, and has already a large and growing reputation in the country, and is not unknown abroad. I congratulate all who are associated in this undertaking for the good work which it is doing in the education of its students to lead lives of honour and usefulness, thus exalting the race for which it was established.
>
> Nowhere, I think, could a more delightful location have been chosen for this unique educational experiment, which has attracted the attention and won the support even of conservative philanthropists in all sections of the country.
>
> To speak of Tuskegee without paying special tribute to Booker T. Washington's genius and perseverance would be impossible. The inception of this noble enterprise was his, and he deserves high credit for it. His was the enthusiasm and enterprise which made its steady progress possible and established in the institution its present high standard of accomplishment. He has won a worthy reputation as one of the great leaders of his race, widely known and much respected at home and abroad as an accomplished educator, a great orator, and a true philanthropist.

The Hon. John D. Long, the Secretary of the Navy, said in part:—

> I cannot make a speech to-day. My heart is too full—full of hope, admiration, and pride for my countrymen of both sections and both colours. I am filled with gratitude and admiration for your work, and from this time forward I shall have absolute confidence in your progress and in the solution of the problem in which you are engaged.
>
> The problem, I say, has been solved. A picture has been presented to-day which should be put upon canvas with the pictures of Washington and Lincoln, and transmitted to future time and

> generations—a picture which the press of the country should spread broadcast over the land, a most dramatic picture, and that picture is this: The President of the United States standing on this platform; on one side the Governor of Alabama, on the other, completing the trinity, a representative of a race only a few years ago in bondage, the coloured President of the Tuskegee Normal and Industrial Institute.
>
> God bless the President under whose majesty such a scene as that is presented to the American people. God bless the state of Alabama, which is showing that it can deal with this problem for itself. God bless the orator, philanthropist, and disciple of the Great Master—who, if he were on earth, would be doing the same work—Booker T. Washington.

Postmaster General Smith closed the address which he made with these words:—

> We have witnessed many spectacles within the last few days. We have seen the magnificent grandeur and the magnificent achievements of one of the great metropolitan cities of the South. We have seen heroes of the war pass by in procession. We have seen floral parades. But I am sure my colleagues will agree with me in saying that we have witnessed no spectacle more impressive and more encouraging, more inspiring for our future, than that which we have witnessed here this morning.

Some days after the President returned to Washington I received the letter which follows:—

> Executive Mansion, Washington, Dec. 23, 1899.
>
> DEAR SIR: By this mail I take pleasure in sending you engrossed copies of the souvenir of the visit of the President to your institution. These sheets bear the autographs of the President and the members of the Cabinet who accompanied him on the trip. Let me take this opportunity of congratulating you most heartily and sincerely upon the great success of the exercises provided for and entertainment furnished us under your auspices during our visit to Tuskegee. Every feature of the programme was perfectly executed and was viewed or participated in with the heartiest satisfaction by every visitor present. The unique exhibition which you gave of your pupils engaged in their industrial vocations was not only artistic but thoroughly impressive. The tribute paid by the President and his Cabinet to your work was none too high, and forms a most encouraging augury, I think, for the future prosperity of your institution. I cannot close without assuring you that the modesty shown by yourself in the exercises was most favourably commented upon by all the members of our party.
>
> With best wishes for the continued advance of your most useful

and patriotic undertaking, kind personal regards, and the compliments of the season, believe me, always,

Very sincerely yours,
JOHN ADDISON PORTER,
Secretary to the President.

To PRESIDENT BOOKER T. WASHINGTON, Tuskegee Normal and Industrial Institute, Tuskegee, Ala.

Twenty years have now passed since I made the first humble effort at Tuskegee, in a broken-down shanty and an old hen-house, without owning a dollar's worth of property, and with but one teacher and thirty students. At the present time the institution owns twenty-three hundred acres of land, one thousand of which are under cultivation each year, entirely by student labour. There are now upon the grounds, counting large and small, sixty-six buildings; and all except four of these have been almost wholly erected by the labour of our students. While the students are at work upon the land and in erecting buildings, they are taught, by competent instructors, the latest methods of agriculture and the trades connected with building.

There are in constant operation at the school, in connection with thorough academic and religious training, thirty industrial departments. All of these teach industries at which our men and women can find immediate employment as soon as they leave the institution. The only difficulty now is that the demand for our graduates from both white and black people in the South is so great that we cannot supply more than one-half the persons for whom applications come to us. Neither have we the buildings nor the money for current expenses to enable us to admit to the school more than one-half the young men and women who apply to us for admission.

In our industrial teaching we keep three things in mind: first, that the student shall be so educated that he shall be enabled to meet conditions as they exist *now*, in the part of the South where he lives—in a word, to be able to do the thing which the world wants done; second, that every student who graduates from the school shall have enough skill, coupled with intelligence and moral character, to enable him to make a living for himself and others; third, to send every graduate out feeling and knowing that labour is dignified and beautiful—to make each one love labour instead of trying to escape it. In addition to the agricultural training which we give to young men, and the training given to our girls in all the usual domestic employments, we now train a number of girls in agriculture each year. These girls are taught gardening, fruit-growing, dairying, bee-culture, and poultry-raising.

While the institution is in no sense denominational, we have a department known as the Phelps Hall Bible Training School, in which a number of students are prepared for the ministry and other forms of

Christian work, especially work in the country districts. What is equally important, each one of these students works half of each day at some industry, in order to get skill and the love of work, so that when he goes out from the institution he is prepared to set the people with whom he goes to labour a proper example in the matter of industry.

The value of our property is now over $700,000. If we add to this our endowment fund, which at present is $1,000,000, the value of the total property is now $1,700,000. Aside from the need for more buildings and for money for current expenses, the endowment fund should be increased to at least $3,000,000. The annual current expenses are now about $150,000. The greater part of this I collect each year by going from door to door and from house to house. All of our property is free from mortgage, and is deeded to an undenominational board of trustees who have the control of the institution.

From thirty students the number has grown to fourteen hundred, coming from twenty-seven states and territories, from Africa, Cuba, Porto Rico, Jamaica, and other foreign countries. In our departments there are one hundred and ten officers and instructors; and if we add the families of our instructors, we have a constant population upon our grounds of not far from seventeen hundred people.

I have often been asked how we keep so large a body of people together, and at the same time keep them out of mischief. There are two answers: that the men and women who come to us for an education are in earnest; and that everybody is kept busy. The following outline of our daily work will testify to this:—

> 5 A.M., rising bell; 5.50 A.M., warning breakfast bell; 6 A.M., breakfast bell; 6.20 A.M., breakfast over; 6.20 to 6.50 A.M., rooms are cleaned; 6.50, work bell; 7.30, morning study hour; 8.20, morning school bell; 8.25, inspection of young men's toilet in ranks; 8.40, devotional exercises in chapel; 8.55, "five minutes with the daily news;" 9 A.M., class work begins; 12, class work closes; 12.15 P.M., dinner; 1 P.M., work bell; 1.30 P.M., class work begins; 3.30 P.M., class work ends; 5.30 P.M., bell to "knock off" work; 6 P.M., supper; 7.10 P.M., evening prayers; 7.30 P.M., evening study hours; 8.45 P.M., evening study hour closes; 9.20 P.M., warning retiring bell; 9.30 P.M., retiring bell.

We try to keep constantly in mind the fact that the worth of the school is to be judged by its graduates. Counting those who have finished the full course, together with those who have taken enough training to enable them to do reasonably good work, we can safely say that at least six thousand men and women from Tuskegee are now at work in different parts of the South; men and women who, by their own example or by direct effort, are showing the masses of our race how to improve their material, educational, and moral and religious life. What is equally important, they are exhibiting a degree of common sense and self-control which is causing better relations to exist between the races, and is causing the Southern white man to learn to believe in the value of educating the men and women of my race. Aside from this, there is the influence that is constantly being exerted through the mothers' meeting and the plantation work conducted by Mrs. Washington.

Wherever our graduates go, the changes which soon begin to appear in the buying of land, improving homes, saving money, in education, and in high moral character are remarkable. Whole communities are fast being revolutionized through the instrumentality of these men and women.

Ten years ago I organized at Tuskegee the first Negro Conference. This is an annual gathering which now brings to the school eight or nine hundred representative men and women of the race, who come to spend a day in finding out what the actual industrial, mental, and moral conditions of the people are, and in forming plans for improvement. Out from this central Negro Conference at Tuskegee have grown numerous state and local conferences which are doing the same kind of work. As a result of the influence of these gatherings, one delegate reported at the last annual meeting that ten families in his community had bought and paid for homes. On the day following the annual Negro Conference, there is held the "Workers' Conference." This is composed of officers and teachers who are engaged in educational work in the larger institutions in the South. The Negro Conference furnishes a rare opportunity for these workers to study the real condition of the rank and file of the people.

In the summer of 1900, with the assistance of such prominent coloured men as Mr. T. Thomas Fortune,[4] who has always upheld my hands in every effort, I organized the National Negro Business League, which held its first meeting in Boston, and brought together for the first time a large number of the coloured men who are engaged in various lines of trade or business in different parts of the United states. Thirty states were represented at our first meeting. Out of this national meeting grew state and local business leagues.

In addition to looking after the executive side of the work at Tuskegee, and raising the greater part of the money for the support of the school, I cannot seem to escape the duty of answering at least a part of the calls which come to me unsought to address Southern white audiences and audiences of my own race, as well as frequent gatherings in the North. As to how much of my time is spent in this way, the following clipping from a Buffalo (N.Y.) paper will tell. This has reference to an occasion when I spoke before the National Educational Association in that city.

4. Timothy Thomas Fortune (1856–1928), editor and owner of the *New York Age*, a leading African American newspaper.

> Booker T. Washington, the foremost educator among the coloured people of the world, was a very busy man from the time he arrived in the city the other night from the West and registered at the Iroquois. He had hardly removed the stains of travel when it was time to partake of supper. Then he held a public levee in the parlours of the Iroquois until eight o'clock. During that time he was greeted by over two hundred eminent teachers and educators from all parts of the United States. Shortly after eight o'clock he was driven in a carriage to Music Hall, and in one hour and a half he made two ringing addresses, to as many as five thousand people, on Negro education. Then Mr. Washington was taken in charge by a delegation of coloured citizens, headed by the Rev. Mr. Watkins, and hustled off to a small informal reception, arranged in honour of the visitor by the people of his race.

Nor can I, in addition to making these addresses, escape the duty of calling the attention of the South and of the country in general, through the medium of the press, to matters that pertain to the interests of both races. This, for example, I have done in regard to the evil habit of lynching. When the Louisiana State Constitutional Convention was in session, I wrote an open letter to that body pleading for justice for the race. In all such efforts I have received warm and hearty support from the Southern newspapers, as well as from those in all other parts of the country.

Despite superficial and temporary signs which might lead one to entertain a contrary opinion, there was never a time when I felt more hopeful for the race than I do at the present. The great human law that in the end recognizes and rewards merit is everlasting and universal. The outside world does not know, neither can it appreciate, the struggle that is constantly going on in the hearts of both the Southern white people and their former slaves to free themselves from racial prejudice; and while both races are thus struggling they should have the sympathy, the support, and the forbearance of the rest of the world.

As I write the closing words of this autobiography I find myself—not by design—in the city of Richmond, Virginia: the city which only a few decades ago was the capital of the Southern Confederacy, and where, about twenty-five years ago, because of my poverty I slept night after night under a sidewalk.

This time I am in Richmond as the guest of the coloured people of the city; and came at their request to deliver an address last night to both races in the Academy of Music, the largest and finest audience room in the city. This was the first time that the coloured people had ever been permitted to use this hall. The day before I came, the City Council passed a vote to attend the meeting in a body to hear me speak. The state Legislature, including the House of Delegates and the Senate, also passed a unanimous vote to attend in a body. In the presence of hundreds of coloured people, many distinguished white citizens, the City Council, the state Legislature, and state officials, I delivered my message, which was one of hope and cheer; and from the bottom of my heart I thanked both races for this welcome back to the state that gave me birth.

Index

CONTEXTS AND COMPOSITION HISTORY

Letters About *Up From Slavery* (1899–1900)

Lyman Abbott to Booker T. Washington †

New York December 9, 1899

My dear Mr. Washington: I have just been reading your volume, and it has renewed and increased my admiration for your work. It is easily within bounds to say that no one in America has thrown so much light or exerted so beneficent an influence upon what we call the negro problem, as you have done. I doubt whether all other influences combined since the close of the Reconstruction period have been as efficient and beneficent as yours.

I hope at an early day to give to our readers what seem to me to be substantial principles which you inculcate, founding that statement upon this volume.

Meanwhile I am minded to write this letter to you, asking of you a service which if I do not misjudge, will be of great use to the cause which you have at heart. This is that you write for us an autobiography or autobiographical reminiscences of about fifteen to twenty thousand words in length. We should probably publish it in three or four parts. My thought is that in such reminiscences you could show our readers by incidents in your own life and career what are the trials, difficulties and obstacles thrown in the way of the progress of your race and how those obstacles may be met and surmounted. Writing as you would necessarily do in an anecdotal and reminiscent mood, your articles would be read by a great many who are not greatly interested in the problem as a problem, and whose interest would be awakened by such a story as you could tell, while at the same time such incidents would necessarily illustrate the principles for which you contend and the solution which you propose to the problem which confronts us.

I know that you are a busy man, and that you may naturally begrudge the time for such an undertaking; but I also am sure that you will appreciate the advantage of enlarging the constituency to which appeal can be made for interest in this problem, and I hope you will see as I do that in no better way could that constituency be enlarged than by such a story of your life.

If the general idea of such a biography strikes you favorably, I should like to have a personal conference with you about length, scope and price (which we should expect to make satisfactory to you) when you next come to New York. Yours sincerely,

Lyman Abbott

† From Louis R. Harlan, ed., *Booker T. Washington Papers* (Urbana: U of Illinois P, 1976) vol. 5, 288–89. Lyman Abbott (1835–1922) was editor of *The Outlook* magazine.

Booker T. Washington to John A. Hertel†

[Tuskegee, Ala.] Sept. 22, 1900

Dear Sir: In addition to the written application which my secretary, Mr. Scott, made to be placed before your company at its next meeting, I wish to say that so far as the mere letter of the law is concerned I feel quite sure I could go ahead and publish the Reminiscences[1] and be sustained in doing so, but it has been my rule to deal frankly and sympathetically with my publishers as well as others with whom I have dealings, and I not only want to obey the letter of the law but have your frank and sympathetic consent in anything that I do, in other words I want to work with you and not in opposition to you and I want you to do the same thing with me.

I am quite sure that, as Mr. Scott stated to you, the two publications will not in any way clash with each other since, in the first place, they are to be on different lines and to be sold in an almost wholly different section of the country and sold by the trade instead of by subscription. I believe that what I have planned to do for the other people will help your book since you know that anything that keeps my name before the public will assist in increasing the sale of your book.

And finally I urge as the strongest point that the work which I am to do for the other people will have for its main advantage the bringing of this institution before a class of people who have money and to whom I must look for money for endowment and other purposes. In proportion as I can get money from these people and keep this institution in a prosperous condition, in the same degree will there be a sale for your book. If this institution were to go down tomorrow, your book would at once become dead property on your hands, so you see it is important that we work wisely and sympathetically together.

I shall hope in the future to do more business with you in regard to publishing books; I don't want this to be the last by any means. This is another reason why I want to keep in close and sympathetic touch with you.

* * *

Booker T. Washington

† From Louis R. Harlan, ed., *Booker T. Washington Papers* (Urbana: U of Illinois P, 1976) vol. 5, 642–43. John A. Hertel, general manager of J. L. Nichols and Company, was the publisher of Washington's first autobiography, *The Story of My Life and Work* (1900).

1. The book that would become *Up From Slavery*.

Lyman Abbott to Booker T. Washington †

New York October 1, 1900

My dear Mr. Washington: I have read with great interest the first pages of your Autobiography, which I return to you herewith. I do not think there is any danger that you will go too much into detailed facts. The pictorial side of your life, the experiences through which you have passed, the incidents which you have seen, out of which your own generalizations have grown, will be of the first interest and the first value to our readers. I, for example, would like very much to know more of your boyhood life in the slave days, if it were possible for you to give it. Did you have any sports, any education, any work to do before emancipation? Probably all this lies back of your recollection, but if it did not, it would be of great interest; and the answer to the same questions within the range of your recollections and after emancipation, would be almost as interesting.

So would your personal recollections of the Reconstruction period and of the way in which that period looked to the just emancipated slave. It is generally looked upon wholly from the white man's point of view, sometimes the Southern white man's, sometimes the Northern white man's. How did it seem then to the Negroes, how does it seem now to one who has the interest of his race at heart and sympathizes with their point of view?

As to style, I have the impression that this manuscript has been dictated, and that if you were to go over it carefully, you would condense it somewhat by cutting out some repetitions. I have hinted at some of these with my own pencil, and I have made a few verbal alterations which I am sure you would approve, and suggested a change in the order of incidents. In order to get this manuscript into The Outlook the first week in November, we ought to have a good instalment in hand by the last of this week, or the first of next week at the latest. Yours sincerely,

Lyman Abbott

Booker T. Washington to Lyman Abbott ††

[Tuskegee, Ala., ca. Oct. 8, 1900]

My dear Dr. Abbott: I have received your kind letter together with the manuscript.

I am grateful to you for the suggestions which you make. I think you will find that the rest of the manuscript will be in better condition as to

† From Louis R. Harlan, ed., *Booker T. Washington Papers* (Urbana: U of Illinois P, 1976) vol. 5, 646.

†† From Louis R. Harlan, ed., *Booker T. Washington Papers* (Urbana: U of Illinois P, 1976) vol. 5, 653–54.

compactness, etc. I think you will find that most of the incidents which you suggest that I bring out more fully are covered in the later manuscript. The matter about which I am most anxious how ever to have an understanding is the order of treatment. When I talked with you and your son I got the impression that you did not care for some of the rather stereotyped styles of autobiographies which as a rule are divided into the periods, of childhood, youth, etc., with each period exhausted before another is begun. This I have sought to avoid not only because I thought you desired it but also because it is in keeping with my own method of writing.

My general plan is to give the *first place* to facts and incidents and to hang the generalizations on to these facts—taking for granted that the average reader is more interested in an interesting fact than in a generalization based on that fact, and for this reason I have sought not to use too many generalizations and when they are used to have them well sugar-coated with some interesting incident.

I think you will find that all my facts are given in chronological order and that the generalizations based upon these facts only go beyond the natural order. For example in giving my experience in entering the Hampton Institute, I describe my first contact with general Armstrong. From this I go on and describe the general influence of general Armstrong—speak of his coming to Tuskegee 18 years later etc. In a word while I am at it I say nearly every thing that I intend saying about general Armstrong. This is the order of treatment in which I feel that I can do my best work. Still I want to be guided by your wishes.

This explanation together with the additional manuscript will enable you to give suggestions for my future work. I fear that you could not get a very correct idea of what I am trying to do from the small amount of man[u]s[c]ript which I sent you. By this mail I send you an additional installment. From this I think you can get a pretty correct idea of what to expect. If after you have gone over this you still feel that the order of treatment is not what you desire, I would suggest one of two things: that you have some one in your office rearrange it or if there is time you return it to me for rearrangement. Yours truly

[Booker T. Washington]

[Review of *Up From Slavery*] †

Up from Slavery: An Autobiography. By Booker T. Washington. Doubleday, Page and Co. 1901.

This book is to be sharply distinguished from another of similar char-

† From *The Nation* 72 (April 4, 1901) 281–82. [Norton Critical Edition page number appears in brackets—*Editor.*]

acter, 'The Life and Work of Booker T. Washington,'[1] a subscription book of the cheapest character which has recently been put upon the market as if it were a new book. It contains a good deal of the matter presented in 'Up from Slavery,' interspersed with illustrations so ill-made and with such offensive titles that they cannot have been approved by Mr. Washington and must give him serious annoyance. 'Up from Slavery' has been published serially in the *Outlook*, where it has been widely read and with much admiration, but it is fully entitled to republication in the attractive volume which now comes to hand, lacking the excellent illustrations which were a notable feature of the *Outlook* serial. Those who would possess themselves fully of Mr. Washington's mind and purpose should supplement 'Up from Slavery' with his 'Future of the American Negro,' published a year ago.

The new book has an accidental timeliness for which we cannot be too glad, coming as it does so close upon the heels of Mr. Thomas's 'American Negro,'[2] recently reviewed in these columns. It is the best kind of answer to that railing accusation, and we hope that Mr. Washington will attempt no other. He has one reference to it, or some earlier deliverance of its author, where he says (p. 32) [113]:

"I have seen the statement made lately, by one who claims to know what he is talking about, that, taking the whole negro race into account, ninety per cent of the negro women are not virtuous. There never was a baser calumny uttered concerning a race, or a statement made that was less capable of being proved by actual facts."

The difference between Mr. Thomas's construction and that of Mr. Washington is not, however, so great as it appears to the more casual reader. For it must be remembered that the negro is for Mr. Thomas, not a body of colored people, but, as certain theologians say of heaven, "a state of mind." His only true negroes are foolish negroes and bad negroes. He adopts a standard which excludes himself and presumably Mr. Washington, seeing that he does not once mention him nor the work which he and his eighty assistants are doing at Tuskegee. Mr. Washington's method is diametrically the opposite of this. He imputes his own work and that of all the better negroes to the race for righteousness. That is to say, in striking the average he does not exclude the better elements. In no other respect is his book more impressive and affecting than in that of his complete identification of himself with his people. His achievements are their possibilities. He delights frankly in the honors paid to him at Atlanta, at Harvard, in Europe, and elsewhere, but always because he is a negro and a representative of the millions who have just escaped from slavery into "a bewildering freedom."

1. Actually, Washington's *The Story of My Life and Work* (1900).
2. William Hannibal Thomas, author of *The American Negro* (1901).

Mr. Washington must have had natural gifts of expression which have been enhanced by careful attention to the principles of good writing. His style is simple and direct, without any of that rhetorical effusion which Mr. Thomas holds to be a negro trait, and grossly illustrates in his own person. His sense of humor is keen, and he has some amusing stories, but they are never lugged in by the ears; they are always pertinent and happy illustrations of particular phases of his thought.

In some degree the book derives its interest from Mr. Washington's low and miserable beginnings contrasting with the successes of his later life. Benjamin Franklin's first arrival in Philadelphia has a worthy pendant in Booker T. Washington's first arrival in Richmond, where he slept under a sidewalk by night, while working by day to earn money to carry him to his destination at the Hampton Institute. It was neither strange nor dishonorable that his mind reverted to those days when he was getting a degree from Harvard or taking tea with Queen Victoria. But his getting on was but the smaller part of his experience—he was bound to do that, he was so ambitious, so thrifty and industrious. Very early in life, however, he developed an ambition to be the helper of his people. Inducements were offered him to seek political preferment, the rewards of which were easily within his grasp, but these he put aside, and at length, in 1881, at the instance of Gen. Armstrong, he went to Tuskegee to begin the work which is so honorably associated with his name.

On his way to this beginning his upward course was marked by many incidents of the *olim meminisse jurabit* kind.[3] In his worst straits at Hampton, while working in a restaurant at Fortress Monroe, he found a new, crisp $10 bill. It would have rescued him from the horrible pit and the miry clay, but his employer decided that the money belonged to himself because it was found on his premises. Trying to be a waiter in New Haven, he failed so egregiously that he was driven off the field by the maledictions of the gentlemen (?) who could not endure his blundering; but he soon made himself efficient. A more significant difficulty was that attending his charge of an Indian student from Hampton to Washington. The Indian had the freedom of the cars and the hotels from which young Washington was excluded. On the other hand, at this early time and later, he had experiences that would have been "wonderful providences" to one more prone to theological interpretations.

The vicissitudes and achievements of the Tuskegee School are exhibited in a series of pictures and contrasts that must sometimes make the reader's heart beat fast and sometimes dim his eyes. Wonderfully pathetic are the reminiscences of students frost-bitten in their beds; of the old colored teachers flocking in and taking a lower rank than their

3. From a longer line by the Latin classical poet Virgil, *forsan et haec olim meminisse jurabit*: "perhaps one day it will be a pleasure to remember these things too."

former pupils; of the disinclination to manual labor which was gradually overcome; of the generous cooperation of the white people of Tuskegee with Mr. Washington and his coworkers. The first animal owned by the school was an old blind horse; now it has over 200 horses, mules, etc., besides 700 pigs, for which creatures Mr. Washington confesses a peculiar admiration. At first there was a stable and a hen-house for housing the pupils; now there are forty buildings, built almost entirely by the students. At first Mr. Washington was the only teacher; now he has a teaching and directing force of eighty men and women. At first there was no money; now the school property is worth $300,000, and there is $250,000 in endowment funds. Mr. Washington's chapter about getting money for the school is one of the most interesting in his book. Many have wondered how he could be away from Tuskegee so much without prejudice to his hold upon the work. We are informed that every day of his absence he receives an account of the work down to the last details—what students are excused from work and why; the bill of fare, and whether certain meats are baked or boiled.

There is scant attention to race problems, but it is not as if Mr. Washington had not written elsewhere of negro lynching and disfranchisement. Here it is only necessary for him to call attention to those utterances which were sufficiently distinct, and absolutely final in their disproof of any willingness on his part to sell the political and social birthrights of his people for any mess of industrial pottage, however wholesome this may be. Of striking episodes there is none superior to that of the Atlanta Exposition speech. In advance of its delivery he was very nervous, but even more so was his friend Mr. William H. Baldwin, Jr., now better known than then, who walked about outside the buildings in a spasm of anxiety until the ordeal was over and a splendid triumph scored. Those who propose skipping the chapter on Mr. Washington's trip to Europe—the chapter on this subject can be so safely skipped in most biographies—would do well to change their minds. What is most interesting about it is the main reason why he feared to go. It was that he might seem "stuck up," trying to "show off," and so give countenance to the idea that the negro cannot bear prosperity without being unduly exalted. What is certain is that Mr. Washington has had successes that would turn the head of many a white man, but his own is right side up. It is kept so by the balance of a heart devoted to the elevation of his race.

W. D. HOWELLS

From An Exemplary Citizen †

* * *

The story of his struggle for an education is the story of Booker Washington's life, which I am not going to spoil for the reader by trying to tell it. He has himself told it so simply and charmingly that one could not add to or take from it without marring it. The part of the autobiography which follows the account of his learning to read and write, in the scanty leisure of his hard work in the West Virginia coal mines, and of his desperate adventure in finding his way into Hampton Institute, is, perhaps, more important and more significant, but it has not the fascination of his singularly pleasing personality. It concerns the great problem, which no man has done more than he to solve, of the future of his race, and its reconciliation with the white race, upon conditions which it can master only through at least provisional submission; but it has not the appeal to the less philosophized sympathies which go out to struggle and achievement. It is not such interesting reading, and yet it is all very interesting; and if the prosperity of the author is not so picturesque as his adversity, still it is prosperity well merited, and it is never selfish prosperity.

Booker Washington early divined the secret of happiness as constant activity for the good of others. This was the first thing he learned from the example of the admirable man who became his ideal and his norm: he formed himself, morally at least, upon General Armstrong, and in a measure he studied his manner—his simple and sincere manner—oratorically.

This must be evident to any one who has heard both men speak. It was most apparent to me when I heard Mr. Washington speak at a meeting which had been addressed by several distinguished white speakers. When this marvellous yellow man came upon the platform, and stood for a moment, with his hands in his pockets, and with downcast eyes, and then began to *talk* at his hearers the clearest, soundest sense, he made me forget all those distinguished white speakers, and he made me remember General Armstrong, from whom he had learned that excellent manner. It was somewhat the manner of Salvini,[1] when, in the character of another colored man, he defends himself to the Venetian Senate for having taken away Brabantio's daughter;[2] and, perhaps, the

† From W. D. Howells, "An Exemplary Citizen," *North American Review* 173 (August 1901): 282–85.

1. Tommasso Salvini, Italian actor, best known for his portrayals of Othello in Shakespeare's play.
2. Desdemona, tragic heroine in Shakespeare's *Othello*.

poet was divining and forecasting the style of the race in the plain, unvarnished reasoning of Othello.

What strikes you, first and last, in Mr. Washington is his constant common sense. He has lived heroic poetry, and he can, therefore, afford to talk simple prose. Simple prose it is, but of sterling worth, and such as it is a pleasure to listen to as long as he chooses to talk. It is interfused with the sweet, brave humor which qualifies his writing, and which enables him, like Dunbar,[3] to place himself outside his race, when he wishes to see it as others see it, and to report its exterior effect from his interior knowledge. To do this may not be proof of the highest civilization, but it is a token of the happiest and usefullest temperament.

III.

The dominant of Mr. Washington's register is *business;* first, last and all the time, the burden of his song is the Tuskegee Industrial Institute. There is other music in him, and no one who reads his story can fail to know its sweetness; but to Tuskegee his heart and soul are unselfishly devoted, and he does not suffer his readers long to forget it. He feels with his whole strength that the hope of his race is in its industrial advancement, and that its education must, above all, tend to that. His people must know how to read and write in order to be better workmen; but good workmen they must be, and they must lead decent, sober, honest lives to the same end. It was the inspiration of this philosophy and experience which enabled him, in his famous speech at the opening of the Atlanta Exposition, to bring the white race into kindlier and wiser relations with the black than they had known before. Social equality he does not ask for or apparently care for; but industrial and economic equality his energies are bent upon achieving, in the common interest of both races. Of all slights and wrongs he is patient, so they do not hinder the negro from working or learning how to work in the best way.

The temper of his mind is conservative, and, oddly enough, that seems to be the temper of the Afro-American mind whenever it comes to its consciousness. The Anglo-American of the South may be, and often has been, an extremist, but the Afro-American, so far as he has made himself eminent, is not. Perhaps, it is his unfailing sense of humor that saves him from extremism. At any rate, cool patience is not more characteristic of Mr. Washington than of Mr. Dunbar or Mr. Chesnutt[4] or of Frederick Douglass himself. Douglass was essentially militant; he was a fighter from 'way back, from the hour when he conceived the notion that if the slave would always fight the man who attempted to whip him, there would be no whipping, and he did fight his master upon this theory, and beat him; his war with slavery was to

3. Paul Laurence Dunbar (1872–1906), the most popular African American poet of the time.
4. Charles Waddell Chesnutt (1858–1932), prominent African American protest fiction writer.

the death. Yet he laid himself open to the blame of certain Abolitionists because he would not go all lengths with them, and he refused to take part in the attempt of John Brown,[5] whom he loved with his whole heart. He kept amidst the tumult of his emotion the judicial mind, and he did not lose his head in the stormy career of the agitator.

This calm is apparently characteristic of the best of the race, and in certain aspects it is of the highest and most consoling promise. It enables them to use reason and the nimbler weapons of irony, and saves them from bitterness. By virtue of it Washington, and Dunbar and Chesnutt enjoy the negro's ludicrous side as the white observer enjoys it, and Douglass could see the fun of the zealots whose friend and fellow-fighter he was. The fact is of all sorts of interesting implications; but I will draw from it, for the present, the sole suggestion that the problem of the colored race may be more complex than we have thought it. What if upon some large scale they should be subtler than we have supposed? What if their amiability should veil a sense of *our* absurdities, and there should be in our polite inferiors the potentiality of something like contempt for us? The notion is awful; but we may be sure they will be too kind, too wise, ever to do more than let us guess at the truth, if it is the truth.

IV.

Mr. Washington's experience of our race has been such as to teach him a greater measure of kindness for it than many of his race have cause to feel. His generous enterprise prospers by our bounty, which he owns, with rather more tolerance for the rich than the New Testament expresses. So far from bidding them "go to and howl," he is disposed to deprecate the censure which some of the public prints (perhaps in too literal a discipleship) heap upon them. With such open hands he believes there must go good hearts, and he finds not excuse only, but justification, for English aristocrats as well as American plutocrats. He does not know but there may be good reasons for the division of society into classes, and for the frank recognition of server and served, as in England. This may be because Mr. Washington's clock does not always strike twelve; and it may be because he and the nobility and gentry are right. In either case, it is interesting in itself and ingenuous in him. It makes assurance doubly sure that the negro is not going to do anything dynamitic to the structure of society. He is going to take it as he finds it, and make the best of his rather poor chances in it. In his heart is no bitterness. If his rights are taken away, he will work quietly on till they are given back. No doubt, it is the wisest way. If he keeps faithfully and quietly at work, he will presently be an owner of the earth and have

5. John Brown (1800–1859), abolitionist leader executed for leading an insurrection at Harpers Ferry, Virginia.

money in the bank, and from such their rights cannot long be withheld. They can buy the strong arm that robs them; they can invoke the law to make the oppressor get off the land. * * *

[An African American Book Review] †

Doubleday, Page and Company, New York, have announced a publication in sets of the two best books by Booker T. Washington. "Up From Slavery" and "Working With The Hands"[1] have been put in uniform edition, and hereafter may be purchased at a very much reduced price.

Dr. Washington's "Up From Slavery," his autobiography, has long ago been adjudged the most interesting life story that has appeared in the last quarter of century, in any land. Indeed so great has been the interest in the work, so widespread the demand for it, that, since its appearance in book form three years ago it has been translated into a dozen tongues, the very latest language to which it has been translated being the Chinese. So much for the outside [of] it.

There is nothing about the style of the book so absorbing; it is the record which it sets down: the simplicity of the life which it records, and the grandeur of character of the man, revealed in the multitudinous activities in which he has engaged for twenty and four years. From the moment one takes up the book, and reads upon the first page Dr. Washington's admission that he does not know when he was born, and his suspicion that he must have been born "somewhere and at some time," until the last page is reached, whereon is breathed a sweet hope for the deliverance of his people, fascination joins with interest in the wade, knee deep and refreshing, through the pages of wit and philosophy, and eloquence of deeds.

The founding of Tuskegee, its subsequent life, or rather struggle, is of course the dominant note in the book. But the good Doctor has set down with accuracy, the part, always prominent, often powerful, he has played in the affairs of the nation, and particularly of his race, since he began his work. It is really as much a surprise as gratification, to learn from his pen, that a man of color has wielded such an influence upon this country where Caste reigns like a ungracious queen, with Dishonor for her aide. For an example, Dr. Washington tells how he was importuned to go with the Atlanta delegation to beseech Congress to aid the Atlanta Exposition; how he spoke and what he said, and the later action of the Committee. It is known of few that Dr. Washington was asked to become the director of the colored exhibit; and that he recommended I. G. Penn, who was appointed.

† From *Colored American Magazine* 8 (March 1905): 161–62.

1. *Working with the Hands* (1905), an exposition of Washington's educational program at Tuskegee Institute.

He treats at length upon his trip to, and reception in England, who he meet and where he dined, when he spoke, and when he refused. He tells in detail of his struggle at Tuskegee, which is unconsciously we know, contrasted in the great honors thrust upon him now and of which he has written.

We have neither time nor space, to dwell further at this late day, upon Washington's autobiography; but it will go down the ages as one of America's great books.

BOOKER T. WASHINGTON

My Larger Education †

The Intellectuals and the Boston Mob

It makes a great deal of difference in the life of a race, as it does in the life of an individual, whether the world expects much or little of that individual or of that race. I suppose that every boy and every girl born in poverty have felt at some time in their lives the weight of the world against them. What the people in the communities did not expect them to do it was hard for them to convince themselves that they could do.

After I got so that I could read a little, I used to take a great deal of satisfaction in the lives of men who had risen by their own efforts from poverty to success. It is a great thing for a boy to be able to read books of that kind. It not only inspires him with the desire to do something and make something of his life, but it teaches him that success depends upon his ability to do something useful, to perform some kind of service that the world wants.

The trouble in my case, as in that of other coloured boys of any age, was that the stories we read in school were all concerned with the success and achievements of white boys and men. Occasionally I spoke to some of my schoolmates in regard to the characters of whom I had read, but they invariably reminded me that the stories I had been reading had to do with the members of another race. Sometimes I tried to argue the matter with them, saying that what others had done some of us might also be able to do, and that the lack of a past in our race was no reason why it should not have a future.

They replied that our case was entirely different. They said, in effect, that because of our colour and because we carried in our faces the brand of a race that had been in slavery, white people did not want us to succeed.

† From Chapter 5, "The Intellectuals and the Boston Mob," in Booker T. Washington, *My Larger Education* (New York: Doubleday, Page, 1911) 102–12.

In the end I usually wound up the discussion by recalling the life of Frederick Douglass, reminding them of the high position which he had reached and of the great services which he had performed for his own race and for the cause of human freedom in the long anti-slavery struggle.

Even before I had learned to read books or newspapers, I remember hearing my mother and other coloured people in our part of the country speak about Frederick Douglass's wonderful life and achievements. I heard so much about Douglass when I was a boy that one of the reasons why I wanted to go to school and learn to read was that I might read for myself what he had written and said. In fact, one of the first books that I remember reading was his own story of his life, which Mr. Douglass published under the title of "My Life and Times." This book made a deep impression upon me, and I read it many times.

After I became a student at Hampton, under Gen. Samuel C. Armstrong, I heard a great deal more about Frederick Douglass, and I followed all his movements with intense interest. At the same time I began to learn something about other prominent and successful coloured men who were at that time the leaders of my race in the United States. These were such men as Congressman John M. Langston, of Virginia; United States Senator Blanche K. Bruce, of Mississippi; Lieut.-Gov. P. B. S. Pinchback, of Louisiana; Congressman John R. Lynch, of Mississippi;[1] and others whose names were household words among the masses of the coloured people at that time. I read with the greatest eagerness everything I could get hold of regarding the prominent Negro characters of that period, and was a faithful student of their lives and deeds. Later on I had the privilege of meeting and knowing all of these men, but at that time I little thought that it would ever be my fortune to meet and know any of them.

On one occasion, when I happened to be in Washington, I heard that Frederick Douglass was going to make a speech in a near-by town. I had never seen him nor heard him speak, so I took advantage of the opportunity. I was profoundly impressed both by the man and by the address, but I did not dare approach even to shake hands with him. Some three or four years after I had organized the Tuskegee Institute I invited Mr. Douglass to make a visit to the school and to speak at the commencement exercises of the school. He came and spoke to a great audience, many of whom had driven thirty or forty miles to hear the great orator and leader of the race. In the course of time I invited all of the prominent coloured men whose names I have mentioned, as well as others,

1. John Roy Lynch (1847–1939), U.S. congressman from Mississippi from 1873 to 1876 and from 1882 to 1883; John M. Langston (1829–1897), U.S. congressman from Virginia from 1890 to 1891; Blanche Kelso Bruce (1841–1898), U.S. senator from Mississippi from 1875 to 1881; Pinkney Benton Stewart Pinchback (1837–1921), lieutenant-governor of Louisiana from 1871 to 1873.

to come to Tuskegee and speak to our students and to the coloured people in our community.

As a matter of course, the speeches (as well as the writings) of most of these men were concerned for the most part with the past history, or with the present and future political problems, of the Negro race. Mr. Douglass's great life-work had been in the political agitation that led to the destruction of slavery. He had been the great defender of the race, and in the struggle to win from Congress and from the country at large the recognition of the Negro's rights as a man and a citizen he had played an important part. But the long and bitter political struggle in which he had engaged against slavery had not prepared Mr. Douglass to take up the equally difficult task of fitting the Negro for the opportunities and responsibilities of freedom. The same was true to a large extent of other Negro leaders. At the time when I met these men and heard them speak I was invariably impressed, though young and inexperienced, that there was something lacking in their public utterances. I felt that the millions of Negroes needed something more than to be reminded of their sufferings and of their political rights; that they needed to do something more than merely to defend themselves.

Frederick Douglass died in February, 1895. In September of the same year I delivered an address in Atlanta at the Cotton States Exposition.

I spoke in Atlanta to an audience composed of leading Southern white people, Northern white people, and members of my own race. This seemed to me to be the time and the place, without condemning what had been done, to emphasize what ought to be done. I felt that we needed a policy, not of destruction, but of construction; not of defence, but of aggression; a policy, not of hostility or surrender, but of friendship and advance. I stated, as vigorously as I was able, that usefulness in the community where we resided was our surest and most potent protection.

One other point which I made plain in this speech was that, in my opinion, the Negro should seek constantly in every manly, straightforward manner to make friends of the white man by whose side he lived, rather than to content himself with seeking the good-will of some man a thousand miles away.

While I was fully convinced, in my own mind, that the policy which I had outlined was the correct one, I was not at all prepared for the widespread interest with which my words were received.

I received telegrams and congratulations from all parts of the country and from many persons whose names I did not know or had heard of only indirectly through the newspapers or otherwise. Very soon invitations began to come to me in large numbers to speak before all kinds of bodies and on all kinds of subjects. In many cases I was offered for my addresses what appeared to me almost fabulous sums. Some of the lecture bureaus offered me as high as $300 and $400 a night for as long a period as I would speak for them. Among other things which came to me was an offer from a prominent Western newspaper of $1000 and all expenses for my services if I would describe for it a famous prize-fight.

I was invited, here and there, to take part in political campaigns, especially in states where the Negro vote was important. Lecture bureaus not only urged upon me the acceptance of their offers through letters, but even sent agents to Tuskegee. Newspapers and magazines made generous offers to me to write special articles for them. I decided, however, to wait until I could get my bearings. Apparently the words which I had spoken at Atlanta, simple and almost commonplace as they were, had touched a deep and responsive chord in the public mind.[2] This gave me much to think about. In the meantime I determined to stick close to my work at Tuskegee.

One of the most surprising results of my Atlanta speech was the number of letters, telegrams, and newspaper editorials that came pouring in upon me from all parts of the country, demanding that I take the place of "leader of the Negro people," left vacant by Frederick Douglass's death, or assuming that I had already taken this place. Until these suggestions began to pour in upon me, I never had the remotest idea that I should be selected or looked upon, in any such sense as Frederick Douglass had been, as a leader of the Negro people. I was at that time merely a Negro school teacher in a rather obscure industrial school. I had devoted all my time and attention to the work of organizing and bringing into existence the Tuskegee Institute, and I did not know just what the functions and duties of a leader were, or what was expected of him on the part of the coloured people or of the rest of the world. It was not long, however, before I began to find out what was expected of me in the new position into which a sudden newspaper notoriety seemed to have thrust me.

I was not a little embarrassed, when I first began to appear in public, to find myself continually referred to as "the successor of Frederick

2. The following is copied from the official history of the exposition:

"Then came Booker T. Washington, who was destined to make a national reputation in the next fifteen minutes. He appeared on the programme by invitation of the directors as the representative of the Negro race. This would appear to have been a natural arrangement, if not a matter of course, and it seems strange now that there should have been any doubt as to the wisdom or propriety of giving the Negro a place in the opening exercises. Nevertheless, there was, and the question was carefully, even anxiously, considered before it was decided. There were apprehensions that the matter would encourage social equality and prove offensive to the white people, and in the end unsatisfactory to the coloured race. But the discussion satisfied the board that this course was right, and they resolved to risk the expediency of doing right. The sequel showed the wisdom of their decision. The orator himself touched upon the subject with great tact, and the recognition that was given has greatly tended to promote good feeling between the races, while the wide and self-respecting course of the Negroes on that occasion has raised them greatly in the estimation of their white fellow-citizens."

In introducing the speaker, Governor Bullock said: "We have with us to-day the representative of Negro enterprise and Negro civilization. I have the honour to introduce to you Prof. Booker T. Washington, principal of the Tuskegee Normal and Industrial College, who will formally present the Negro exhibit."

Professor Washington was greeted with applause, and his speech received marked attention [*Washington's note*].

Douglass." Wherever I spoke—whether in the North or in the South—I found, thanks to the advertising I had received, that large audiences turned out to hear me.

It has been interesting, and sometimes amusing, to note the amount and variety of disinterested advice received by a man whose name is to any extent before the public. During the time that my Atlanta address was, so to speak, under discussion, and almost every day since, I have received one or more letters advising me and directing my course in regard to matters of public interest.

One day I receive a letter, or my attention is called to some newspaper editorial, in which I am advised to stick to my work at Tuskegee and put aside every other interest that I may have in the advancement of my race. A day or two later I may receive a letter, or read an editorial in a newspaper, saying that I am making a mistake in confining my attention entirely to Tuskegee, to Negro education, or even to the Negro in the United States. It has been frequently urged upon me, for example, that I ought, in some way or other, to extend the work that we are trying to do at Tuskegee to Africa or to the West Indies, where Negroes are a larger part of the population than in this country.

There has been a small number of white people and an equally small number of coloured people who felt, after my Atlanta speech, that I ought to branch out and discuss political questions, putting emphasis upon the importance of political activity and success for the members of my race. Others, who thought it quite natural that, while I was in the South, I should not say anything that would be offensive, expected that I would cut loose in the North and denounce the Southern people in a way to keep alive and intensify the sectional differences which had sprung up as a result of slavery and the Civil War. Still others thought that there was something lacking in my style of defending the Negro. I went too much into the facts and did not say enough about the Rights of Man and the Declaration of Independence.

When these people found that I did not change my policy as a result of my Atlanta speech, but stuck to my old line of argument, urging the importance of education of the hand, the head, and the heart, they were thoroughly disappointed. So far as my addresses made it appear that the race troubles in the South could be solved by education rather than by political measures, they felt that I was putting the emphasis in the wrong place.

I confess that all these criticisms and suggestions were not without effect upon my mind. But, after thinking the matter all over, I decided that, pleasant as it might be to follow the programme that was laid out for me, I should be compelled to stick to my original job and work out my salvation along the lines that I had originally laid down for myself.

* * *

CRITICISM

W. E. B. DU BOIS

Of Mr. Booker T. Washington and Others †

From birth till death enslaved; in word, in deed, unmanned!

. . . .

Hereditary bondsmen! Know ye not
Who would be free themselves must strike the blow?

BYRON.

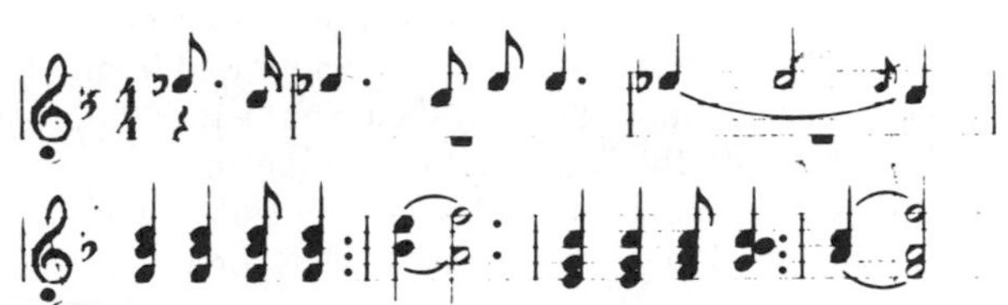

Easily the most striking thing in the history of the American Negro since 1876 is the ascendancy of Mr. Booker T. Washington. It began at the time when war memories and ideals were rapidly passing; a day of astonishing commercial development was dawning; a sense of doubt and hesitation overtook the freedmen's sons,—then it was that his leading began. Mr. Washington came, with a simple definite programme, at the psychological moment when the nation was a little ashamed of having bestowed so much sentiment on Negroes, and was concentrating its energies on Dollars. His programme of industrial education, conciliation of the South, and submission and silence as to civil and political rights, was not wholly original; the Free Negroes from 1830 up to war-time had striven to build industrial schools, and the American Missionary Association had from the first taught various trades; and Price[1] and others had sought a way of honorable alliance with the best of the Southerners. But Mr. Washington first indissolubly linked these things; he put enthusiasm, unlimited energy, and perfect faith into this programme, and changed it from a by-path into a veritable Way of Life. And the tale of the methods by which he did this is a fascinating study of human life.

It startled the nation to hear a Negro advocating such a programme after many decades of bitter complaint; it startled and won the applause of the South, it interested and won the admiration of the North; and

† From W. E. B. Du Bois, *The Souls of Black Folk* (Chicago: A. C. McClurg, 1903) 392–404.

1. Joseph Charles Price (1854–1893), Southern orator, educator, African Methodist Episcopal Zion church leader, and moderate civil rights spokesman.

after a confused murmur of protest, it silenced if it did not convert the Negroes themselves.

To gain the sympathy and coöperation of the various elements comprising the white South was Mr. Washington's first task; and this, at the time Tuskegee was founded, seemed, for a black man, well-nigh impossible. And yet ten years later it was done in the word spoken at Atlanta: "In all things purely social we can be as separate as the five fingers, and yet one as the hand in all things essential to mutual progress." This "Atlanta Compromise" is by all odds the most notable thing in Mr. Washington's career. The South interpreted it in different ways: the radicals received it as a complete surrender of the demand for civil and political equality; the conservatives, as a generously conceived working basis for mutual understanding. So both approved it, and to-day its author is certainly the most distinguished Southerner since Jefferson Davis, and the one with the largest personal following.

Next to this achievement comes Mr. Washington's work in gaining place and consideration in the North. Others less shrewd and tactful had formerly essayed to sit on these two stools and had fallen between them; but as Mr. Washington knew the heart of the South from birth and training, so by singular insight he intuitively grasped the spirit of the age which was dominating the North. And so thoroughly did he learn the speech and thought of triumphant commercialism, and the ideals of material prosperity, that the picture of a lone black boy poring over a French grammar amid the weeds and dirt of a neglected home soon seemed to him the acme of absurdities. One wonders what Socrates and St. Francis of Assisi would say to this.

And yet this very singleness of vision and thorough oneness with his age is a mark of the successful man. It is as though Nature must needs make men narrow in order to give them force. So Mr. Washington's cult has gained unquestioning followers, his work has wonderfully prospered, his friends are legion, and his enemies are confounded. To-day he stands as the one recognized spokesman of his ten million fellows, and one of the most notable figures in a nation of seventy millions. One hesitates, therefore, to criticise a life which, beginning with so little, has done so much. And yet the time is come when one may speak in all sincerity and utter courtesy of the mistakes and shortcomings of Mr. Washington's career, as well as of his triumphs, without being thought captious or envious, and without forgetting that it is easier to do ill than well in the world.

The criticism that has hitherto met Mr. Washington has not always been of this broad character. In the South especially has he had to walk warily to avoid the harshest judgments,—and naturally so, for he is dealing with the one subject of deepest sensitiveness to that section. Twice—once when at the Chicago celebration of the Spanish-American War he alluded to the color-prejudice that is "eating away the vitals of the

South," and once when he dined with President Roosevelt—has the resulting Southern criticism been violent enough to threaten seriously his popularity. In the North the feeling has several times forced itself into words, that Mr. Washington's counsels of submission overlooked certain elements of true manhood, and that his educational programme was unnecessarily narrow. Usually, however, such criticism has not found open expression, although, too, the spiritual sons of the Abolitionists have not been prepared to acknowledge that the schools founded before Tuskegee, by men of broad ideals and self-sacrificing spirit, were wholly failures or worthy of ridicule. While, then, criticism has not failed to follow Mr. Washington, yet the prevailing public opinion of the land has been but too willing to deliver the solution of a wearisome problem into his hands, and say, "If that is all you and your race ask, take it."

Among his own people, however, Mr. Washington has encountered the strongest and most lasting opposition, amounting at times to bitterness, and even to-day continuing strong and insistent even though largely silenced in outward expression by the public opinion of the nation. Some of this opposition is, of course, mere envy; the disappointment of displaced demagogues and the spite of narrow minds. But aside from this, there is among educated and thoughtful colored men in all parts of the land a feeling of deep regret, sorrow, and apprehension at the wide currency and ascendancy which some of Mr. Washington's theories have gained. These same men admire his sincerity of purpose, and are willing to forgive much to honest endeavor which is doing something worth the doing. They coöperate with Mr. Washington as far as they conscientiously can; and, indeed, it is no ordinary tribute to this man's tact and power that, steering as he must between so many diverse interests and opinions, he so largely retains the respect of all.

But the hushing of the criticism of honest opponents is a dangerous thing. It leads some of the best of the critics to unfortunate silence and paralysis of effort, and others to burst into speech so passionately and intemperately as to lose listeners. Honest and earnest criticism from those whose interests are most nearly touched,—criticism of writers by readers, of government by those governed, of leaders by those led,—this is the soul of democracy and the safeguard of modern society. If the best of the American Negroes receive by outer pressure a leader whom they had not recognized before, manifestly there is here a certain palpable gain. Yet there is also irreparable loss,—a loss of that peculiarly valuable education which a group receives when by search and criticism it finds and commissions its own leaders. The way in which this is done is at once the most elementary and the nicest problem of social growth. History is but the record of such group-leadership; and yet how infinitely changeful is its type and character! And of all types and kinds, what can be more instructive than the leadership of a group within a group?—

that curious double movement where real progress may be negative and actual advance be relative retrogression. All this is the social student's inspiration and despair.

Now in the past the American Negro has had instructive experience in the choosing of group leaders, founding thus a peculiar dynasty which in the light of present conditions is worth while studying. When sticks and stones and beasts form the sole environment of a people, their attitude is largely one of determined opposition to and conquest of natural forces. But when to earth and brute is added an environment of men and ideas, then the attitude of the imprisoned group may take three main forms,—a feeling of revolt and revenge; an attempt to adjust all thought and action to the will of the greater group; or, finally, a determined effort at self-realization and self-development despite environing opinion. The influence of all of these attitudes at various times can be traced in the history of the American Negro, and in the evolution of his successive leaders.

Before 1750, while the fire of African freedom still burned in the veins of the slaves, there was in all leadership or attempted leadership but the one motive of revolt and revenge,—typified in the terrible Maroons, the Danish blacks, and Cato of Stono,[2] and veiling all the Americas in fear of insurrection. The liberalizing tendencies of the latter half of the eighteenth century brought, along with kindlier relations between black and white, thoughts of ultimate adjustment and assimilation. Such aspiration was especially voiced in the earnest songs of Phyllis, in the martyrdom of Attucks, the fighting of Salem and Poor, the intellectual accomplishments of Banneker and Derham, and the political demands of the Cuffes.[3]

Stern financial and social stress after the war cooled much of the previous humanitarian ardor. The disappointment and impatience of the Negroes at the persistence of slavery and serfdom voiced itself in two movements. The slaves in the South, aroused undoubtedly by vague rumors of the Haytian revolt, made three fierce attempts at insurrection,—in 1800 under Gabriel in Virginia, in 1822 under Vesey in

2. Fugitive slaves in the South sometimes found refuge in secluded communities known as maroons, from which they raided nearby farms and plantations. In 1723, when the Virgin Islands were known as the Danish West Indies, insurrectionary slaves took control of the island of St. John and held it for six months. Cato of Stono led an insurrection of slaves in Stono, South Carolina, in 1739.

3. Paul Cuffe (1759–1817), merchant-mariner, author, and promoter of the emigration of African Americans to West Africa. In 1780 with his brother John he protested Massachusetts laws that withheld the vote from African Americans and American Indians; Phillis Wheatley (c. 1753–1784), internationally acclaimed African-born poet who grew up a slave in Boston; Crispus Attucks (1723?–1770), believed to have been an escaped slave, was the first man to die in the Boston Massacre, a prelude to the American Revolution; Peter Salem (1750–1816), distinguished slave-born American Revolutionary War soldier from Massachusetts; Salem Poor (1758–?), distinguished free-born American Revolutionary War soldier from Massachusetts; Benjamin Banneker (1731–1806), surveyor, mathematician, astronomer, and almanac maker; James Durham (or Derham, 1762–?), earliest known African American physician.

Carolina, and in 1831 again in Virginia under the terrible Nat Turner. In the Free States, on the other hand, a new and curious attempt at self-development was made. In Philadelphia and New York color-prescription led to a withdrawal of Negro communicants from white churches and the formation of a peculiar socio-religious institution among the Negroes known as the African Church,—an organization still living and controlling in its various branches over a million of men.

Walker's wild appeal[4] against the trend of the times showed how the world was changing after the coming of the cotton-gin. By 1830 slavery seemed hopelessly fastened on the South, and the slaves thoroughly cowed into submission. The free Negroes of the North, inspired by the mulatto immigrants from the West Indies, began to change the basis of their demands; they recognized the slavery of slaves, but insisted that they themselves were freemen, and sought assimilation and amalgamation with the nation on the same terms with other men. Thus, Forten and Purvis of Philadelphia, Shad of Wilmington, Du Bois of New Haven, Barbadoes of Boston,[5] and others, strove singly and together as men, they said, not as slaves; as "people of color," not as "Negroes." The trend of the times, however, refused them recognition save in individual and exceptional cases, considered them as one with all the despised blacks, and they soon found themselves striving to keep even the rights they formerly had of voting and working and moving as freemen. Schemes of migration and colonization arose among them; but these they refused to entertain, and they eventually turned to the Abolition movement as a final refuge.

Here, led by Remond, Nell, Wells-Brown,[6] and Douglass, a new period of self-assertion and self-development dawned. To be sure, ultimate freedom and assimilation was the ideal before the leaders, but the assertion of the manhood rights of the Negro by himself was the main reliance, and John Brown's raid was the extreme of its logic. After the war and emancipation, the great form of Frederick Douglass, the greatest of American Negro leaders, still led the host. Self-assertion, especially in political lines, was the main programme, and behind Douglass came Elliot,[7] Bruce, and Langston, and the Reconstruction politicians,

4. David Walker (1785–1830), author of *David Walker's Appeal* (1829), a revolutionary antislavery tract.
5. James G. Barbadoes (c. 1796–1841), abolitionist and leader among the free African Americans of Boston; James Forten, Sr. (1766–1842), wealthy Philadelphia businessman, abolitionist, and civil rights activist; Robert Purvis, Sr. (1810–1898), wealthy Philadelphia reformer and one of the founders of the American Anti-Slavery Society; Mary Ann Shad (or Shadd; 1823–1893), newspaper editor, antislavery lecturer, and Civil War recruiting agent; Alexander Du Bois, W. E. B. Du Bois's grandfather.
6. William Wells Brown (c. 1814–1884), internationally famous fugitive slave, abolitionist lecturer, and author; Charles Lenox Remond (1810–1874), Massachusetts-born journalist and lecturer for the American Anti-Slavery Society; William C. Nell (1816–1874), abolitionist journalist and lecturer and active participant in the Underground Railroad.
7. Robert Brown Elliott (1842–1884), newspaper editor and Reconstruction politician from South Carolina.

and, less conspicuous but of greater social significance Alexander Crummell and Bishop Daniel Payne.[8]

Then came the Revolution of 1876, the suppression of the Negro votes, the changing and shifting of ideals, and the seeking of new lights in the great night. Douglass, in his old age, still bravely stood for the ideals of his early manhood,—ultimate assimilation *through* self-assertion, and on no other terms. For a time Price arose as a new leader, destined, it seemed, not to give up, but to re-state the old ideals in a form less repugnant to the white South. But he passed away in his prime. Then came the new leader. Nearly all the former ones had become leaders by the silent suffrage of their fellows, had sought to lead their own people alone, and were usually, save Douglass, little known outside their race. But Booker T. Washington arose as essentially the leader not of one race but of two,—a compromiser between the South, the North, and the Negro. Naturally the Negroes resented, at first bitterly, signs of compromise which surrendered their civil and political rights, even though this was to be exchanged for larger chances of economic development. The rich and dominating North, however, was not only weary of the race problem, but was investing largely in Southern enterprises, and welcomed any method of peaceful coöperation. Thus, by national opinion, the Negroes began to recognize Mr. Washington's leadership; and the voice of criticism was hushed.

Mr. Washington represents in Negro thought the old attitude of adjustment and submission; but adjustment at such a peculiar time as to make his programme unique. This is an age of unusual economic development, and Mr. Washington's programme naturally takes an economic cast, becoming a gospel of Work and Money to such an extent as apparently almost completely to overshadow the higher aims of life. Moreover, this is an age when the more advanced races are coming in closer contact with the less developed races, and the race-feeling is therefore intensified; and Mr. Washington's programme practically accepts the alleged inferiority of the Negro races. Again, in our own land, the reaction from the sentiment of war time has given impetus to race-prejudice against Negroes, and Mr. Washington withdraws many of the high demands of Negroes as men and American citizens. In other periods of intensified prejudice all the Negro's tendency to self-assertion has been called forth; at this period a policy of submission is advocated. In the history of nearly all other races and peoples the doctrine preached at such crises has been that manly self-respect is worth more than lands and houses, and that a people who voluntarily surrender such respect, or cease striving for it, are not worth civilizing.

In answer to this, it has been claimed that the Negro can survive only

8. Daniel A. Payne (1811–1893), African Methodist Episcopal church leader, educator, and president of Wilberforce University in Ohio; Alexander Crummell (1819–1898), Episcopal minister, abolitionist, and missionary to Liberia.

through submission. Mr. Washington distinctly asks that black people give up, at least for the present, three things,—

First, political power,

Second, insistence on civil rights,

Third, higher education of Negro youth,—

and concentrate all their energies on industrial education, the accumulation of wealth, and the conciliation of the South. This policy has been courageously and insistently advocated for over fifteen years, and has been triumphant for perhaps ten years. As a result of this tender of the palm-branch, what has been the return? In these years there have occurred:

1. The disfranchisement of the Negro.
2. The legal creation of a distinct status of civil inferiority for the Negro.
3. The steady withdrawal of aid from institutions for the higher training of the Negro.

These movements are not, to be sure, direct results of Mr. Washington's teachings; but his propaganda has, without a shadow of doubt, helped their speedier accomplishment. The question then comes: Is it possible, and probable, that nine millions of men can make effective progress in economic lines if they are deprived of political rights, made a servile caste, and allowed only the most meagre chance for developing their exceptional men? If history and reason give any distinct answer to these questions, it is an emphatic *No*. And Mr. Washington thus faces the triple paradox of his career:

1. He is striving nobly to make Negro artisans business men and property-owners; but it is utterly impossible, under modern competitive methods, for workingmen and property-owners to defend their rights and exist without the right of suffrage.
2. He insists on thrift and self-respect, but at the same time counsels a silent submission to civic inferiority such as is bound to sap the manhood of any race in the long run.
3. He advocates common-school and industrial training, and depreciates institutions of higher learning; but neither the Negro common-schools, nor Tuskegee itself, could remain open a day were it not for teachers trained in Negro colleges, or trained by their graduates.

This triple paradox in Mr. Washington's position is the object of criticism by two classes of colored Americans. One class is spiritually descended from Toussaint the Savior,[9] through Gabriel, Vesey, and Turner, and they represent the attitude of revolt and revenge; they hate the white South blindly and distrust the white race generally, and so far as they agree on definite action, think that the Negro's only hope lies in emigration beyond the borders of the United States. And yet, by the

9. Toussaint L'Ouverture (c. 1744–1803), leader of the successful Haitian slave revolt in 1791.

irony of fate, nothing has more effectually made this programme seem hopeless than the recent course of the United States toward weaker and darker peoples in the West Indies, Hawaii, and the Philippines,—for where in the world may we go and be safe from lying and brute force?

The other class of Negroes who cannot agree with Mr. Washington has hitherto said little aloud. They deprecate the sight of scattered counsels, of internal disagreement; and especially they dislike making their just criticism of a useful and earnest man an excuse for a general discharge of venom from small-minded opponents. Nevertheless, the questions involved are so fundamental and serious that it is difficult to see how men like the Grimkes, Kelly Miller, J. W. E. Bowen,[1] and other representatives of this group, can much longer be silent. Such men feel in conscience bound to ask of this nation three things:

1. The right to vote.
2. Civic equality.
3. The education of youth according to ability.

They acknowledge Mr. Washington's invaluable service in counselling patience and courtesy in such demands; they do not ask that ignorant black men vote when ignorant whites are debarred, or that any reasonable restrictions in the suffrage should not be applied; they know that the low social level of the mass of the race is responsible for much discrimination against it, but they also know, and the nation knows, that relentless color-prejudice is more often a cause than a result of the Negro's degradation; they seek the abatement of this relic of barbarism, and not its systematic encouragement and pampering by all agencies of social power from the Associated Press to the Church of Christ. They advocate, with Mr. Washington, a broad system of Negro common schools supplemented by thorough industrial training; but they are surprised that a man of Mr. Washington's insight cannot see that no such educational system ever has rested or can rest on any other basis than that of the well-equipped college and university, and they insist that there is a demand for a few such institutions throughout the South to train the best of the Negro youth as teachers, professional men, and leaders.

This group of men honor Mr. Washington for his attitude of conciliation toward the white South; they accept the "Atlanta Compromise" in its broadest interpretation; they recognize, with him, many signs of promise, many men of high purpose and fair judgment, in this section; they know that no easy task has been laid upon a region already tottering under heavy burdens. But, nevertheless, they insist that the way to truth

1. John Wesley Edward Bowen (1855–1933), Methodist church leader, theology professor, and popular lecturer, the second black Ph.D. recipient in the United States; Archibald H. Grimké (1849–1930), attorney and journalist, and Francis J. Grimké (1850–1937), Presbyterian clergyman and educator, were civil rights activists in the North; Kelly Miller (1863–1939), professor and dean at Howard University in Washington, D.C., and an intellectual leader and mediator between the conservative and militant camps in the African American community.

and right lies in straightforward honesty, not in indiscriminate flattery; in praising those of the South who do well and criticising uncompromisingly those who do ill; in taking advantage of the opportunities at hand and urging their fellows to do the same, but at the same time in remembering that only a firm adherence to their higher ideals and aspirations will ever keep those ideals within the realm of possibility. They do not expect that the free right to vote, to enjoy civic rights, and to be educated, will come in a moment; they do not expect to see the bias and prejudices of years disappear at the blast of a trumpet; but they are absolutely certain that the way for a people to gain their reasonable rights is not by voluntarily throwing them away and insisting that they do not want them; that the way for a people to gain respect is not by continually belittling and ridiculing themselves; that, on the contrary, Negroes must insist continually, in season and out of season, that voting is necessary to modern manhood, that color discrimination is barbarism, and that black boys need education as well as white boys.

In failing thus to state plainly and unequivocally the legitimate demands of their people, even at the cost of opposing an honored leader, the thinking classes of American Negroes would shirk a heavy responsibility,—a responsibility to themselves, a responsibility to the struggling masses, a responsibility to the darker races of men whose future depends so largely on this American experiment, but especially a responsibility to this nation,—this common Fatherland. It is wrong to encourage a man or a people in evil-doing; it is wrong to aid and abet a national crime simply because it is unpopular not to do so. The growing spirit of kindliness and reconciliation between the North and South after the frightful differences of a generation ago ought to be a source of deep congratulation to all, and especially to those whose mistreatment caused the war; but if that reconciliation is to be marked by the industrial slavery and civic death of those same black men, with permanent legislation into a position of inferiority, then those black men, if they are really men, are called upon by every consideration of patriotism and loyalty to oppose such a course by all civilized methods, even though such opposition involves disagreement with Mr. Booker T. Washington. We have no right to sit silently by while the inevitable seeds are sown for a harvest of disaster to our children, black and white.

First, it is the duty of black men to judge the South discriminatingly. The present generation of Southerners are not responsible for the past, and they should not be blindly hated or blamed for it. Furthermore, to no class is the indiscriminate endorsement of the recent course of the South toward Negroes more nauseating than to the best thought of the South. The South is not "solid"; it is a land in the ferment of social change, wherein forces of all kinds are fighting for supremacy; and to praise the ill the South is to-day perpetrating is just as wrong as to condemn the good. Discriminating and broad-minded criticism is what the

South needs,—needs it for the sake of her own white sons and daughters, and for the insurance of robust, healthy mental and moral development.

To-day even the attitude of the Southern whites toward the blacks is not, as so many assume, in all cases the same; the ignorant Southerner hates the Negro, the workingmen fear his competition, the money-makers wish to use him as a laborer, some of the educated see a menace in his upward development, while others—usually the sons of the masters—wish to help him to rise. National opinion has enabled this last class to maintain the Negro common schools, and to protect the Negro partially in property, life, and limb. Through the pressure of the money-makers, the Negro is in danger of being reduced to semi-slavery, especially in the country districts; the workingmen, and those of the educated who fear the Negro, have united to disfranchise him, and some have urged his deportation; while the passions of the ignorant are easily aroused to lynch and abuse any black man. To praise this intricate whirl of thought and prejudice is nonsense; to inveigh indiscriminately against "the South" is unjust; but to use the same breath in praising Governor Aycock, exposing Senator Morgan, arguing with Mr. Thomas Nelson Page, and denouncing Senator Ben Tillman, is not only sane, but the imperative duty of thinking black men.

It would be unjust to Mr. Washington not to acknowledge that in several instances he has opposed movements in the South which were unjust to the Negro; he sent memorials to the Louisiana and Alabama constitutional conventions, he has spoken against lynching, and in other ways has openly or silently set his influence against sinister schemes and unfortunate happenings. Notwithstanding this, it is equally true to assert that on the whole the distinct impression left by Mr. Washington's propaganda is, first, that the South is justified in its present attitude toward the Negro because of the Negro's degradation; secondly, that the prime cause of the Negro's failure to rise more quickly is his wrong education in the past; and, thirdly, that his future rise depends primarily on his own efforts. Each of these propositions is a dangerous half-truth. The supplementary truths must never be lost sight of: first, slavery and race-prejudice are potent if not sufficient causes of the Negro's position; second, industrial and common-school training were necessarily slow in planting because they had to await the black teachers trained by higher institutions,—it being extremely doubtful if any essentially different development was possible, and certainly a Tuskegee was unthinkable before 1880; and, third, while it is a great truth to say that the Negro must strive and strive mightily to help himself, it is equally true that unless his striving be not simply seconded, but rather aroused and encouraged, by the initiative of the richer and wiser environing group, he cannot hope for great success.

In his failure to realize and impress this last point, Mr. Washington is especially to be criticised. His doctrine has tended to make the whites, North and South, shift the burden of the Negro problem to the Negro's shoulders and stand aside as critical and rather pessimistic spectators; when in fact the burden belongs to the nation, and the hands of none of us are clean if we bend not our energies to righting these great wrongs.

The South ought to be led, by candid and honest criticism, to assert her better self and do her full duty to the race she has cruelly wronged and is still wronging. The North—her co-partner in guilt—cannot salve her conscience by plastering it with gold. We cannot settle this problem by diplomacy and suaveness, by "policy" alone. If worse come to worst, can the moral fibre of this country survive the slow throttling and murder of nine millions of men?

The black men of America have a duty to perform, a duty stern and delicate,—a forward movement to oppose a part of the work of their greatest leader. So far as Mr. Washington preaches Thrift, Patience, and Industrial Training for the masses, we must hold up his hands and strive with him, rejoicing in his honors and glorying in the strength of this Joshua called of God and of man to lead the headless host. But so far as Mr. Washington apologizes for injustice, North or South, does not rightly value the privilege and duty of voting, belittles the emasculating effects of caste distinctions, and opposes the higher training and ambition of our brighter minds,—so far as he, the South, or the Nation, does this,—we must unceasingly and firmly oppose them. By every civilized and peaceful method we must strive for the rights which the world accords to men, clinging unwaveringly to those great words which the sons of the Fathers would fain forget: "We hold these truths to be self-evident: That all men are created equal; that they are endowed by their Creator with certain unalienable rights; that among these are life, liberty, and the pursuit of happiness."

KELLY MILLER

Radicals and Conservatives†

When a distinguished Russian was informed that some American Negroes are radical and some conservative, he could not restrain his laughter. The idea of conservative Negroes was more than the Cossack's risibilities could endure. "What on earth," he exclaimed with astonishment, "have they to conserve?"

According to a strict use of terms, a "conservative" is one who is satisfied with existing conditions and advocates their continuance; while a

† From Kelly Miller, *Race Adjustment* (New York: Neale, 1908), 11–12, 17–20, 21–22, 23–27.

"radical" clamors for amelioration of conditions through change. No thoughtful Negro is satisfied with the present status of his race, whether viewed in its political, its civil or general aspect. He labors under an unfriendly public opinion, one which is being rapidly crystallized into a rigid caste system and enacted into unrighteous law. How can he be expected to contemplate such oppressive conditions with satisfaction and composure? Circumstances render it imperative that his attitude should be dissentient rather than conformatory. Every consideration of enlightened self-respect impels him to unremitting protest, albeit the manner of protestation may be mild or pronounced, according to the dictates of prudence. Radical and conservative Negroes agree as to the end in view, but differ as to the most effective means of attaining it. The difference is not essentially one of principle or purpose, but point of view. All anti-slavery advocates desired the downfall of the iniquitous institution, but some were more violent than others in the expression of this desire. Disagreement as to method led to personal estrangement, impugnment of motive, and unseemly factional wrangle. And so, colored men who are alike zealous for the betterment of their race, lose half their strength in internal strife, because of variant methods of attack upon the citadel of prejudice. Mr. Booker T. Washington is, or has been, the storm-center about which the controversy rages, and contending forces have aligned themselves in hostile array as to the wisdom or folly of the doctrine of which he is the chief exponent. * * *

The radical and conservative tendencies of the Negro race cannot be better described than by comparing, or rather contrasting, the two superlative colored men in whom we find their highest embodiment—Frederick Douglass and Booker Washington, who were both picked out and exploited by white men as the mouthpiece and intermediaries of the black race. The two men are in part products of their times, but are also natural antipodes. Douglass lived in the day of moral giants; Washington lives in the era of merchant princes. The contemporaries of Douglass emphasized the rights of man; those of Washington, his productive capacity. The age of Douglass acknowledged the sanction of the Golden Rule; that of Washington worships the Rule of *Gold*. The equality of men was constantly dinned into Douglass's ears; Washington hears nothing but the inferiority of the Negro and the dominance of the Saxon. Douglass could hardly receive a hearing today; Washington would have been hooted off the stage a generation ago. Thus all truly useful men must be, in a measure, time-servers; for unless they serve their time, they can scarcely serve at all. But great as was the diversity of formative influences that shaped these two great lives, there is no less opposability in their innate bias of character. Douglass was like a lion, bold and fearless; Washington is lamblike, meek and submissive. Douglass escaped from personal bondage, which his soul abhorred; but for Lincoln's proclamation, Washington would probably have arisen to esteem and favor in the eyes of his master as a good and faithful servant. Douglass insisted upon rights; Washington insists upon duty. Douglass held up to public scorn the sins of the white man; Washington portrays the faults of his own race. Douglass spoke what he thought the world should hear; Washington speaks only what he feels it is disposed to listen to. Douglass's conduct was actuated by principle; Washington's by prudence. Douglass had no limited, copyrighted programme for his race, but appealed to the Decalogue, the Golden Rule, the Declaration of Independence, the Constitution of the United States; Washington, holding these great principles in the shadowy background, presents a practical expedient applicable to present needs. Douglass was a moralist, insisting upon the application of righteousness to public affairs; Washington is a practical opportunist, accepting the best terms which he thinks it possible to secure.

Booker T. Washington came upon the public stage at the time when the policies which Douglass embodied had seemed to fail. Reconstruction measures had proved abortive; Negro politicians, like Othello, had lost their occupation, and had sought asylum in the Government departments at Washington; the erstwhile advocates of the Negro's cause had grown indifferent or apologetic, and the plain intent of the Constitution had been overborne in the South with the connivance of the North. The idea of lifting the Negro to the plane of equality with the white race, once so fondly cherished, found few remaining advocates. Mr. Washington sized up the situation with the certainty and celerity of a genius. He based his policy upon the ruins of the policy that had been exploited. He avoided controverted issues, and moved, not along the line of least resistance, but of no resistance at all. He founded his creed upon construction rather than upon criticism. He urged his race to do the things possible rather than whine and pine over things prohibited. According to his philosophy, it is better to build even upon the shifting sands of expediency than not to build at all simply because you cannot secure a granite foundation. He thus hoped to utilize for the betterment of the Negro whatever residue of good feeling there might be in the white race. Tuskegee Institute, which is in itself a marvelous achievement, is only the pulpit from which Mr. Washington proclaims his doctrine. Industrial education has become so intricately interwoven into his policy that his critics are forced into the ridiculous attitude of opposing a form of training essential to the welfare of any people. For reasons of policy, Mr. Washington has been provokingly silent as to the claim of higher education, although his personal actions proclaim loudly enough the belief that is in his heart. The subject of industrial and higher education is merely one of ratio and proportion, and not one of fundamental controversy.

Mr. Washington's bitterest opponents cannot gainsay his sincerity or doubt that the welfare of his race is the chief burden of his soul. He follows the leading of his own light. Few men of this generation have shown such signal devotion, self-abnegation and strenuous endeavor for an altruistic cause.

One of the chief complaints against the Tuskegeean is lack of definite statement upon questions of vital concern. Mr. Washington is a diplomat, and a great one. He sinks into sphinxlike silence when the demands of the situation seem to require emphatic utterance. His carefully studied deliverances upon disputed issues often possess the equivocalness of a Delphic oracle. While he does not openly avow, yet he would not disclaim, in distinct terms, a single plank in the platform of Douglass. The white race saddles its own notions and feelings upon him, and yet he opens not his mouth. His sagacious silence and shrewdly measured assertions must be taken, if not with the traditional grain of salt, at least with a goodly lump of diplomatic allowance. We do not usually associate deep moral conviction with the guileful arts of diplomacy, but we must remember that the delicate rôle of race statesmanship cannot be played without rare caution and tactful prudence.

Mr. Washington's popularity and prominence depend largely upon the fact that his putative policy is acceptable to the Southern whites, because he allows them to believe that he accepts their estimate of the Negro's inferior place in the social scheme. He is quiescent, if not acquiescent, as to the white man's superior claims. He shuts his eyes to many of the wrongs and outrages heaped upon the Negro race. He never runs against the Southerner's traditional prejudices, and even when he protests against his practices the protestation is so palliatory that, like a good conscience, it is void of offence. Equality between the races, whether social, political, or civil, is an unsavory term to the white man's palate, and, therefore, Mr. Washington obliterates it from his vocabulary. The higher education of the Negro is in general disfavor, so Mr. Washington gives the approval of his silence to the charge that such pure and devoted philanthropists as President Ware of Atlanta, Patton of Howard, Tupper of Shaw, and Cravath of Fisk, who did more than all others to quicken and inspire the Negro race, have lived, loved, labored, and died in vain. Nor is Washington objectionable to the white man by reason of his self-assertive personality. He is an exact modern counterpart of Chaucer's knight: "Curteys he was, lowly, and servysable." Even when he violates the sacred code of the whites by dining with the President or mingling on easy terms with ultra-fashionable circles, they lash themselves into momentary fury, but straightway proceed to laud and glorify his policy. The North applauds and sustains his propagandism because he strives to be at peace with all men. He appeals to the amity and not the enmity of both races. We are in the midst of an era of good feeling, and must have peace at any price. It is interesting to witness how many of the erstwhile loud-voiced advocates of the Negro's rights have seized upon Mr. Washington's pacific policy as a graceful recession from the former position. The whites have set up Booker Washington as in a former day they set up Frederick Douglass, as the divinely appointed and anointed leader of his race, and regard as sacrilege all criticism and even candid discussion on the part of those whom he has been sent to guide. They demand for him an exemption which they have never accorded their own leaders, from George Washington to Theodore Roosevelt. Nothing could be further from Mr. Washington's thoughts than the assumption of divine commission which the whites seek to impose upon him. He makes no claim to have received a revelation, either from burning bush or mountain top. He is a simple, sincere, unsophisticated colaborer with his brethren; a single, though signal, agency for the betterment of his race.

Mr. Washington did not start out as a leader of his people's own choosing; he did not command an enthusiastic and spontaneous following. He lacks that magnetic personality that would cause men to love him and women to adore him. His method is rather that of a missionary seeking the material and moral betterment of an unfortunate people, than of a spontaneous leader voicing their highest self-expression. He is deficient in the fearlessness, the self-assertion, the aggressive and heroic spirit necessary to quicken and inspire. Such a leader must not hold up for painful contemplation or emphasize to the outside world the repugnant, grotesque and ludicrous faults and foibles of his own people, but he must constantly direct their attention to higher and better ideals. His dominant note must be pitched in the major key. He must not be of the earth earthy, with range of vision limited to the ugliness of untoward conditions, but must have the power of idealization and spiritual vista. Exaggerated self-importance is deemed an individual fault, but a racial virtue. It has been the chief incentive of every race or nation that has ever gained prominence in the world's affairs. The triumphant, God-sent leader of any people must be the exponent and expounder of their highest aspirations and feelings, and must evoke their manhood and self-esteem, yea, even their vanity and pride.

Mr. Washington's following was at first very largely prudential and constrained; it lacked spontaneousness and joyance. He was not hailed with glad acclaim as the deliverer of his people. He brought good gifts rather than glad tidings. Many believed in him for his work's sake; some acquiesced rather than antagonize one who had gained so large a measure of public confidence; others were willing to co-operate in the accomplishment of good deeds, though they inwardly detested his doctrine; while those of political instinct sought his favor as a pass-key to prestige and place. Few thoughtful colored men espoused what passed as Mr. Washington's "policy" without apology or reserve. Many of the more dispassionate and thoughtful are disposed to yield to his primacy because he has such a hold on the sentiment and imagination of the white race that, if for any reason the spell should be broken, no other colored man could ever hope for like consideration and esteem.

Mr. Washington's critics assert that his leadership has been barren of good results to the Negro race, unmindful of the magnitude of the contract he has promised the American people that he would solve the race problem. Under his regnancy it is claimed that the last vestige of political power has been swept away. Civil privileges have been restricted, educational opportunities, in some States at least, have been curtailed; the industrial situation, the keystone of his policy, has become more ominous and uncertain, while the feeling between the races is constantly growing more acute and threatening. In answer to this it is averred that no human power could stay the wave of race hatred now sweeping over the country, but that the Tuskegeean's pacific policy will serve to relieve the severity of the blow. All of the leaders before him essayed the task in vain, and gave up in despair.

The majority of thoughtful men range between these wide-apart views, appreciating the good and the limitations of both. They believe in neither surrender nor revolution, and that both forces have their place and function in the solution of the race problem. They are joint factors of a common product, whose relative strength and importance may increase or diminish with the shifting exigencies of conditions. While it would be unseemly for those who breathe the free air of New England to remain silent concerning the heavy burden borne by their brethren in the South, yet we must not forget that Frederick Douglass himself could not to-day build up an institution in Alabama, nor do the imperative constructive work in that section. The progress of all peoples is marked by alternations of combat and contention on the one hand, and compromise and concession on the other, and progress is the result of the play and counterplay of these forces. Colored men should have a larger tolerance for the widest latitude of opinion and method. Too frequently what passes as "an irrepressible conflict" is merely difference in point of view.

The Negro's lot would be sad indeed if, under allurement of material advantage and temporary easement, he should sink into pliant yieldance to unrighteous oppression; but it would be sadder still if intemperate insistence should engender ill will and strife, when the race is not yet ready to be "battered with the shocks of doom." The words of Guizot never found a more pertinent application than to the present circumstances and situation of the Negro race:

> We continually oscillate between an inclination to complain without sufficient cause and to be too easily satisfied. We have extreme susceptibility of mind, an inordinate craving, an ambition in our thoughts, in our desires, and in the movements of our imagi-

> nation; yet when we come to practical life, when trouble, when sacrifices, when efforts are required for the attainment of our object, we sink into lassitude and inactivity. Let us not, however, suffer ourselves to be invaded by either of these vices. Let us estimate fairly what our abilities, our knowledge, our power enable us to do lawfully, and let us aim at nothing that we cannot lawfully, justly and prudently—with a proper respect for the great principles upon which our social system, our civilization, is based—attain.

Mr. Booker T. Washington's later career is exemplifying more and more the philosophy of this sentiment.

Under the spur of adverse criticism and the growing sense of responsibility which his expanding opportunities impose, Mr. Washington has become so enlarged that his leadership is universally conceded, and well-nigh universally accepted. Few men have shown such power of enlargement. Even those who continue to challenge his primacy confess that they are opposing the Washington of long ago rather than the Washington of to-day. He rises triumphantly on stepping-stones of his dead self to higher things. He began his career with a narrow educational bias and a one-sided championship of industrial training, as offset to the claims of literary culture which had hitherto absorbed the substance of Northern philanthropy. But he has grown so far in grasp and in breadth of view that he advocates all modes of education in their proper place and proportion. He at first deprecated the Negro's active participation in politics, but with broadening vision and increasing courage he now serves as consulting statesman touching all political interests of the race.

Washington's equability of temper is most remarkable. He receives a bequest of a million dollars, dines with the President, listens to the adulation of half the world or the bitter abuse of those whom he strives to serve, with the same modest and unruffled demeanor. His sanity and poise are unsurpassed. In a toast at a banquet given in honor of Mr. Washington in the city of Washington, the present writer proclaimed his conditional leadership, which the Negro race is now accepting with lessening reserve:

"We have as our guest to-night one who has come up from slavery, up from the coal caverns of West Virginia, struggling up against narrow theories, lack of early education and bias of environment, tactfully expanding the prudential restraints of a delicate and critical situation, rising upon successive stepping-stones of past achievements and past mistakes, but ever planting his feet upon higher and higher ground. Sir, you enjoy a degree of concrete achievement and personal distinction excelled by few men now living on this planet. You are not only the foremost man of the Negro race, but one of the foremost men of all the world. We did not give you that 'glad eminence' and we cannot take it away, but we would utilize and appropriate it to the good of the race. You have the attention of the white world; you hold the pass-key to the heart of the great white race. Your commanding position, your personal prestige, and the magic influence of your illustrious name entail upon you the responsibility to become the leader of the people, to stand as daysman between us and the great white God, and lay a propitiating hand upon us both. Some have criticised in the past, and reserve the right to do so in the future. A noble soul is big enough to invite candid criticism, and eschew sycophantic adulation.

"Sir, if you will stand upon the granite pedestal of truth and righteousness, and pursue policies that are commensurate with the entire circle of our needs, and which are broad-based upon the people's will, and advocate the fullest opportunity of Negro youth to expand and exploit their faculties, if you will stand as the fearless champion of the Negro's political rights before the law and behind the law, then a united race will rise up and join in gladsome chorus:

" 'Only thou our leader be,
And we still will follow thee.' "

AUGUST MEIER

Booker T. Washington: An Interpretation †

Booker T. Washington had assiduously cultivated a good press and from time to time had received the attention accorded leaders who were, as the phrase went, "succeeding." Yet it was with relative suddenness that he emerged at the Atlanta Exposition in September 1895 as a figure of national reputation and the acknowledged leader of Negroes in America.

To Washington the solution of the race problem lay essentially in an application of the gospel of wealth, and he opened and closed his address that memorable afternoon with references to material prosperity. He urged Negroes to stay in the South, since when it came to business, pure and simple, it was in the South that the Negro was given a man's chance. Whites were urged to lend a helping hand in the uplifting of the Negroes in order to further the prosperity and well-being of their region. Coupled with this appeal to the self-interest of the white South

† From August Meier, *Negro Thought in America, 1880–1915* (Ann Arbor: U of Michigan P, 1963), 100–102, 103–106, 110–112, 113–118. Copyright © by the University of Michigan, 1963. Copyright © renewed in the name of August Meier, 1992. Reprinted by permission. Except where otherwise noted, all works cited in this article are by Booker T. Washington, and all citations to correspondence are to the Booker T. Washington Papers.

was a conciliatory phraseology and a criticism of Negroes. Washington deprecated politics and the Reconstruction experience. He criticized Negroes for forgetting that the masses of the race were to live by the production of their hands and for permitting their grievances to overshadow their opportunities. He grew lyrical in reciting the loyalty and fidelity of Negroes—"the most patient, faithful, law-abiding and unresentful people that the world had seen." He denied any interest in social equality when he said: "In all things that are purely social we can be as separate as the five fingers, yet one as the hand in all things essential to mutual progress." In conclusion he asked for justice and an elimination of sectional differences and racial animosities, which, combined with material prosperity would usher in a new era for "our beloved South."[1]

Washington's emphasis upon economic prosperity was the hallmark of the age. The pledges of loyalty to the South and the identification of Negro uplift with the cause of the New South satisfied the "better class" of Southern whites and Northern investors; the generalities about justice to the Negro, of interracial co-operation in things essential to mutual progress, coupled with a denial of interest in social equality, encompassed a wide range of views that could be satisfied by ambiguous phraseology. Washington's generalized references to justice and progress and uplift soothed the pallid consciences of the dominant groups in the nation and at the same time allowed the white South to assume that justice could be achieved without granting Negroes political and civil rights. Yet a careful reading of the address indicates that it could also be interpreted as including ultimate goals more advanced than white Southerners could possibly support. Negroes must begin at the bottom, but surely Washington believed that eventually they would arrive at the top. Most Negroes interpreted social equality as meaning simply intimate social relationships which they did not desire, though most whites interpreted it as meaning the abolition of segregation. Even though Washington said that "it is important and right that all privileges of the law be ours; but it is vastly more important that we be prepared for the exercise of these privileges," and that "the opportunity to earn a dollar in a factory just now is worth infinitely more than the opportunity to spend a dollar in an opera house," his Negro supporters emphasized the future implications of his remarks, and his statement that "no race that has anything to contribute to the markets of the world is long in any degree ostracized." Unlike Negroes, the dominant whites were impressed by his conciliatory phraseology, confused his means for his ends, and were satisfied with the immediate program that he enunciated.

1. *Address . . . Delivered at the Opening of the Cotton States and International Exposition, 1895* (no imprint, n.d.), 6–11.

Washington captured his audience and assured his ascendancy primarily because his ideas accorded with the climate of opinion at the time. His association with industrial education, his emphasis upon the economic, and his conciliatory approach were undoubtedly important reasons why he was selected to speak on this prominent occasion. As Charles S. Johnson has suggested, Washington was effectively manipulating the symbols and myths dear to the majority of Americans.[2] It cannot be overemphasized that Washington's philosophy represents in large measure the basic tendencies of Negro thought in the period under consideration. * * *

The central theme in Washington's philosophy was that through thrift, industry, and Christian character Negroes would eventually attain their constitutional rights. To Washington it seemed but proper that Negroes would have to measure up to American standards of morality and material prosperity if they were to succeed in the Social Darwinist race of life. Just as the individual who succeeds can do something that the world wants done well, so with a race. Things would be on a different footing if it became common to associate the possession of wealth with a black skin. "It is not within the province of human nature that the man who is intelligent and virtuous, and owns and cultivates the best farm in his county, shall very long be denied the proper respect and consideration."[3]

Consequently Negroes, he felt, must learn trades in order to compete with whites. He blamed Negroes for neglecting skills acquired under slavery, for the loss of what had been practically a monopoly of the skilled labor in the South at the close of the Civil War. He feared that unless industrial schools filled the breach, the next twenty years would witness the economic demise of the Negro. He was often critical of higher education. He never tired of retelling the anecdotes about the rosewood piano in the tumble-down cabin, or about the young man he found sitting in an unkempt cabin, studying from a French grammar. He denied that he intended to minimize the value of higher education, and his own children in fact enjoyed its advantages, but practical education, he believed, should come first in the rise of a people toward civilization. Occasionally, he praised higher education, but he often cited cases of college graduates who were accomplishing nothing, and once at least he referred to "the college bacillus."[4]

Fundamentally, Washington did not think in terms of a subordinate place in the American economy for Negroes. Though his language was ambiguous, he thought in terms of developing a substantial propertied

2. Johnson, "The Social Philosophy of Booker T. Washington," 1940, MS lent to the author by the late Dr. Johnson.
3. *Future of the American Negro*, 176.
4. "A University Education for Negroes," *Independent*, 68 (March 24, 1910), 613–18; "What I am Trying to Do," *World's Work*, 27 (Nov., 1913), 103.

class of landowners and businessmen. There was, as he often put it, a great need for "captains of industry." He felt a deep sympathy with the wealthy, and he preferred to talk most of all to audiences of businessmen who, he found, were quick to grasp what he was saying. In all this he was thoroughly in accord with the New South philosophy. He praised Robert C. Ogden of Wanamaker's (a trustee of Tuskegee and Hampton and chairman of the General Education Board) and H. H. Rogers, the Standard Oil and railroad magnate, as men whose interest in uplifting the Negro was partly motivated by their desire to develop one of the neglected resources of the South.[5]

Part of Washington's outlook toward capital and the New South was his antagonistic attitude toward labor unions. He recollected that before the days of strikes in the West Virginia coal mines where he had worked, he had known miners with considerable sums in the bank, "but as soon as the professional labor agitators got control, the savings of even the more thrifty ones began disappearing." To some extent, he felt, the loss of the Negro's hold on the skilled trades was due to the unions. He boasted that Negro labor was, if fairly treated, "the best free labor in the world," not given to striking. Later, writing in the *Atlantic Monthly* in 1913, Washington, though still basically hostile, appeared somewhat more favorable toward unions. He admitted that there were cases in which labor unions had used their influence on behalf of Negroes even in the South, and he knew of instances in which Negroes had taken a leading part in the work of their unions. Nevertheless, he felt that unions would cease to discriminate only to the extent that they feared Negro strikebreakers.[6]

Exceedingly important in Washington's outlook was an emphasis on agriculture and rural landownership that has ordinarily been overlooked. He constantly deprecated migration to cities where, he said, the Negro was at his worst and insisted that Negroes should stay on the farmlands of the South. Since all peoples who had gained wealth and recognition had come up from the soil, agriculture should be the chief occupation of Negroes, who should be encouraged to own and cultivate the soil. While he called Negroes the best labor for Southern farms, he optimistically looked forward to an independent yeomanry, respected in their communities.

Also associated with Washington's middle-class and Social Darwinist philosophy were the ideas of the value of struggle in achieving success, of self-help, and of "taking advantage of disadvantages." As he put it, "No race of people ever got upon its feet without severe and constant struggle, often in the face of the greatest disappointment."[7] He turned

5. *My Larger Education*, 72–73, 76–77.
6. *Up From Slavery*, 68–69; "The Best Free Labor in the World," *Southern State Farm Magazine* (Jan., 1898), 496–98 (clipping in BTW Papers); "The Negro and the Labor Unions," *Atlantic Monthly*, CXI (June, 1913), 756–67.
7. *The Case of the Negro*, 2.

misfortune into good fortune, and middle-class rationalization of the strenuous life into an accommodating rationalization of the Negro's status. Paradoxical as it might seem, the difficulties facing the Negro had on the whole helped him more than they had hindered him, for under pressure the Negro had put forth more energy which, constructively channeled, had been of untold value.

While whites had some responsibility, the most important part in the Negro's progress was to be played by the Negro himself; the race's future recognition lay within its own hands. On the negative side this emphasis on self-help involved a tendency to blame Negroes for their condition. Washington constantly criticized them for seeking higher rather than practical education, for their loss of places in the skilled trades, for their lack of morality and economic virtues, and for their tendency toward agitation and complaint. But in its positive aspects this emphasis involved race pride and solidarity. Negroes should be proud of their history and their great men. For a race to grow strong and powerful it must honor its heroes. Negroes should not expect any great success until they learned to imitate the Jews, who through unity and faith in themselves were becoming more and more influential. He showed considerable pride in the all-Negro communities. At times he espoused a high degree of racial solidarity and economic nationalism. On one occasion he declared: "We are a nation within a nation." While Negroes should be the last to draw the color line, at the same time they should see to it that "in every wise and legitimate way our people are taught to patronise racial enterprises."[8]

If emphasis upon racial pride and self-help through economic and moral development formed one side of Washington's thinking, another was his insistence that interracial harmony and white good will were prerequisite to the Negro's advancement. In appealing to whites Washington spoke in both moral and practical terms. Southern whites should aid Negroes out of economic self-interest and should act justly since to do less would corrupt their moral fiber. Washington constantly reiterated his love for the South, his faith in the Southern white man's sense of justice, his belief that the South afforded Negroes more economic opportunity than the North. In 1912, answering the question "Is the Negro Having a Fair Chance?" he did go so far as to admit the existence of the standard grievances, but declared that nowhere were there ten million black people who had greater opportunities or were making greater progress than the Negroes of the South; nowhere had any race "had the assistance, the direction, and the sympathy of another race in all its efforts to rise to such an extent as the Negro in the United States." Washington devoted one whole book, *The Man Farthest Down* (1912), to the thesis that American Negroes were better off than the depressed

8. Detroit *Leader*, Sept. 8, 1911 (in BTW Clipping Books).

classes in Europe. In general, Washington appealed to the highest sentiments and motives of the whites and brushed lightly over their prejudices and injustices in an attempt to create the favorable sentiment without which Negro progress was doomed. He frequently referred to the friendship Southern whites exhibited toward Negroes and constantly cited examples of harmonious relations between the races. At a time when Mississippi was notorious for "whitecapping" (the attacking of business establishments owned by prosperous Negroes who were then run out of town), he opined that "there, more than anywhere else, the colored people seem to have discovered that, in gaining habits of thrift and industry, in getting property, and in making themselves useful, there is a door of hope open for them which the South has no disposition to close." He was incurably optimistic in his utterances—as he said, "We owe it not only to ourselves, but to our children, to look always upon the bright side of life."[9]

* * *

Although overtly Washington minimized the importance of the franchise and civil rights, covertly he was deeply involved in political affairs and in efforts to prevent disfranchisement and other forms of discrimination.

For example, he lobbied against the Hardwick disfranchisement bill in Georgia in 1899. While his public ambiguities permitted Southern whites to think that he accepted disfranchisement if they chose to, through the same ambiguities and by private communications Washington tried to keep Negroes thinking otherwise. In 1903 when the Atlanta editor Clark Howell implied that Washington opposed Negro officeholding, he did not openly contradict him, but asked T. Thomas Fortune to editorialize in the *Age* that Howell had no grounds for placing Washington in such a position, for it was "well understood that he, while from the first deprecating the Negro's making political agitation and office-holding the most prominent and fundamental part of his career, has not gone any farther."[1] Again, while Washington opposed proposals to enforce the representation provisions of the fourteenth amendment (because he felt that the South would accept reduction in representation and thus stamp disfranchisement with the seal of constitutionality), he was secretly engaged in attacking the disfranchisement constitutions by court action. As early as 1900 he was asking certain philanthropists for money to fight the electoral provisions of the Louisiana constitution. Subsequently, he worked secretly through the finan-

9. "Is the Negro Having a Fair Chance?" *Century*, 85 (Nov., 1912), 50–55, 46; *My Larger Education*, 189, 197–98; "Fundamental Needs for the Progress of the Race" (1904, MS at Tuskegee Institute Department of Records and Research).
1. BTW [Booker T. Washington] to Garrison, Nov. 28, 1899 in Garrison Papers; BTW to T. Thomas Fortune, Nov. 10, 1899, June 23, 1903.

cial secretary of the Afro-American Council's legal bureau, personally spending a great deal of money and energy fighting the Louisiana test case.[2] At the time of the Alabama Constitutional Convention in 1901 he used his influence with important whites in an attempt to prevent discriminatory provisions that would apply to Negroes only.[3] He was later deeply involved in testing the Alabama disfranchisement laws in the federal courts in 1903 and 1904. So circumspect was he in this instance that his secretary, Emmett J. Scott, and the New York lawyer Wilford Smith corresponded about the cases under pseudonyms and represented the sums involved in code. Washington was also interested in efforts to prevent or undermine disfranchisement in other states. For example, in Maryland, where disfranchisement later failed, he had a Catholic lawyer, F. L. McGhee of St. Paul, approach the Catholic hierarchy in an attempt to secure its opposition to disfranchisement and urged the Episcopal divine George Freeman Bragg of Baltimore to use his influence among important whites.[4] Washington contributed money generously to the test cases and other efforts, though, except in the border states, they were unsuccessful. In 1903 and 1904 he personally "spent at least four thousand dollars in cash, out of my own pocket . . . in advancing the rights of the black man."[5]

Washington's political involvement went even deeper. Although he always discreetly denied any interest in politics, he was engaged in patronage distribution under Roosevelt and Taft, in fighting the lily-white Republicans, and in getting out the Negro vote for the Republicans at national elections. He might say that he disliked the atmosphere at Washington because it was impossible to build up a race whose leaders were spending most of their time and energy in trying to get into or stay in office,[6] but under Roosevelt he became the arbiter of Negro appointments to federal office. Roosevelt started consulting Washington almost as soon as he took office, and later claimed that Washington had approved of his policy of appointing fewer but better-qualified Negroes.[7] Numerous politicians old and new were soon writing to Tuskegee for favors, and in a few cases Roosevelt consulted Washington in regard to

2. BTW to Garrison, Feb. 27, and March 11, 1900, Garrison Papers; Jesse Lawson to BTW, March 29, June 26, July 30, Oct. 2, Dec. 30, 1901; April 30, June 24, 1902; BTW to Lawson, Dec. 11, 1903. On BTW's opposition to reduced representation for Southern states, see BTW to R. C. Ogden, May 15, 1903; BTW to W. H. Baldwin, March 4, 1904.
3. E.g., Correspondence with A. D. Wimbs, 1901.
4. Correspondence of Wilford Smith (alias J. C. May) and Emmett J. Scott (alias R. C. Black) 1903 and 1904; F. L. McGhee to BTW, Jan. 12, 1904; BTW to George F. Bragg, March 10, 1904. For fuller documentation of this and other points made in this section see August Meier, "Toward a Reinterpretation of Booker T. Washington," *JSH*, 23 (May, 1957), 220–27.
5. BTW to J. W. E. Bowen, Dec. 27, 1904.
6. *My Larger Education*, 159.
7. See especially Roosevelt to BTW, Sept. 14, Dec. 12, 1901; and Roosevelt to James Ford Rhodes, Dec. 15, 1905, in Elting E. Morison, ed., *The Letters of Theodore Roosevelt* (Cambridge, 1951–54), IV, 1072; Roosevelt to Richard Watson Gilder, Nov. 16, 1908, in Roosevelt Papers, Library of Congress.

white candidates.[8] Ex-Congressman George H. White unsuccessfully appealed to Washington after the White House indicated that "a letter from you would greatly strengthen my chances." Scott reported that the President's assertion to one office seeker that he would consider him only with Washington's endorsement, had "scared these old fellows as they never have been scared before." Washington had at his disposal a number of collectorships of ports and internal revenue, receiverships of public monies in the land office, and several diplomatic posts, as well as the positions of auditor of the Navy, register of the Treasury and recorder of the deeds. As Roosevelt wrote to a friend in 1903, his Negro appointees "were all recommended to me by Booker T. Washington."[9] Furthermore, Roosevelt sought Washington's advice on presidential speeches and messages to Congress and consulted him on most matters concerning the Negro. Every four years also Washington took charge of the Negro end of the Republican presidential campaign.[1]

* * *

Of special interest are Washington's efforts against railroad segregation. At Washington's suggestion Giles B. Jackson of Richmond undertook the legal fight against the Jim Crow Law in Virginia in 1901.[2] When Tennessee in 1903 in effect prohibited Pullman accommodations for Negroes by requiring that such facilities be entirely separate, he stepped into the breach. He worked closely with Napier in Nashville and enlisted the aid of Atlanta leaders like W. E. B. Du Bois. This group, however, did not succeed in discussing the matter with Pullman Company president Robert Todd Lincoln, in spite of the intercession of another railroad leader, William H. Baldwin, president of the Long Island Railroad, an important figure in the Pennsylvania and Southern systems, and Washington's closest white friend. And, though Washington wanted to start a suit, the Nashville people failed to act.[3] Again, in 1906, employing the Howard University Professor Kelly Miller and the Boston lawyer Archibald W. Grimké as intermediaries, Washington discreetly supplied funds to pay ex-Senator Henry W. Blair of New Hampshire to lobby against the Warner-Foraker Amendment to the Hepburn

8. Samuel R. Spencer, Jr., *Booker T. Washington and the Negro's Place in American Life* (Boston, 1955), 136, 138; two letters of BTW to Roosevelt dated Nov. 4, 1902; Roosevelt to John Graham Brooks, Nov. 13, 1908, in Roosevelt Papers.
9. White to BTW, Oct. 7, 1901; Scott to BTW, July 2, 1902; Roosevelt to Silas McBee, Feb. 3, 1903, in Morison, *Letters of Theodore Roosevelt*, 3, 419.
1. The correspondence concerning Washington's political activities during the Roosevelt and Taft administrations is enormous. See especially correspondence with Roosevelt, James R. Clarkson, George Cortelyou, William Loeb, and Charles W. Anderson during Roosevelt's presidency, and with Taft, C. D. Norton, C. D. Hilles, and Anderson during Taft's.
2. Jackson to BTW, Jan. 24, 1901.
3. Napier to BTW, Oct. 28, Dec. 11, 1903; BTW to Napier, No. 2, 1903; BTW to Lawson, Nov. 5, 1903; BTW to Du Bois, Dec. 14, 1903, Feb. 27, June 4, 1904; Baldwin to BTW, Jan. 7, 1904.

Railway Act.[4] This amendment, by requiring equality of accommodations in interstate travel, would have impliedly condoned segregation throughout the country, under the separate-but-equal doctrine. The amendment was defeated, but whether due to Blair's lobbying or to the protests of Negro organizations is hard to say.

Thus, in spite of his accommodating tone and his verbal emphasis upon economy as the solution to the race problem, Washington was surreptitiously engaged in undermining the American race system by a direct attack upon disfranchisement and segregation, and in spite of his strictures against political activity he was a powerful politician in his own right.

Comparable to Washington's influence in politics was his position with the philanthropists. He wielded an enormous influence in appropriations made by Carnegie, Rosenwald, the General Education Board, and the Phelps-Stokes and Jeanes Funds. Negro schools that received Carnegie libraries received them at Washington's suggestion, and even applied for them upon his advice.[5] Contributors sought his advice on the worthiness of schools; college administrators asked his advice on personnel. His weight was especially appreciated by the liberal arts colleges. Washington accepted a place on the boards of trustees of Howard University in 1907 and Fisk University in 1909. In the case of Fisk he proved exceedingly helpful in attracting philanthropic contributions.[6] So complete was Washington's control over educational philanthropy that John Hope, president of Atlanta Baptist College, and a member of the anti-Bookerite Niagara Movement, found the doors of the foundations entirely closed to him. Only through the intercession of his friend Robert Russa Moton, a member of the Hampton circle and Washington's successor at Tuskegee, was Hope able to obtain Washington's necessary endorsement of his school to philanthropists such as Carnegie.[7]

Washington's popularity with leading whites and his power in philanthropic and political circles enhanced his prestige and power within the Negro community. His influence was felt in multifarious ways beyond his control, over philanthropy and political appointments. His power over the Negro press was considerable and in large measure stifled criticism of his policies. His influence extended into the Negro churches, and his friendship and assistance were eagerly sought by those seeking positions in the church. Between 1902 and 1904 and perhaps longer,

4. Miller to BTW, May 22, 1906; Grimké to BTW, May 25, June 10, 1906; BTW to Grimké, June 2, 4, 10, 1906; Scott to Thompson, June 5, 1906.
5. See correspondence with various college presidents 1904 and 1905.
6. BTW to President J. G. Merrill of Fisk, April 26, 1905; James C. Bertram (Carnegie's secretary) to BTW, Jan. 15, 1908; BTW to Carnegie, Oct. 18, 1910; BTW to Bertram, April 28, 1913, etc.
7. Ridgely Torrence, *The Story of John Hope* (New York, 1948), 159–63; correspondence between Hope and BTW, 1909.

Washington controlled the avowedly protest Afro-American Council, the leading Negro rights organization prior to 1905. Whether or not Washington was a " benevolent despot" as one recent biographer has asserted,[8] is an open question, but that he wielded enormous power over the Negro community is undeniable.

It was this quasi-dictatorial power as much as anything else that alienated W. E. B. Du Bois from Washington and his program. Once Washington had achieved eminence he grew extremely sensitive to adverse criticism from Negroes. From the first some had opposed his viewpoint, and while many rushed to his support after he became the puissant adviser to Theodore Roosevelt, somehow "the opposition" (as Washington often referred to his critics) grew apace. Objections were raised to the arbitrary power of the "Tuskegee machine," as Du Bois called it, and to Washington's soft-pedaling of political and civil rights. From 1903 on Washington found himself increasingly under attack. He used every means at his disposal to combat his critics—his influence with the press, placing spies in the opposition movements, depriving their members of church and political positions. The high point of the attack on Washington, the formation of the National Association for the Advancement of Colored People in 1909–10, came at the very time when his political power was slipping, and after 1913 he had no political influence at all, while the N.A.A.C.P. was becoming stronger. By the time he died Washington had lost much of his power.

Washington's struggle against the various protest groups is interesting in that they had the same ultimate goal as he did, and came out frankly for the very things for which he was working surreptitiously. Yet Washington appears to have regarded them as more dangerous to the welfare of the race than "friends" like Carnegie, Taft, and Roosevelt, who were not genuine equalitarians and who thought Negroes should not emphasize politics and civil rights. Washington sincerely believed that his program would be the most effective in the long run, but he did not object too much to militance and agitation in the newspapers that supported him. His attacks upon "the opposition" suggest that something more than tactics or ideologies was at stake. It appears that Washington feared the effect of his critics on his personal power and prestige. He did not object to protest too much as long as it was not aimed at him and his policies. As he wrote R. C. Ogden, "wise, conservative agitation looking toward securing the rights of colored people on the part of the people of the North is not hurtful."[9]

It would appear to this author that a large part of Washington's motivation was his desire for power. To a large extent he had to be satisfied with the substance rather than the symbols of power. His desire for

8. Spencer, *Booker T. Washington*, chap. x.
9. BTW to Ogden, May 1, 1903.

power and prestige, however, does not necessarily indicate insincerity or hypocrisy. It is usually hard to distinguish where altruism ends and self-interests begins. So thoroughly and inextricably bound together in Washington's mind were his program for racial elevation and his own personal career, that he genuinely thought that he and only he was in the best position to advance the interests of the race.

Thus, although Washington held to full citizenship rights and integration as his objective, he masked this goal beneath an approach that satisfied influential elements that were either indifferent or hostile to its fulfillment. He was not the first to combine a constructive, even militant emphasis upon self-help, racial co-operation and economic development with a conciliatory, ingratiating, and accommodating approach to the white South. But his name is the one most indissolubly linked with this combination. He was, as one of his followers put it, attempting to bring the wooden horse within the walls of Troy.

Washington apparently really believed that in the face of an economic and moral development that assimilated Negroes to American middle-class standards, prejudice would diminish and the barriers of discrimination would crumble. He emphasized duties rather than rights; the Negro's faults rather than his grievances; his opportunities rather than his difficulties. He stressed means rather than ends. He was optimistic rather than pessimistic. He stressed economics above politics, industrial above liberal education, self-help above dependence on the national government. He taught that rural life was superior to urban life. He professed a deep love for the South and a profound faith in the goodness of the Southern whites—at least of the "better class." He appealed more to the self-interest of the whites—their economic and moral good—than to their sense of justice.

The ambiguities in Washington's philosophy were vital to his success. Negroes who supported him looked to his tactfully, usually vaguely worded expression on ultimate goals. Conservative Southerners were attracted by his seeming acceptance of disfranchisement and segregation, and by his flattery. Industrialists and philanthropists appreciated his petit bourgeois outlook. Washington's skillful manipulation of popular symbols and myths like the gospel of wealth and the doctrines of Social Darwinism enhanced his effectiveness. Terms like "social equality," "civil relations," "constitutional rights," "Christian character," "industrial education," and "justice" were capable of a wide variety of interpretations. The Supreme Court, for example, did not appear to think that the fourteenth and fifteenth amendments prohibited segregation and the use of various subterfuges that effected disfranchisement. Washington shrewdly used these ambiguities, and they were an important source both of his popularity and of the acrimonious discussion over his policy that occupied Negroes for many years.

Washington did not appeal to all groups. Extremists among white Southerners liked him no more than did the Negro "radicals." Men such as Governor Vardaman of Mississippi and the author Thomas Dixon, who feared any Negro advancement, opposed the Tuskegeean's program of elevation and uplift. Washington basically appealed to conservative, propertied elements both North and South. His stress upon the economic rather than the political was parallel to the New South philosophy of emphasizing industry rather than politics as a way of advancing the South in the councils of the nation. Yet he also capitalized on the myth of the small farmer, and the romantic agrarian traditions of the South. His call for a justly applied property and educational test that would disfranchise ignorant and poor Negroes and whites alike, and enfranchise the propertied, taxpaying, conservative Negroes, met the approval of important elements in the Black Belt plantation and urban areas of the south, who had no more love for the "poor whites" than Washington did. Again, Washington espoused a Social Darwinism of competition between individuals and races, of uplifting backward races, that was congenial to his age. He conveniently put Negro equality off into a hazy future that did not disturb the "practical" and prejudiced men of his generation. At the same time, by blaming Negroes for their condition, by calling them a backward race, by asserting that an era of justice would ultimately be ushered in, by flattering the whites for what little they had done for Negroes, he palliated any pangs of conscience that the whites might have had.

His program also appealed to a substantial group of Negroes—to those Negroes who were coming to count for most—in large part to a rising middle class. In fact, stress upon economics as an indirect route to the solution of the race problem, interest in industrial education, the appeal to race pride and solidarity, and denial of any interest in social equality were all ideas that had become dominant in the Negro community. The older upper-class Negroes in certain Northern centers, who had their economic and sometimes their social roots in the white communities, were less sympathetic to Washington. But to self-made middle-class Negroes, and to lower middle-class Negroes on the make, to the leaders and supporters of Negro fraternal enterprises, to businessmen who depended on the Negro community for their livelihood, Washington's message seemed common sense. Interestingly enough, this group, especially in the North, did not always express Washington's conciliatory tone, but assumed that Washington was using it to placate the white South.

To what extent Washington directly influenced Negro thought is difficult to evaluate. Washington was acceptable to Negroes partly because of the prestige and power he held among whites, and partly because his views—except for his conciliatory phraseology—were dominant in the Negro community throughout the country, and his accommodating approach was general throughout the South. Then, too, his Negro supporters read a great deal into his generalizations about eventual justice and constitutional rights. The fact that Negroes tended to see in his words what they already believed would appear to minimize his direct influence. Yet his prestige, the teachers sent out by Tuskegee and her daughter schools, and the widespread publicity generated by the National Negro Business League of which Washington was the founder and president, undoubtedly had a significant impact on Negro thought, reinforcing tendencies already in the foreground.

LOUIS R. HARLAN

Booker T. Washington in Biographical Perspective †

In the current vogue of black history Booker T. Washington has been a figure to ignore rather than to grapple with, an anomaly, an embarrassment. This is partly because his methods were too compromising and unheroic to win him a place in the black pantheon, but it is also because he was so complex and enigmatic that historians do not know what to make of him. We have lost the thread we used to believe would guide us through his labyrinth. When his rich private collection of papers was opened to scholars two decades ago, historians had to abandon the simpler picture of Washington presented in his autobiography. They generally seized upon the concept that Washington was a symbol of his age in race relations, a representative figure whose actions and philosophy were pragmatically adjusted to the demands of an era of sharply worsening race relations. He was the type of Negro leader that the age of Jim Crow would throw to the top. There is something to be said for this view, and certainly Washington was delicately attuned to his age. From the biographical perspective, however, Washington seems thoroughly consistent throughout a life that spanned from the slavery era into the twentieth century. In the period of his leadership after 1895 he followed the lessons he had learned at Hampton Institute in the seventies and practiced at Tuskegee in the eighties.

In his mature years Washington's life became extremely complex. There was first of all the public image, that of a race leader who told his people to accommodate themselves to the realities of white power, and whose own personal success illustrated that such a course could be personally rewarding. In the Atlanta Address in 1895, the year the old militant leader Frederick Douglass died, Washington stated the formula: "In

† From Louis R. Harlan, "Booker T. Washington in Biographical Perspective," *American Historical Review*, vol. 75, no. 4 (Oct. 1970), 1581–86, 1587–90, 1592–93, 1594–95, 1596–99. Reprinted by permission.

all things that are purely social we can be as separate as the fingers, yet one as the hand in all things essential to mutual progress." Put down your buckets where they are, make peace and common cause with your white neighbor, seek a white patron, but also improve yourself slowly through education and property, through "severe and constant struggle rather than . . . artificial forcing."[1] A few years later Washington's success story, *Up from Slavery*, a worldwide best seller, further buttressed the accommodation formula. It described, somewhat mythically, his rise from a slave cabin to the middle class, the inculcation at Hampton Institute of Puritan virtues, and their practice through a useful and successful life. It was a comforting witness that even the American race system could not keep a good man down. Tuskegee Institute, which he founded in a Negro church and a henhouse and built into one of the largest and best-endowed schools in the South, was a monument to the effectiveness of his approach.

Though Washington never made another speech of the significance of the Atlanta Address nor wrote another book equal to *Up from Slavery*, he remained throughout his life a popular platform speaker and magazine article writer. He expressed what John Kenneth Galbraith calls "the conventional wisdom" of his day in race relations and social thought. He was the apostle of things as they were. He had to employ a series of ghost writers to meet the demand for books and articles. Unfortunately, however, under his instructions the ghost writers merely paraphrased Washington's earlier utterances, thus freezing his public thought in outmoded patterns. His mind as revealed in formal public expression became a bag of clichés.

Washington's mind or psyche as the directing force of his private actions, on the other hand, was kaleidoscopic in its changing patterns and apparent lack of a central design. The source of this complexity, no doubt, was being a black man in white America, with the attendant dualism and ambivalence that black people feel. Washington's life and thought were layered into public, private, and secret and also segmented according to which subgroup of black or white he confronted. For each group he played a different role, wore a different mask. Like the proverbial cat, Washington lived nine lives, but he lived them all at once. Yet there were so few slips of the mask that it is no wonder his intimates called him "the wizard."

One of Washington's private roles was that of master of the Tuskegee plantation. From his big house, "The Oaks," Washington ran his school without delegation of authority and with infinite attention to detail. Even during his absences in the North, he continued to direct affairs closely through the confidential reports of his brother, private secretary,

1. "The Atlanta Exposition Address," Sept. 18, 1895, in Booker T. Washington (hereafter BTW), *Up from Slavery* (Bantam ed., New York, 1963), 153–58.

and other informers. He saw the sparrow's fall. Faculty members dreaded the crunch of carriage wheels that signaled his return, for each morning he toured the campus on horseback and noted every scrap of trash, every stray chicken, every dirty plate, every evidence of student waste or neglect. It all went into his little red notebook,[2] from which flowed a thousand memoranda reminding errant faculty members of their high duty to make of Tuskegee a black utopia, a proof that Negroes were capable of the petit bourgeois life.

In the radically different world of the white philanthropists Washington showed his appealing mask, deferential but dignified. At first, following the example of Hampton Institute, he made Boston his Northern headquarters and the church and Sunday-school philanthropy of New England small towns his principal philanthropic target. At the turn of the century, however, he began spending his winters and summers in New York, center of the new wealth of industry and finance. Showing that there can be a subtlety even in platitudes, Washington gradually modified his rhetoric from the style of Puritan homiletics to that of the "gospel of wealth." His principal appeal to businessmen, however, was that he seemed so much like them, not only in his attitude toward labor, property, public order, and other questions but in the earnestness, diligence, and energy with which he conducted his school. What struck Andrew Carnegie, when he gave Tuskegee a library, was Washington's ability, through the cheap labor of students, to get so much building for so little money. He was a safe, sane, self-made man who could be trusted with one's money. Moving freely in the offices, homes, and summer resorts of the wealthy, Washington constantly crossed the color line in the North, riding first-class cars and staying at first-class hotels. Though he had dinner at the White House only once, that was no measure of his dining habits among the Northern elite, who accepted him on perhaps more completely equal terms than any other black American in history.

Among Southern whites Washington was more circumspect. He made a point of not crossing the color line while in the South. He sought to reduce social friction by what Southerners called keeping his place. Washington divided white Southerners into two classes: employers who were the benefactors of Negroes and fit allies of Northern philanthropists, and poor whites, who were enemies of the black people and of a harmonious social order. Washington's strategy of partnership with the Southern white elite was notably unsuccessful in halting the tide of white racial aggression, violence, disfranchisement, discrimination, and segregation in his day. The white planters and businessmen turned out to be not as benevolent as expected and nowhere near as powerful, and

2. See, for example, the red notebook of 1887, Booker T. Washington Papers, Library of Congress, Container 949 (hereafter these papers will be cited as BTW Papers, LC, with container number in parentheses).

the Southern political system and to some extent its economy fell into the hands of whites in whose lives of hardship and disappointment in a depressed Southern economy the Negro served as a convenient scapegoat. Washington refused to face this worsening of race relations realistically, refused to doubt the viability of his Atlanta Compromise. In 1908, after a tour of Mississippi, then in the throes of Vardaman's demagoguery, he wrote to Oswald Garrison Villard: "I was surprised to find a large number of white men and women who, close down in their hearts, I am sure are all right, but only need encouragement and help to lead them to the point where they will speak out and act more bravely." When a white mob at Lula, Mississippi, hanged two Negroes where Washington could see them as his train passed, he assured Villard that this episode was not significant "outside of the ordinary disgraceful lynchings that so frequently occur in that state."[3]

Among Southern blacks Washington presented a fatherly image. He was of the same rural Southern peasant origins and could speak to them in their own language. They responded also to the peasant conservatism of his economic program, with its emphasis on the basic needs of a rural people—small property accumulation, education of a practical sort, recognition of the dignity of toil, doing the common, everyday things of life "uncommonly without a murmur." Washington conceived of Tuskegee as "a school built around a social problem." He thought that all his compromises would be justified if his industrial school, located like a settlement house in the middle of a rural slum, could transform the lives of the black sharecroppers of Macon County, Alabama, and the surrounding Black Belt. So he not only trained teachers and skilled farmers and tradesmen to return to these communities, but he offered them schemes to improve their lives. The Jesup Wagon, an agricultural classroom on wheels, toured the back roads; an annual Negro Conference brought farmers from Alabama and neighboring states for lessons in scientific agriculture and the economics of landownership. Tuskegee managed several loan funds to aid local farmers to buy their land.[4] It is easy to see now that Washington's plan for economic progress was bound to fail because he sought to build through small business institutions in a day when big business was sweeping all before it. Worse yet, it was in agriculture, the sickest industry in America, and in the South, the nation's sickest region, and in certain obsolescent trades such as blacksmithing that Washington sought to work his economic wonders. All that was less clear in his day, however, and besides he had an emotional commitment to "keep them down on the farm," for he hated and feared the city.

Despite his Southern rural distrust of the city and particularly the

3. BTW to Oswald Garrison Villard, Oct. 30, 1908, BTW Papers, LC (42).
4. These included the Dizer, Cockran, and Milholland Funds, the Southern Improvement Company, and Baldwin Farms.

Negro intellectuals and professional men of the Northern cities, Washington used the power that white approval and financing gave him to dominate also the Northern black ghetto-dwellers. As August Meier has shown so convincingly, he even bound a large segment of the "talented tenth," the professional-class elite, to him by patronage and mutual interest rather than common ideology.[5] He was the founder and president of the National Negro Business League, an organization he shrewdly used to create a nucleus of conservative blacks in all the Northern cities. He could not completely control Negro journalistic expression, but he did dominate it by a combination of ownership of some newspapers and advertising subsidies to others, and by paying a Negro syndicated columnist to follow the Tuskegee line. Black professors were kept under control by college presidents who recognized that Washington could reward or punish them when philanthropists asked his advice. His smile or frown could govern the fate of a college library, and he personally dispensed much of the Negro philanthropy of Carnegie, Schiff, and Rosenwald. His white friends patronized the black painters, singers, and writers whom he favored. His friends infiltrated the leading black church denominations and even the Negro Odd Fellows and Prince Hall Masons in his interest. In all the activity of this Tuskegee Machine was a determination to crush rash militants who were more and more openly denouncing him as a traitor to his race.

Despite his public advice to Negroes to abandon voting and officeholding as a solution of their problems, Washington became the leading Negro political broker in the era of Theodore Roosevelt and Taft. The constituency of black politicians was dissolving in those years because of disfranchisement in the South, while the Northern ghetto populations were still too small to have much political weight. The trend in Negro patronage positions, therefore, was downward, and Washington could do little to reverse its course. He simply secured places for his friends, particularly Negro businessmen in the South and well-trained lawyers in the North. He also helped Roosevelt pick white Southerners as judges, revenue collectors, and marshals who gave evidence of conservatism and a paternalistic sympathy for Negroes. Washington used his position as a Negro political boss to try to curb the lily-white Republican movement in the South, to moderate the Republican platforms and presidential utterances on racial matters, and to dampen Negro protest against the wholesale dismissal of Negro troops accused of rioting in Brownsville, Texas, in 1906. Although Washington supported Taft in 1908, he was subsequently dismayed by the president's rapid removal of nearly all Southern Negro officeholders. The Wilson administration continued this trend and increased segregation in

5. See particularly the chapter "Booker T. Washington and the 'Talented Tenth,' " in August Meier, *Negro Thought in America, 1880–1915: Racial Ideologies in the Age of Booker T. Washington* (Ann Arbor, 1963), 207–47.

the federal civil service. By the end of his life Boss Washington's political machine was in a state of nearly complete breakdown.

Finally, Washington had an elaborate secret life. In his civil rights activity he presented himself publicly as a social pacifist and accommodationist, while secretly he financed and generaled a series of court suits challenging the grandfather clause, denial of jury service to Negroes, Jim Crow cars, and peonage. Working sometimes with the Negro lawyers of the Afro-American Council, sometimes through his own personal lawyer Wilford H. Smith, and sometimes with sympathetic Southern white lawyers, Washington took every precaution to keep his collaboration a secret. He used his private secretary and a Tuskegee faculty member as go-betweens, and in the Alabama suffrage cases that were carried to the United States Supreme Court he had his secretary and the lawyer correspond using the code names R. C. Black and J. C. May.[6]

It cannot be said that Washington's secret militancy had much effect against the downtrend of race relations. Another secret activity, however, that of espionage against his Negro enemies, sometimes had devastating effect. When the Boston black radical William Monroe Trotter began openly to denounce Washington and created a disturbance known as the Boston Riot, Washington employed a spy named Melvin J. Chisum to infiltrate Trotter's New England Suffrage League. Chisum acted as a provocateur and informed Washington of secret meetings so that Washington could counter their strategy. Washington also planted a Boston lawyer, Clifford Plummer, in the Trotter organization and arranged with a Yale student to sue Trotter's paper for libel. When W. E. B. Du Bois and some thirty of his friends met at Niagara Falls in 1905 to found the Niagara Movement, Washington paid Plummer to go there and spy on the meeting and to stop the Associated Press from giving it publicity. The following year Washington used a distinguished old Negro, who hoped Washington would help him regain his political appointment, to infiltrate the Niagara Movement at Harper's Ferry. Washington had many other agents, including Pinkerton detectives and paid and unpaid Negro informers. Melvin Chisum worked for years as Booker Washington's spy in New York and Washington, infiltrating the Niagara Movement and the NAACP, holding meetings with Washington on park benches to disclose his findings, and obviously enjoying his work. "I am your obedient humble servant, Chisum," he roguishly ended one letter, "your own property, to use as your Eminence desires, absolutely."[7]

In each of these compartmentalized worlds Washington displayed a different personality, wore a different mask, played a different role. At

6. *Ibid.*, 100–18.
7. See the author's article, "The Secret Life of Booker T. Washington," in *Journal of Southern History* [37 (August 1971), 393–416].

Tuskegee he was a benevolent despot. To Northern whites he appeared a racial statesman; to Southern whites he was a safe, sane Negro who advised blacks to "stay in their place." To Southern Negroes he was a father, to Northern blacks a stepfather; to politicians he was another political boss. In his paradoxical secret life he attacked the racial settlement that he publicly accepted, and he used ruthless methods of espionage and sabotage that contrasted sharply with his public Sunday-school morality.

Perhaps psychoanalysis or role psychology would solve Washington's behavioral riddle, if we could only put him on the couch. If we could remove those layers of secrecy as one peels an onion, perhaps at the center of Booker T. Washington's being would be revealed a person single-mindedly concerned with power, a minotaur, a lion, fox, or Br'er Rabbit, some frightened little man like the Wizard of Oz, or, as in the case of the onion, nothing, a personality disintegrated by the frenzied activity of being all things to all men in a multifaceted society. He "jumped Jim Crow" so often that he lost sight of the original purposes of his motion.

It is possible to explain many of the seeming contradictions in Washington's mature life by examining his biography. A biographical approach may counterbalance a slight distortion introduced by the historical approach. Historians have tended to see Washington's accommodationist behavior as of its time, that is, of the period of his leadership after 1895, and as a deliberate, realistic, pragmatic response to the black man's "time of troubles." While C. Vann Woodward, for example, recognizes that Washington "dealt with the present in terms of the past," he says that "it is indeed hard to see how he could have preached or his people practiced a radically different philosophy in his time and place."[8] The biographical evidence, on the other hand, shows that all the hallmarks of Washington's style of leadership—his conservative petit bourgeois social philosophy, his accommodation to white supremacy and segregation, and his employment of secret weapons against his adversaries—were well developed prior to the 1890's. They were a response to precepts and pressures of the 1870's and 1880's. These decades turn out on close examination to have been not as different from the period after 1890 as some historians have assumed. Perhaps we have too sharply periodized the history of American race relations and have exaggerated the differences between one decade and another. This is not to say that the Progressive era was not characterized by racial violence, disfranchisement, and segregation, but so were the seventies, the age of the Ku Klux Klan and the abandonment of Reconstruction, and the eighties, the era of reversal of civil rights legislation.

Knowledge of Washington's early life is based primarily on his two

8. C. Vann Woodward, *Origins of the New South, 1877–1913* (Baton Rouge, 1951), 367.

autobiographies. *Up from Slavery* is more detailed and better written but distorted by its success-story formula. *The Story of My Life and Work*, written a year earlier primarily for the Negro subscription book market, reveals facets of his career ignored in *Up from Slavery*. These works are supplemented, however, by other contemporary evidence and the reminiscences of a number of close associates of Washington's youth.

Washington was born on a small Virginia farm, the child of a slave cook and a white man of the neighborhood. His birth occurred prior to his mother's marriage to Washington Ferguson, the slave of a neighboring farmer, and prior to the birth of the darker half-sister Amanda. It was a common pattern of slavery that house servants, because of higher status, lighter work load, closeness to the master class, and, sometimes, lighter color often identified themselves in attitude as well as mutual interest with the master and his family. They learned by daily study to interpret and respond to the whims and desires of the white owners. Because he had the softer life and better food of a house servant's child, because he was only five when his master died and only nine when he was freed, because he lived on a small farm instead of a large plantation, Washington never experienced slavery in its harshest forms. He later recalled his horror at seeing a grown man whipped for a minor infraction, but he also recalled "Christmas Days in Old Virginia" with a curious sentimentality, telling how grown slaves hung their stockings on Christmas Eve on the mantel of the master's or mistress' bedroom, and came in next morning shouting "Christmas gift," singing, and bearing the Yule log.[9] One day in 1909, while speaking to the Republican Club at the Waldorf-Astoria, Washington saw in the audience the grandson of his former owner and recalled:

> He and I played together as children, fought and wept, laughed and sobbed together. He was the white boy, I was the black boy, on that old plantation.
>
> He liked me then and he likes me yet. I liked him then and I like him now. But until this week I have not met Abe Burroughs since one day away back in 1863 it came to my frightened ears that old "Massa" Burroughs, his grandfather and my owner, had been killed.
>
> There was a skirmish and the Federal troops, I was told, had shot him. I was frightened. I rushed home and told Abe and he and I cried together. Our hearts were broken. That is a long while ago.[1]

Washington probably exaggerated the hardness of his early life for purposes of contrast in conformity with a literary convention of the success-story genre. He recalled in *Up from Slavery* the hard physical

9. BTW, "Christmas Days in Old Virginia," *Suburban Life*, 5 (1907), 336–37.
1. Quoted in New York *Age*, Feb. 18, 1909, BTW Papers, LC, clipping (1052). James Burroughs actually died of "lung disease" in 1861, but several of his sons died in Confederate service.

work of the salt furnace and coal mine, and he rejected both the work and the exploitative black stepfather who forced him into it, probably within a few months of his arrival in the little West Virginia town of Malden. He moved out of the home occupied by his mother, stepfather, half-brother, and half-sister. He moved into the mansion of General Lewis Ruffner, the leading citizen of the village and perhaps its richest man. "Booker Washington came to me about 1865 as servant," the general's wife Viola later recalled, "and as there was little for him to do, he had much spare time which I proposed he should use by learning to read, which he readily accepted." If Mrs. Ruffner was a godsend to Booker Washington, so was he to her. A Yankee schoolteacher who had married the widowed general after teaching his younger children, Mrs. Ruffner was ostracized by the general's family because of her alien background and sharp tongue, and she threw all the frustrated energies of a New England do-gooder into the training of Booker Washington. She as well as he later recalled his strenuous efforts to meet her exacting demands. "I would help and direct, and he was more than willing to follow direction," she remembered. "There was nothing peculiar in his habits, except that he was always in his place and never known to do anything out of the way, which I think has been his course all thru life. His conduct has always been without fault, and what more can we wish?" And yet there was something more. "He was ever restless, uneasy, as if knowing that contentment would mean inaction. 'Am I getting on?'—that was his principal question."[2] A neighbor similarly recalled: "The reported hard times that he underwent, never really occurred. He lived a thoroughly easy life with General Ruffner."[3]

The general himself was a prototype of those Southerners "of the better class" whom Washington later sought as allies. Of a distinguished Virginia family that owned the Luray Caverns and pioneered in the salt industry of West Virginia, General Ruffner had owned slaves and worked them in his mines and furnaces but believed slavery retarded Southern economic growth and therefore opposed it. He supported the Union and the new state of West Virginia and became a militia general and Republican leader. One day the young houseboy Booker witnessed a riot that dramatized the struggles of race and class with which he would have to live for the rest of his life. A group of whites, largely of the working class, began meeting in the hills at night and called themselves Gideon's Band or the Ku Klux Klan. One day General Ruffner heard

2. See letters of William Henry Ruffner to his wife written in 1865–66 from the home of his uncle Lewis Ruffner, in Ruffner Family Papers, Presbyterian Historical Foundation, Montreat, N.C.; Viola Ruffner to Gilson Willetts, May 29, 1899, in Willetts, "Slave Boy and Leader of His Race," *The New Voice*, 16 (June 24, 1899), 3. It was actually in 1867 or later, rather than in 1865, that Washington became the Ruffners' houseboy.

3. William A. MacCorkle, *Recollections of Fifty Years* (New York, 1928), 569. A Democratic governor of West Virginia, MacCorkle knew Washington well in his mature years.

the shots of a melee between the Klansmen and the black workers of Malden. The Klansmen were trying to prevent the blacks from testifying about the Klan's activities. Running past the blacks, the general shouted, "Put down that revolver you scoundrel," and was obeyed. When he moved on to reason with the whites, however, a brick one of them had hurled hit him on the back of the head. Relatives dragged the general away unconscious as the battle resumed, and the old man never completely recovered. "It seemed to me as I watched this struggle between members of the two races that there was no hope for our people in this country," Washington later recalled.[4] That there were dangers in transgressing white racial codes was certainly one of the lessons of this incident, but another was that the white paternalist was the black man's only friend, albeit never a perfect one and in this case an ineffectual one.

Not many black boys had an early life as full of generals as Booker T. Washington. He found his beau ideal in General Samuel Chapman Armstrong, the principal of Hampton Institute in Virginia, the Christian soldier, the great white father for whom Washington had long been searching. He began to model his own conduct and thought on Armstrong's. Washington described him as "the most perfect specimen of man, physically, mentally and spiritually" that he had ever seen, and he considered the best part of his education to have been the privilege of being permitted to look upon General Armstrong each day.[5] The general was the child of missionaries in Hawaii, a graduate of the Williams College of Mark Hopkins, and a commander of black troops in the Civil War. One of the war's youngest generals, Armstrong had a quick, nervous, but unhesitating manner, what might appropriately be called a commanding presence; he was the very model of a modern major general. Washington had the opportunity of observing the general closely, for throughout the black youth's three years at Hampton he was janitor in the academic building. Close to the general and the white teachers, picking up all they had to teach, he impressed them as ingratiating, ambitious, and quick to learn.

It was from Hampton and General Armstrong that Washington borrowed what became known in his day as "the Tuskegee idea." Armstrong seems sincerely to have believed that the Polynesians among whom he had grown up and the Negroes and Indians at Hampton were lower on the evolutionary scale than the white race, not so much inferior as

4. Charleston *West Virginia Journal*, Dec. 15, 22, 1869, Mar. 30, 1870; BTW, *Up from Slavery*, 54–55. Washington concluded, from the perspective of 1900: "There are few places in the South now where public sentiment would permit such organizations to exist."

5. BTW, *Up from Slavery*, 37–40; BTW, *The Story of My Life and Work* (rev. ed., Naperville, Ill., 1915), 41–42. BTW said of Armstrong: "I shall always remember that the first time I went into his presence he made the impression upon me of being a perfect man: I was made to feel that there was something about him that was superhuman." *Up from Slavery*, 37.

"backward."[6] They were children who must crawl before they could walk, must be trained before they could be educated. Their moral training was much more important than their intellectual instruction, for it was only after the backward people, as individuals and races, put away childish things, stilled their dark laughter, and learned self-discipline through the imposition of the morning inspection and close-order drill that they would be ready for higher things. Armstrong would not discourage a bright young man from higher education, but he believed that the black race should abstain from politics and civil rights agitation until industrial education should have done its work. Industrial education as Armstrong conceived it was not so much technical as moral, a training in industriousness, abstinence, thrift, in short, the Protestant ethic, the virtues that helped a man get ahead, mankind progress, and the world turn. The bluff General Armstrong was unaware of the cultural and racial arrogance of his faith and program. He was benevolent and earnest, toiling all his life amid the alien corn, a missionary to the benighted blacks. He slept well because his soul was daily cleansed by good works.[7] The contradictions and inner tensions came when one of his black pupils, Booker T. Washington, eager to please and eager to learn all that it took to be a General Armstrong, incorporated not only the method but the rationale and values of this benevolent white racist, and then went forth to preach the gospel of industrial education.

* * *

When Washington established his own school in 1881 in Alabama, he deliberately followed the Hampton model not only in educational philosophy and industrial features but in accommodation to the conditions of Southern life. Samuel R. Spencer, Jr., has pointed out that in his first major national speech, before the National Education Association at Madison, Wisconsin, in 1884, Washington clearly foreshadowed the Atlanta Compromise address in all of its major elements.[8] He was so complimentary of the local white people that a member of the audience, a white woman teacher in a Tuskegee female seminary, wrote a glowing report of it back to her girls. "He represented things as they are at the South, and said some nice things of the Tuskegee citizens," she said.[9] The Civil Rights Act of 1875 had been declared unconstitutional

6. Samuel C. Armstrong, "Lessons from the Hawaiian Islands," *Journal of Christian Philosophy*, 3 (1884), 200–29.
7. On Armstrong's thought and attitudes, see Suzanne Carson [Lowitt], "Samuel Chapman Armstrong: Missionary to the South," Ph.D. dissertation, The Johns Hopkins University, 1952; Meier, *Negro Thought in America, 1880–1915*, 88–90, 95–99; Samuel C. Armstrong, *Armstrong's Ideas on Education for Life* (Hampton, Va., 1940); Edith Armstrong Talbot, *Samuel Chapman Armstrong* (New York, 1904).
8. Samuel R. Spencer, Jr., *Booker T. Washington and the Negro's Place in American Life* (Boston, 1955), 91–94; reprint of speech in *Selected Speeches of Booker T. Washington*, ed. E. Davidson Washington (New York, 1932), 1–11.
9. "M. A. O.," letter in Tuskegee *Macon Mail*, July 23, 1884.

only a year before Washington's speech, but he took the complacent view that good schoolteachers and money to pay them "will be more potent in settling the race question than many civil rights bills." "Brains, property, and character" were the forces that would win, he said. At the bottom of everything "for our race, as for all races, an economic foundation, economic prosperity, economic independence."[1]

That nothing could shake this faith was illustrated in 1885, when a wedding party of Tuskegee teachers of "brains, property, and character" tried to ride a first-class railroad car through Alabama. They were insulted, physically assaulted, and twice forced into the Jim Crow car. Finally they were ejected from the train in a small town where they were arrested and fined. They completed their journey on horseback.[2] Washington wrote a letter of protest to the state's leading newspaper, the Montgomery *Advertiser*, but his first sentences were: "I wish to say a few words from a purely business standpoint. It is not a subject with which to mix social equality or anything bordering on it. To the negro it is a matter of dollars and cents." Washington's complaint was not against separation itself but against the crowded, old, uncarpeted cars, in which drunken or slovenly whites felt free to slouch when ostracized from the white first-class cars. If railroad officials did not want blacks in the first-class cars occupied by whites, said Washington, "let them give us a separate one just as good in every particular and just as exclusive, and there will be no complaint." "If the railroads will not give us first-class accommodations," he added, "let them sell us tickets at reduced rates." He expressed doubt that national legislation or outside attempts would succeed and agreed to wait with "a wise patience" for an equitable adjustment from within the South that would end what he called "these jars in our business relations." He concluded the letter with a remarkable anticipation of the Atlanta Address: "We can be as separate as the fingers, yet one as the hand for maintaining the right."[3]

* * *

All through the eighties, both locally and regionally, Washington made common cause with the Southern conservative establishment. He exchanged letters with Henry Grady, the principal spokesman of the New South, in which they agreed that "there need be no hostility between the white and the colored people in the South," their interests being "identical."[4] In his solicitation for funds in the North, he carried letters of endorsement from a succession of Alabama governors and superintendents of education, and he seems to have mesmerized the

1. *Selected Speeches*, ed. Washington, 3.
2. Samuel E. Courtney, interview, Boston *Journal*, Mar. 29, 1896, BTW Papers, LC, clipping (6).
3. Letter in Montgomery *Advertiser*, Apr. 30, 1885.
4. Henry W. Grady to BTW, Jan. 10, 1887, in Montgomery *Advertiser*, Jan. 15, 1887.

local bankers, businessmen, and planters, for whom Tuskegee Institute was both an economic stimulant and a social tranquilizer. Local white approval constantly soothed him like a balm, and when he said, as he frequently did, that the race problem had been solved in the city of Tuskegee, he generalized from his own experience. He was "one of the best men in the United States," said a visiting legislator. "His influences have all been for the best interest of his own race," said the Montgomery *Advertiser*, "and for peace and good feeling between the whites and blacks."[5] It was not merely that Washington was circumspect, that the mask he turned to Southern whites was a mirror. In many cases Washington not only seemed to agree with those whites who were moderate in their racial views and conservative in their economic views, he actually did agree with them, and they correctly sensed his response.

* * *

The clearest illustration of Washington's predicament as a Negro spokesman in the South occurred when, only a few months before the Atlanta Compromise, a wounded black militant, Thomas A. Harris, sought refuge on the Tuskegee campus from a lynch mob.

Tom Harris' problem stemmed from his decision in middle age to practice law in Tuskegee, a town that took pride in its toleration of black farmers, teachers, and businessmen but could not accept black lawyers or editors. Formerly a slave and a Confederate officer's body servant, during and after Reconstruction he was a Republican politician. The local white newspaper described him as "rather a seditious character," "a very ambitious and rather an idle negro man, extremely unpopular with his own race on account of his airs of superiority" and obnoxious to whites because of his "impudent utterances and insolent bearing." Booker T. Washington called him "worthless and very foolish." Yet he appeared before the Alabama bar in 1890 with testimonials to his character and probity from the leading conservative lawyers of Tuskegee, was admitted to the bar, practiced for a time in Birmingham, and then returned to Tuskegee.[6] He had the temerity to entertain an itinerant white preacher in his home. A white mob forced the minister to leave and then sent a note to Harris giving him a deadline for leaving town.

By the time Harris received the note the deadline had already passed. As Harris crossed the street to ask his white neighbor's advice, the lynch mob came down the road with blazing torches. "There they are now, coming to kill me!" Harris shouted, entering John H. Alexander's front yard in an attempt to escape by running through the house and out the

5. Montgomery *Advertiser*, Nov. 22, Dec. 13, 1890.
6. Tuskegee *News*, May 8, 1890, June 13, 1895; BTW to Rev. Francis J. Grimké, Nov. 27, 1895, Booker T. Washington Collection, Moorland Foundation, Howard University, Container 1 (hereafter this collection will be cited as BTW Collection, Howard, with container number in parentheses); Montgomery *Advertiser*, Apr. 30, May 13, 1890.

back door. Fearful for his daughters seated on the porch, Alexander wrestled with Harris at his front gate until the lynch mob arrived. As Harris frenziedly burst into the yard, one of the mob rushed behind him and in the light of the moon put his pistol within a foot of Harris and fired with intent to kill. The black man squatted in time to avert the shot, which struck Alexander in the throat and lodged in his spinal column. Other shots rang out, one wounding Harris in the leg as he ran down the road toward his own house. His leg bone shattered, Harris lay in the dirt road within a few feet of his gate, screaming for help. Several white physicians in the crowd rushed past the black man to render Alexander all the assistance in their power. Though first thought mortally wounded, he recovered after the lead ball was found and removed.

Since Tom Harris needed medical attention, his son Wiley brought him in the dead of night to Booker T. Washington's home, "where however he was not received," according to the local newspaper, "for Booker T. Washington . . . has ever conducted himself and his school in the most prudent manner, and learning that a mob was in pursuit of Harris he told him that he could not be admitted there."[7]

The report that Washington had turned away Harris pleased local whites but brought much criticism from the Negro press all over the country. In a debate on the Atlanta Compromise at the Bethel Literary and Historical Society in Washington, an important forum of black expression, the Harris affair was characterized as "hypocritical and showing the natural bent of the man." The house roared its approval when a speaker said: "Mr. Washington, the negro head of a negro institute refused a fellow negro admittance to his negro college, thereby denying the right of medical assistance."[8]

The Reverend Francis J. Grimké, pastor of the Fifteenth Street Presbyterian Church, left the Bethel Literary meeting very disturbed at the conflict the incident created between his friendship for Washington and his commitment to Negro rights. Writing a letter of inquiry, he received from Washington a detailed explanation:

> After the man was shot his son brought him to my house for help and advice, (and you can easily understand that the people in and about Tuskegee come to me for help and advice in all their troubles). I got out of bed and went out and explained to the man and his son that . . . I could not take the wounded man into the school and endanger the lives of students entrusted by their parents to my care to the fury of some drunken white men. Neither did I for the same reason feel that it was the right thing to take him into my own house. For as much as I love the colored people in that section, I

7. Tuskegee *News*, June 13, 1895; Birmingham *Age-Herald*, June 10, 1895; Montgomery *Advertiser*, June 11, 13, 1895.
8. George W. Lovejoy to BTW, July 17, 1895, BTW Papers, LC (862); Washington *Bee*, Oct. 26, 1895.

> can not feel that I am in duty bound to shelter them in all their personal troubles any more than you would feel called on to do the same thing in Washington.

Washington then told Grimké what he said he had told no one else:

> I helped them to a place of safety and paid the money out of my own pocket for the comfort and treatment of the man while he was sick. Today I have no warmer friends than the man and his son. They have nothing but the warmest feelings of gratitude for me and are continually in one way or another expressing this feeling. I do not care to publish to the world what I do and should not mention this except for this false representation. I simply chose to help and relieve this man in my own way rather than in the way some man a thousand miles away would have had me do it.[9]

Washington was, of course, a genius at self-justification, but his other correspondence confirms his statements to Grimké. In September 1895, about ten days after the Atlanta Address, Tom Harris wrote him from Selma: "Dear friend, I remember all of your kindnesses to me, I will not take time to mention them, as you know them all." He was getting well. "I think I will be able one day to walk on my leg as well as ever," he reported. "It will be a little shorter than the other."[1]

A chastened Tom Harris was eventually allowed to return to Tuskegee, George Lovejoy became a successful lawyer in Mobile, and Hiram Thweatt became the head of an industrial school modeled after Tuskegee. In a physical sense at least, none of these men was victimized by Washington's conservative approach. On the other hand, it is also clear that in his years of power Washington was neither a fragmented personality pursuing contradictory and unclear goals nor an illusion-free pragmatist coolly adjusting his program to a realistic view of a worsening racial situation. He confronted a threatening social environment in 1895, but so did he in 1875 and 1885.

If we read Washington's life from front to back, we find that his life was of a piece. Perhaps the clearest characterization of his program would be "Uncle Tom in his own cabin," peasant conservatism, originating in the experience of slavery—the central life experience being emancipation itself—and practiced in a nation and by a race still overwhelmingly rural and agricultural. Perhaps because there were few black models in his life with the charisma of success, Washington from early life became inordinately attached to a succession of fatherly white men, white racists all, but mild and benevolent in their racism: General Ruffner, General Armstrong, William H. Baldwin, Jr., Theodore Roosevelt.

9. BTW to F. J. Grimké, Nov. 27, 1895, BTW Collection, Howard (1).
1. Thomas A. Harris to BTW, Sept. 29, 1895, BTW Papers, LC (862). See also Harris to Warren Logan, Dec. 18, 1895, from Okolona, Miss., BTW Papers, Tuskegee (7); Harris to BTW, Oct. 27, 1902, from Anniston, Ala., BTW Papers, LC (229).

All his life Washington followed the precepts that Hampton Institute taught and all these men subscribed to: a nineteenth-century faith in individual initiative and self-help, an accommodationist strategy toward Southern and American white racism that Armstrong believed to be the lesson taught by Reconstruction, and a faith that men like these could be his effective partners in counteracting Southern proscription and discrimination. Whenever his identity with the black community or his own interest impelled him to actions of which these white counselors and benefactors would not approve, he resorted to secrecy. Some complexities and inner tensions inevitably resulted. Washington's experiences in the 1880's and his responses to them suggest that historians have generally exaggerated the cyclical pattern of race relations in the period after Reconstruction or that Washington's life was more consistent and in a way more principled than we have assumed. If by 1895 he had become a "white man's black man," considering his background it is hard to see how he could have been anything else.

SIDONIE SMITH

[Casting Down] †

Booker T. Washington was probably the first well-known black Horatio Alger. "By the beginning of the new century, Washington," explains John Hope Franklin in an introduction to one edition of the autobiography,

> . . . was one of the most powerful men in the United States. Great philanthropists and industrialists such as Andrew Carnegie and John D. Rockefeller listened to him courteously and were influenced by his advice. Presidents such as Theodore Roosevelt and William Howard Taft depended on him for suggestions regarding the resolution of problems involving race. Southern whites in high places knew that a good word in their behalf by Washington would open doors previously closed to them.[1]

After achieving such stature and power in American society, Washington was urged by others to write his autobiography. The popularity of *Up From Slavery*, which became a best seller soon after publication,

† From Sidonie Smith, *Where I'm Bound: Patterns of Slavery and Freedom in Black American Autobiography* (Westport, CT: Greenwood, 1974), 30–44. Reprinted with permission of Greenwood Publishing Group, Inc., Westport, CT.

1. John Hope Franklin, ed., *Three Negro Classics*, p. xi.

indicated how inspiring his rise to fame had been.[2] His life was an embodiment of the possibility of self-improvement, made powerful and tangible by his preference for objective reality. "I have great faith in the power and influence of facts," writes Washington early in the work.[3]

> I have found, too, that it is the visible, the tangible, that goes a long ways in softening prejudice. The actual sight of a first-class house that a Negro has built is ten times more potent than pages of discussion about a house that he ought to build, or perhaps could build. (154) [71–72]

His exemplary life is just such a tangible "house," and the narrative of his rise to fame is designed to relate the material facts of its evolutionary construction within society.

A sense of mystery pervades the first paragraph of the autobiography. Washington does not know the exact place or date of his birth; he "suspects [he] must have been born somewhere and at some time" (1) [7]. To this initial sense of mystery, the second paragraph adds the quality of life—desolate poverty—and the third paragraph his anonymous ancestry. Although Washington knew his mother's name, he admits: "Of my father I knew even less than of my mother. I do not even know his name" (2) [7]. The prominent leader enters the drama of life as a semi-orphan, spawned mysteriously from nowhere, secured by no ancestral roots, environed by humble conditions. This beginning sharpens the contrast with his social position fifty years later at the time of writing and underscores the fact that whatever he achieved he achieved single-handedly.

Soon after emancipation, Washington, as did other former slaves, named himself. The child's choice of name is particularly revealing: by naming himself "Washington"—a name associated with patriotism, American democracy, social prominence, and leadership—Booker, prompted by a belief in the society into which he was born and a need to be a part of and a leader in that society, creates an ideal identity which embodies his personal vision of himself. Naming becomes a prophetic, baptismal ritual.

The next rite of passage of Washington's journey is the "effort to fit [himself] to accomplish the most good in the world" (51) [28]. The early part of his narrative, therefore, centers on his struggle to secure an education, first at Kanawha Valley school and then at Hampton Institute, which, interestingly enough, he describes as "the promised land." Thereafter, the autobiography becomes the narrative of Washington's work, an open-ended exposition of his public efforts to better the condi-

2. Emmett J. Scott and Lyman Beecher Stowe, *Booker T. Washington: Builder of a Civilization*, p. 264. Between 1901 and 1917, 110,000 copies were sold, and the book was translated into French, Spanish, German, Hindustani, and braille.
3. Booker T. Washington, *Up From Slavery*, p. 32 [20]. Further citations will appear in the text. [Norton Critical Edition page numbers appear in brackets—*Editor.*]

tions of his race, especially through the founding and growth of Tuskegee Institute. He focuses his narrative, as he did his life, on the material obstacles he had to overcome—money to finance new buildings, furniture, clothing for the students, and so on and on. In the process of surmounting these obstacles, Washington assumes the position of leadership which fulfills the destiny inherent in the name.

The many parallels between Washington's success story and that of Benjamin Franklin are striking and suggest the degree to which Washington is simply giving us the black version of a well-known formula. Both men, growing restless at an early age because their overwhelming need for self-improvement remains unsatisfied, journey to a distant city that offers them an opportunity to fulfill that need. Both describe their entry into the city similarly, stressing, by implication, the disparity between their early status and their prominence at the moment of writing. Here is Franklin's entrance into Philadelphia in 1723:

> I have been the more particular in this description of my journey, and shall be so of my first entry into that city, that you may in your mind compare such unlikely beginnings with the figure I have since made there. I was in my working dress, my best clothes being to come round by sea. I was dirty from my journey; my pockets were stuffed out with shirts and stockings; I knew no soul, nor where to look for lodging. Fatigued with walking, rowing, and want of rest, I was very hungry, and my whole stock of cash consisted of a Dutch dollar and about a shilling in copper coin, which I gave to the boatmen for my passage. At first they refused it on account of my having rowed; but I insisted on their taking it. A man is sometimes more generous when he has little money than when he has plenty, perhaps through fear of being thought to have but little. I walked towards the top of the street, gazing about till near Market Street, where I met a boy with bread. I have often made a meal of dry bread, and inquiring where he had bought it, I went immediately to the baker's he directed me to. I asked for bisket, meaning such as we had in Boston; but that sort, it seems, was not made in Philadelphia. I then asked for a three penny loaf and was told they had none such. Not knowing the different prices nor the names of the different sorts of bread, I told him to give me three pennyworth of any sort. He gave me accordingly three great puffy rolls. I was surprised at the quantity but took it, and having no room in my pockets, walked off with a roll under each arm and eating the other. Thus I went up Market Street as far as Fourth Street, passing by the door of Mr. Read, my future wife's father; when she, standing at the door, saw me, and thought I made—as I certainly did—a most awkward, ridiculous appearance. Then I turned and went down Chestnut Street and part of Walnut Street, eating my roll all the way, and coming round, found myself again at Market Street wharf near the boat I came in, to which I went for a draught of the

> river water, and being filled with one of my rolls, gave the other two to a woman and her child that came down the river in the boat with us and were waiting to go farther.[4]

Washington's description of his entry into Richmond in 1872 echoes Franklin's self-portraiture and his chronology of concerns:

> By walking, begging rides both in wagons and in the cars, in some way, after a number of days, I reached the city of Richmond, Virginia, about eighty-two miles from Hampton. When I reached there, tired, hungry, and dirty, it was late in the night. I had never been in a large city, and this rather added to my misery. When I reached Richmond, I was completely out of money. I had not a single acquaintance in the place, and, being unused to city ways, I did not know where to go. I applied at several places for lodging, but they all wanted money, and that was what I did not have. Knowing nothing else better to do, I walked the streets. In doing this I passed by many foodstands where fried chicken and half-moon apple pies were piled high and made to present a most tempting appearance. At that time it seemed to me that I would have promised all that I expected to possess in the future to have gotten hold of one of those chicken legs or one of those pies. But I could not get either of these, nor anything else to eat.
>
> I must have walked the streets till after midnight. At last I became so exhausted that I could walk no longer. I was tired, I was hungry, I was everything but discouraged. Just about the time when I reached extreme physical exhaustion, I came upon a portion of a street where the board sidewalk was considerably elevated. I waited for a few minutes, till I was sure that no passers-by could see me, and then crept under the sidewalk and lay for the night upon the ground, with my satchel of clothing for a pillow. (48–49) [26–27]

Both men go on to describe their gradual rise to social prominence and focus on their endeavors in behalf of others, Franklin with his social projects for Philadelphia and the nation, Washington with his program for Negro betterment.

Even this brief summary of parallels is sufficient to rearticulate the fundamental ethos behind the Horatio Alger myth, whether black or white. This hero is an economic materialist, an industrious, self-made businessman who views the world as material to be conquered in his rise to success. He is a public man, a man of action whose sense of identity and self-fulfillment derive from his social usefulness. He is a virtuous man who upholds middle-class mores and morals. The ethos of Washington's life journey mirrors the predominant ethos of the time; therein lies its power and its influence. *Up From Slavery* is a businessman's

4. Benjamin Franklin, *The Autobiography of Benjamin Franklin*, A *Restoration of a "Fair Copy" by Max Farrand* (Berkeley: University of California Press, 1949), pp. 30–31.

autobiography, which is one reason why it met such success in the United States and abroad at a time when business was becoming big business and when the Horatio Alger myth itself was extremely popular, embodied as it was in current fiction and such autobiographies as that of Andrew Carnegie. But it met with success primarily because Washington responded as a businessman would to the social climate of the late nineteenth century—a time when the black American was being systematically deprived of political and civil rights—by adopting a pragmatic stance that mirrored the white attitudinal climate. The exuberant hope of postwar Reconstruction had been shattered; a more realistic hope, deriving from a program of self-help, of assimilation into and accommodation with the dominant culture, replaced it.

The situations that Washington and Franklin describe above, however, are only almost identical, and the differences that lie in the "almost" embody the essential disparity between the white and black versions of the journey of the Horatio Alger hero. Franklin had some money and his good clothes were being sent to him; Washington had neither. Franklin could give food away; Washington could buy none at all. Franklin did not worry about lodging; Washington could find none but the space beneath the boardwalk. The obstacles along the black Horatio Alger's way, whether social, economic, or political, radically limit the fluidity of his movement in American society. They are literally antagonistic and potentially destructive. Nevertheless, through a strict moral rectitude, Washington does manage to transform even this radical difference from a liability into an asset:

> With few exceptions, the Negro youth must work harder and must perform his task even better than a white youth in order to secure recognition. But out of the hard and unusual struggle which he is compelled to pass, he gets a strength, a confidence, that one misses whose pathway is comparatively smooth by reason of birth and race. (40) [23]

In the end, Washington's optimism and faith in the system are reaffirmed in his appropriation of an autobiographical form that embodies the traditional American myth of social success. *Up From Slavery*, articulated in the formal language of the dominant culture, serves as a vehicle for discussing a philosophy acceptable to the dominant culture and for dramatizing, to both blacks and whites, the success of that philosophy.

II

There is yet another sharp difference between Washington's autobiographical life and the prototypical life of the Horatio Alger hero, whether Franklin's or certain later black autobiographers'. This difference is made clear in the following passage:

> In order to be successful in any kind of undertaking, I think the main thing is for one to grow to the point where he completely forgets himself; that is, to lose himself in a great cause. In proportion as one loses himself in this way, in the same degree does he get the highest happiness out of his work. (181) [83]

The fundamental paradox of Christian invisibility—that in order to find oneself, one must lose oneself—apparently controls Washington's drama of selfhood. Life becomes a journey of self-sacrifice and self-effacement, characterized by the sublimation of selfish desires in the embracement of social causes. Fame and fortune are merely the results—not the primary goals—of Washington's exemplary life of self-sacrifice, which finds fruition in the improvement of the conditions of his race. In this respect, Washington's autobiography contrasts with Franklin's and the rise of the traditional Horatio Alger hero: there is no such tendency to self-effacement in Franklin's narrative. Franklin's cause is his own, although after he gains success he devotes himself to public betterment.

The point is that there are complexities in the situation of the black American that Franklin did not have to be self-conscious about. The slave narrator testified to the self-destruction consequent upon any expression of self-assertion, whether real or imagined, whether conspicuous or inconspicuous, which made it necessary for him to fabricate a mask in order to survive. The Civil War did not end the need for the mask because it did not end imprisonment. Washington was a child of a Reconstruction that promised much in the way of freedom but delivered little, if anything, in fact. He, too, had to survive—in life as well as in autobiography. And one prerequisite was successfully met by means of the mask of Christian invisibility; for one of the "obstacles" Washington had to overcome was his audience. That audience, a major determinant of Washington's approach to his life story, was, for the most part, composed of white southerners and northerners, in contrast to the slave narrator's, which had been entirely a northern one before which he could adopt a critical attitude toward his experience in the South. Washington's approach toward his experience and that of blacks in general therefore had to be responsive to the nature of such an audience.

The first paragraphs of the autobiography establish his assumed point of view. Bitterness and vindictiveness are nonexistent; Christian love and forgiveness prevail. Of his father, a white man, he says: "But I do not find especial fault with him. He was simply another unfortunate victim of the institution which the Nation unhappily had engrafted upon it at that time" (3) [8]. He avoids retributive judgment, emphasizes "understanding." Thus, he comments about the South as a region:

> I have long since ceased to cherish any spirit of bitterness against the Southern white people on account of the enslavement of my

> race. No one section of our country was wholly responsible for its introduction, and, besides, it was recognized and protected for years by the General Government. Having once got its tentacles fastened on to the economic and social life of the Republic, it was no easy matter for the country to relieve itself of the institution. (16) [13]

Because the system is to blame, no one is accountable. Circumspect in order not to antagonize his white audience, Washington touches only peripherally on the brutal realities of life for the black American. He devotes the last three paragraphs of chapter 4 to these realities, concluding once again by exonerating white complicity.

> I have referred to this unpleasant part of the history of the South simply for the purpose of calling attention to the great change that has taken place since the days of the "Ku Klux." Today there are no such organizations in the South, and the fact that such ever existed is almost forgotten by both races. There are few places in the South now where public sentiment would permit such organizations to exist. (71) [40]

In his avid tendency to extol the efforts of whites, especially southern whites, he is the epitome of the loving, charitable Christian. His mask assures his survival in the South. But it does more. It is central to Washington's role as a black leader, functioning as a shrewd business means to achieve his ends, a tactic earlier employed by the slave who was often successful in avoiding work, getting food, pulling easy jobs, if he knew how to manipulate the mask of the "darky" effectively. It was good business to assure southerners that they were fine people, that everything was improving, that the South was the place where the Negroes should "cast down [their] buckets." In this way, too, Washington could lead members of his own race as well as whites. He described, for example, his practice at Tuskegee of asking students and faculty for suggestions and criticisms. His motivation is preeminently practical:

> Few things help an individual more than to place responsibility upon him, and to let him know that you trust him. . . . Every individual responds to confidence, and this is not more true of any race than of the Negroes. Let them once understand that you are unselfishly interested in them, and you can lead them to any extent. (172) [79]

Washington's choice of the word "lead" is illuminating, for he implies an intimate relationship between the ability to play the benign, "humble" role—"Let[ting] them . . . understand that you are unselfishly interested in them"—and the ability to lead others successfully. Such a role is extremely useful to a leader and to a con man.

Leadership, of course, implies power over those led. Washington's consciousness of and pride in such power, betrayed in his propensity for inserting in the text of the autobiography newspaper reviews praising him for a speech or other accomplishment, belie the self-effacement of the mask of Christian invisibility. One such review reads: "All the speeches were enthusiastically received, but the colored man carried off the oratorical honors, and the applause which broke out when he had finished was vociferous and long-continued" (302) [137]. In his description of the acceptance speech he made when Harvard awarded him an honorary degree in 1896, he does not include one, but four, reviews; in his description of his University of Chicago speech, he refers to the praise he received from President McKinley:

> The part of the speech which seemed to arouse the wildest and most sensational enthusiasm was that in which I thanked the President for his recognition of the Negro in his appointments during the Spanish-American war. The President was sitting in a box at the right of the stage. When I addressed him I turned toward the box, and as I finished the sentence thanking him for his generosity, the whole audience rose and cheered again and again, waving handkerchiefs and hats and canes, until the President arose in the box and bowed his acknowledgements. At that the enthusiasm broke out again, and the demonstration was almost indescribable. (255) [117]

This passage suggests the manipulative quality of Washington's flattering and deferential mask.

Ultimately, the mask of Christian invisibility is a means to triumph over and manipulate others. Washington's mentor General Samuel C. Armstrong had advised him "that great men cultivate love, and that only little men cherish a spirit of hatred" (165) [76]. His use of the word "cultivate," whether it is his own choice or whether he remembers the exact words of General Armstrong (the act of memory is itself revealing) implies, like the use of "lead," a self-conscious rather than a selfless response. Washington "cultivated" love as one cultivates a pose or fabricates a mask and, in so doing, gained control over others—both black and white.

The moral ambiguity inherent in Washington's use of the mask will concern certain writers of later generations such as Ralph Ellison, who explores such ambiguity in his novel *Invisible Man* when he reincarnates Washington as Dr. Bledsoe, the sycophantic southern educator who "cultivates" the mask of humility in order to manipulate white men.[5] The protagonist recalls that "he was the only one of us whom I knew—except perhaps a barber or a nursemaid—who could touch a white man with impunity."[6] The privilege of touch symbolizes Bledsoe's

5. Ralph Ellison's *Invisible Man*, although a novel, proved invaluable in this study because it explores in a fictional autobiography so many of the central structural and thematic motifs that concerned me here.
6. Ellison, *Invisible Man*, p. 89.

real power and authority over the white man: his ostensible mask of self-abnegating humility conceals a covetous ego whose self-fulfillment derives from oblique mastery. This power he reveals to the protagonist as he expels him from the college:

> "I's big and black and I say 'Yes, suh' as loudly as any burr-head when it's convenient, but I'm still the king down here. I don't care how much it appears otherwise. Power doesn't have to show off. Power is confident, self-assuring, self-starting and self-stopping, self-warming and self-justifying. When you have it, you know it. Let the Negroes snicker and the crackers laugh! Those are the facts, son. The only ones I even pretend to please are *big* white folk, and even those I control more than they control me. This is a power set-up, son, and I'm at the controls."[7]

In order to maintain such control, Bledsoe must sacrifice the naive youth who has threatened his power structure; in other words, he must betray his own community. A leader may thus become more a tyrant than a savior, more a jailor than a liberator, a possibility W. E. B. Du Bois recognized clearly when he chose to criticize Washington's program and his influence.

From another point of view, the leader may himself be the imprisoned victim, for the mask may be a form of oppression that forces the black self to deny its authentic impulses, a negative possibility apparent in the slave narratives. For the slave, the mask, a necessity for survival, could not be freely chosen. So, too, Washington, in order to be successful, must sacrifice himself to his social mask, a victimization that certainly limits his narrative art and may have limited him as a person. Not only is he not free to choose his mask; he is not free to examine that mask consciously in his autobiography. Thus, the self-portrait that emerges from the passage above describing his entry into Richmond lacks the self-parody of Franklin's portrait of himself. Unlike Franklin who was a master of the pose, Washington is mastered by the pose since it is a necessary response to his audience. And because he is not really free to control his material by maintaining a conscious distance between himself as autobiographer and himself as protagonist, his narrative is literal, unironic, unreflective.

Franklin, in contrast, was free to choose his pose, a freedom reflected in his description of the entry into Philadelphia and in subsequent descriptions of his early experimentation with various poses until he finally chose the one that would serve him best—the "plain dress" of "Benjamin Franklin of Philadelphia, Printer"—but a freedom reflected finally in the ironic distance which allows him, for example, to articulate and reexamine the advantages of his chosen pose:

7. Ibid., p. 109–110.

> I took care not only to be in *reality* industrious and frugal, but to avoid all *appearances* of the contrary. I dressed plain and was seen at no places of idle diversion . . . and to show that I was not above my business, I sometimes brought home the paper I purchased at the stores thro' the streets on a wheelbarrow.[8]

In recreating his past life, Franklin achieves sophisticated control of his narrative by remaining outside his materials and maintaining a distance between himself as autobiographer and his younger self as protagonist. Washington does not or cannot and so is forced to narrate a two-dimensional tale of the facts of his education and his work, not a self-conscious or self-analytical (three-dimensional) tale of the choice of a mask, for the black self-assertion his mask of Christian invisibility conceals must remain concealed if he is to be successful. From this point of view, Washington is ultimately imprisoned in his social identity. * * *

JAMES M. COX

Autobiography and Washington†

Up from Slavery is a resistant text. The autobiography of a prominent public figure, it almost affronts the literary critic with the bleak inertia of its prose. Its content is equally resistant—its didacticism, its self-gratulation, its facts, and its policies are all but in front of its form. Thus cultural historians will see it as representative of a time which they hope history has transcended; black militants will see it as the record of an Uncle Tom who made his way at the expense of his people; white liberals will see it in a light much the same but weaker. Representatives of all these constituencies would inevitably choose W. E. B. Du Bois's *Souls of Black Folk* (1903) as a stronger piece of writing. Du Bois's eloquence and poetic presentation would satisfy the literary critic; his scholarship would please the historian; his intellectual and moral grasp of the racial question would gratify the cultural critic. Yet the cultural fact to remember is that Du Bois knew how powerful Booker T. Washington was, and in powerfully risking a counterview to Washington's life and vision he initiated a dialectic upon the racial question which has no more been settled than the racial question itself has been settled.

More important for my immediate purposes than the actual controversy between two black views of the racial question is the resistance which Washington's text raises against my own reflections on autobiog-

8. Franklin, *Autobiography*, p. 32.

† First published in the *Sewanee Review*, vol. 85, no. 2, Spring 1977. Reprinted with the permission of the editor.

raphy. It is not, first of all, Washington's only autobiography. A year before he published it, he had published *The Story of My Life and Work* (1900). It is not uncommon for an autobiographer to write two versions of his life. Du Bois was to write at least three in his long life; so did Sherwood Anderson; so did Frederick Douglass. Edward Gibbon never could settle on a version of his life, and left behind him six manuscript versions of his memoirs. If Gibbon's multiversion manuscripts indicate an unwillingness to stabilize (and thereby finish) his life in a text—here he would be similar to Wordsworth, who kept the *Prelude* from publication for forty-five years, revising it throughout his long, dying poetic life—Du Bois, Anderson, and Douglass would in their triply published versions be recasting their lives in order to render each prior version less final. Though such strategies allow the writer a chance for revision, each succeeding effort throws more and more into doubt his capacity for any secure point of view. The insecurity may keep him alive, but it diminishes the finality of each life that he writes.

Even here Washington is different. He wrote neither of his lives alone. Instead he supervised them, something in the manner of an overseer. *The Story of My Life and Work* was, as Louis Harlan points out in his biography of Washington, actually written by Edgar Webber, a black journalist whom Washington brought to Tuskegee in 1897 largely for the purpose of assisting him in his life story. But Washington was so busy and so exhausted that he took his first vacation, a trip to Europe, and did not oversee the final chapters of the manuscript. Webber on his part proved inadequate to the task, making many errors and resorting to the short-cut methods of padding the book with schedules, letters, and copies of speeches, which are in reality substitutions for the text rather than fulfillments or extensions of it. Published by J. L. Nichols & Company, a subscription house of Naperville, Illinois, which catered to a black audience, the book was so full of typographical errors that Washington fired Webber and in subsequent editions removed his picture from the photographs in the book.

Even before Webber had finished the book, Washington was, according to Harlan, already planning another book, this time for the regular rather than the subscription trade; and this time he got a white journalist, Max Thrasher from St. Johnsbury, Vermont, to help him with the project. This time, too, Washington supervised the work every inch of the way, leaving Thrasher practically no freedom. He dictated to Thrasher on trains, took Thrasher's notes and in turn wrote his own draft of the autobiography, letting Thrasher check the manuscript. I have on occasion heard scholars of black studies point gloatingly to Thrasher's presence in the project as evidence of Washington's having been a captive to the white mind. It would actually be difficult to imagine a more reduced role than Thrasher was forced to play; even to call him a ghost, as Harlan does, is to use the term loosely. He seems much more like a slave to Washington's narrative. That fact, concealed from the text, provides both a starting point and index for scrutinizing the life story which Washington ordered for himself.

That story is, as everyone knows, one of the great success-stories of American history. Washington tells in the simplest, most straightforward terms of his rise from slavery to a position as leader of his people. He begins his life as a slave in Franklin County, Virginia, is taken by his mother to Malden, West Virginia, after the slaves are freed, works first in the salt mines and then in the coal mines near Malden, but does manage to go to school. From that meager beginning he determines to go to Hampton Institute in Virginia, where he makes a sufficient impression on General Samuel Armstrong, head of the school, to be recommended to go to Alabama "to take charge of what was to be a normal school for the coloured people in the little town of Tuskegee in that state." By dint of hard work, ceaseless diplomacy with the white population of Macon County, and unremitting perseverance in the face of ignorance, poverty, inertia, and doubt, he builds Tuskegee from nothing but dilapidated out-buildings of a ruined plantation into Tuskegee Normal and Industrial Institute. Money for the school comes primarily from white northern philanthropists; students come from the black population of the United States, though largely from the South; survival comes from Washington's carefully orchestrated interdependence between Tuskegee and the dominant southern whites. The climax of Washington's career, as he narrates it, is his speech at the Atlanta Exposition in 1895. That speech not only represents the achievement of an ex-slave addressing a largely white southern audience; it also marks Booker T. Washington's emergence as a national leader of his people.

That is the barest outline of Washington's story—or the story he chooses to tell. The way he tells it is simple and unadorned. His prose is reduced to an almost impoverished simplicity; metaphor is sparse; eloquence is all but absent; there is neither richness of texture nor complication of consciousness; even the simplicity never condenses into the energy of compression but retains an air of immobility being put into slow and steady motion. Although Washington was a successful public speaker and although the Atlanta speech (which he quotes in full in his text) shows oratorical flourish and declamatory urgency, the narrative throughout is characterized by what can best be called almost pure inertia.

In calling Washington's style purely inertial, I mean that he writes as if language were matter rather than energy. The words are things which, added one to another, do not record so much as they build the narrative life upon the line that the structure of his life has taken. Thus the events which Washington recounts are not so much dramatized as deadened into matter with which to make the narrative. They are being set steadily in place by the narrator, as if he were constructing the model of his life. The pain, fear, anguish, self-doubt, and anxiety which attended Washington's life are there, of course; but they are muted into the very matter of the narrative. This tendency to treat language as material causes Washington's narrative consciousness to seem literally housed in his narrative. If Washington is moving the blocks of his life into position, they seem to rest in place by their own weight.

That solid stability is one aspect of Washington's inertial style; but there is also motion—for Washington is moving his material into place. Yet here again he seems to be following the course of his life rather than directing it. The relatively strict chronology of autobiographical convention to which he adheres provides the form that draws him along. If he drove himself to make his actual life—and he explicitly indicates that he did—his belief in the existence of that life gives him the powerful illusion that it has created him as the narrator of it. This combination of conventional form and self-belief conveys the strong sense that Washington is pursuing the slow and steady motion of his life.

His use of chronological convention to order his life is but a reflection of his capacity to use time to make his life into a book just as he had used it to make his life as a man. His belief in the weight of his life puts all his language into a rhetorical rather than a dramatic or imaginary relation to that life. The solid reality to which his language refers now exists for language to use. If it was the result of desire, ambition, and fierce determination, it now becomes the matter from which Washington will read higher laws. Here again Washington's book is conventional, embracing as it does the moral and exemplary fatalities of autobiography. The exemplary autobiography is the secularized version of the Christian confessional form. The confessional form (with the exception of the revolutionary Rousseau!) denigrates the man by relating his conversion into God; the exemplary form converts godlike achievement into a model for man to follow. The one portrays the fallen child attaining to the spirit of the Father; the other becomes the model father to provide principles for the children. The one seeks goodness as truth, the other goodness as conduct. Franklin's *Autobiography* is a classic example of the exemplary convention, and Washington is clearly Franklin's descendant. Having achieved success, he publishes his life as an example of the virtues he believes that he practiced in gaining the high ground from which he writes.

If Franklin is almost disarmingly simple in his exemplary narrative, Washington is dismayingly simple in his. Franklin enunciates principles with sufficient ease to disclose the possibility that he lacks principle altogether; he can thus reveal an implicit amusement in his life of himself. Washington clings almost desperately to his virtues. What for Franklin is policy becomes gospel for Washington. Keeping his life under much stricter control than that of Franklin, Washington is constrained to reiterate his smaller number of principles—the principle of constant work, the principle of helping others to help themselves, and the principle of building a life from the ground up. Thus where Franklin takes pleasure in the disclosure of his principles—he even writes the autobiography in moments of leisure—Washington's principles are themselves his only pleasure. He hardly knows how to play. If Franklin's very model of himself is a gift that he easily bequeaths to posterity, Washington's life is all but asking for the reader's charity—as if he were waiting in the parlor for one more contribution.

Then one must confront Washington's idea of education. It is as single-minded as his adherence to the Protestant work ethic—and as unpopular to critics of his life and work. Believing that education for people on the bottom of society has to begin at the bottom, Washington wants the body and hands cleaned and disciplined before he cultivates the head. Foreign languages and even books themselves have little benefit in his eyes unless students are able to command a trade. He championed industrial education, and particularly he champions it in his autobiography, as a means of teaching his people how to work. This philosophy of education, reiterated throughout the book, galled blacks in Washington's own time, and it galls them all the more in our time when they can see, just as white readers can see, that this was a means of placating whites. Washington was assuring them, in effect, that Tuskegee graduates would know how to work more than they would know how to think.

These aspects of Washington's narrative make it singularly unprepossessing for both the literary and the cultural critic. They are there, and I could not wish them away even if I would. Yet a reader willing to encounter the book and give it a degree of consciousness—Washington's book, like his life philosophy, is going to ask for something—has a chance for revelations in Washington's inertial narrative.

First of all, there is the fact that Washington was born in *Franklin* County, Virginia. That inertial fact reveals its energy once we think of the book in relation to Franklin's autobiography. He was born a slave, but does not know his father, who is said to be a white man. Thus he has white blood from an unknown father. When he goes to Malden he has no name—but names himself Booker Washington, in a schoolroom. For all his matter-of-factness Washington does note that one of the advantages of having been a slave was his freedom to name himself. He even mentions other slaves taking names such as John S. Lincoln. But he chose Washington; at the time he did it he was no doubt attempting to follow a pattern he saw others pursuing. Yet in light of all that he was to do, the early act is charged with significance—a significance which Washington never stresses because he does not need to. George Washington was, after all, a Virginian who owned slaves yet was the father of his country. Booker Washington is also a Virginian who has been a slave and has an unknown white father. In naming himself he lays claim to the white blood in him and relates himself to the father of his country. He himself clearly sees his original naming of himself as a promise of being a father to his people.

As for Washington's actual call to his vocation, here is what he says about it:

> One day, while working in the coal mine, I happened to overhear two miners talking about a great school for coloured people somewhere in Virginia. That was the first time I had ever heard anything about any kind of school or college that was more pretentious than the little coloured school in our town.
>
> In the darkness of the mine I noiselessly crept as close as I could to the two men who were talking. I heard one tell the other that not only was the school established for the members of my race, but that opportunities were provided by which poor but worthy students could work out all or part of the cost of board, and at the same time be taught some trade or industry.
>
> As they were describing the school, it seemed to me that it must be the greatest place on earth, and not even Heaven presented more attractions for me at that time than did the Hampton Normal and Agricultural Institute in Virginia, about which these two men were talking. I resolved at once to go to that school, although I had no idea where it was, or how I was going to reach it. I remembered only that I was on fire constantly with one ambition, and that was to go to Hampton.

That quotation stands out in my context much more than it does in Washington's text. I have seen students read right through it, numbed by the patient plod of Washington's inertial style. Yet it is Washington's *calling,* as he make unmistakably clear. The whole episode may be a fiction; certainly there would be no way to prove its actual existence, since the two men conversing were unaware of Washington's secret presence. In any event here is a *black boy in a coal mine* hearing his life's direction named, and any wish to call it a fiction seems to me merely a weak theoretical formulation in the face of Washington's capacity, from the established ground he has come to hold, to *make the facts of his life.* If his identity as ex-slave gave him the freedom to name himself and make that name a fact, his achievement as founder of Tuskegee gives him the freedom to make the fact of his call. He even shows that he is creating the fact when he intrudes the full name of Hampton, which the two men could hardly have named. When we consider that it is a coal mine, that he is black, that both he and the coal possess the implicit or inertial energy, we begin to see both the act and style of *Up from Slavery.* The inertia of the style produces the effect of an indeterminate consciousness on the part of Washington, the autobiographer. If I say that he intended the significance that I see, both the style and the skeptical readers reading it almost smile in my face, implicitly accusing me of trying to make a "symbol" of that passage. And of course the accusation is to a large extent right. That is why I am willing to leave it as a made or earned fact—inertial in its existence until it is put into relation to a consciousness prepared to invest it with dynamic energy.

Such a consciousness, once attracted to that inertia, feels the whole possibility of Washington's life about to come to life; relationships start up like rabbits from a blackberry patch. It was Henry Adams, after all, who in his dynamic *Education* determined to measure the line of force of American history in terms of coal production. And it is coal which to this very moment holds the inertial energy of all the weight of geological ages pressing down upon it to create the potential fire of civilization. Set against Henry Adams's autobiography of a failed education, Washington's calling to a successful education strikes sparks. Yet the very critic who would write a book on Henry Adams's art would likely smile indulgently at the comparison.

But let that go. The point is that coal is in the earth. It is the earth into which Booker T. Washington's life is driven and out of which it stands. In his slave cabin, which had no wooden floors, he tells us, there had been a hole where sweet potatoes were kept. When he comes up out of the coal mine to go to Hampton Institute, he makes his way to Richmond where, without enough money to get a meal or a room, he sleeps under a board sidewalk on the ground. Though beneath the pedestrians, he is yet on the earth. And when he ultimately goes to Tuskegee, the first thing he does is to acquire land on which to build his school from the ground up. He helps clear the fields of this farm—it is actually a ruined plantation—which his school is to occupy. The first building takes the place of the burned-down ruin of the original plantation house; he and his students "dig out the earth" where the foundations are to be laid. Washington is proud that the cornerstone is grounded in the great "black belt" of the South; he knows, and says, that the black belt refers both to the dark soil of the deep South and to the dark people who live there. All this is the ground of Washington's world—the ground where slavery had existed and the ground in which he is determined to found his school. Both his act of life and his vision of education are rooted in this land.

The purchase and possession of this land are the very base of Washington's whole program of education. It is there that Washington means to teach his people that freedom means freedom to labor, not freedom from labor. As Washington sees the time he has lived through, he regrets that the trades and skills which were taught in slavery have been denigrated by a vision of education as an escape from labor. School for Washington means being able to build a school, to acquire land and clear it, to make bricks and lay them, to get lumber and measure it, to build beds and make mattresses for them, to grow food on the acquired land and cook it. His own transition from an unlettered to a lettered society is scarcely ever defined in the books that he has read. It has instead involved learning to clean a room, as Mrs. Ruffner had taught him to do. That background enabled him to pass the examination for entry to Hampton, which was cleaning a classroom. He had to learn how to sleep between sheets, how to wear clothes, how to eat a balanced diet; and he knows that these acts cannot be taken for granted in teaching blacks in the unreconstructed South. Yankee women, Mrs. Ruffner of Charleston and Mary Mackie of Hampton, have taught him these rudimentary but utterly essential lessons, and Washington clings to such discipline as if it were a lifeline. He teaches the "gospel of the toothbrush" at Tuskegee, as if the toothbrush were a synecdoche for civilization. Keeping clean is not a ritual but a rule, a discipline which Washington enforces with a master hand. Traveling through the South where there are often no bathing facilities, Washington makes his way to nature, to bathe in streams. When one sees all this, it is possible to be condescending; it is also possible to see that Washington has discovered the root meaning of the name he has chosen. No wonder, with such a name, he criticizes the city of Washington, where black women have lost the skills of washing clothes. Such an emphasis on these aspects of education may make, and has made, readers lament this educator's bare mention of books. Again it is well to remember that his name is *Booker*. If the cleanliness is contained in his last name, the books are contained in his first. He knows books—he says that he likes biography and dislikes fiction; he claims to have read everything written about Abraham Lincoln. But he does not emphasize his bookishness. He does not have to, since he is making and writing his own book, a fact which a reader shouldn't be blind to. His strategy does well enough, particularly when compared to the books which Harvard, Yale, and Dartmouth presidents have written.

All this is not to praise Washington's vision of education but to see that vision. His discipline is the measure of the rudimentary struggle to gain the ground on which education can be founded. That ground is in the South, under the political sway of whites who, having been dispossessed of their slave world, have nonetheless ridden out reconstruction to regain their damaged dominion. Washington is placating them. He has to; to do otherwise would be to abandon his school or go north to relocate it. His whole theory of education can justifiably be viewed as a promise to southern whites that Tuskegee graduates will not have big ideas; but it cannot justifiably be seen as simply that. The desperate order of the skilled hand, the toothbrush, the clean body, and the clean school is a great hope rooted in a great fear.

We might want to say that the hope represses the fear, but that simply isn't true. Fear is everywhere present in Washington's narrative. When he was a slave boy bringing food home late from the mill he feared that he would be caught in the dark and have his ears cut off by deserting soldiers. On the way to West Virginia with his mother and brothers, the family spent the night in an abandoned house, only to be frightened away by a blacksnake. Even when he names himself, he is in anxiety at not having a name as the teacher begins to call the roll. There is fear present in being "called" in the coal mine; thus he noiselessly creeps to hear the two men talking. He is glad to be called to be a teacher—partly out of fear of being called to be a preacher. He is afraid of the whites around Tuskegee and afraid of the whites in the North from whom he has to beg money, but most of all he is afraid of the psychological space he occupies between the two hostile camps. The space and the fear are almost one and the same thing. Riding on a train in Alabama, he is trapped into eating with two northern white liberal ladies, and he suffers the anxiety of knowing the hostility his presence in the dining car may provoke.

This fear never diminishes with Washington's success; if anything, it increases—not in intensity, since the inertial style precludes emotional crescendo, but in presence. For as Washington gains recognition, he is more and more exposed. Beyond fearing lack of money for Tuskegee from the North or resistance to the school from the South, he has to fear how his action as a public figure will be interpreted by his conflicting constituencies. In preparing to speak at Atlanta, he faces fear on every hand—fear of what southern whites may say, fear of whether he will hurt his school, fear of the visiting northern whites, and fear of the speaking act itself. That fear is, to be sure, a rhetorical background for the success of the speech, but it is also one of the great facts in Washington's book. He discusses his profound fear of public speaking—the fear that some single member of the audience may walk out, the performer's fear of going on stage, the gnawing anxiety of eating a multicourse dinner with the knowledge of having to give an after-dinner speech. When he at last takes his first vacation—the trip to Europe—he fears the luxuries, the dinners, the society, and the possible misunderstandings the Tuskegee community may have about his absence. As he ends the book he is very much on the defensive. He knows that Du Bois and hundreds of northern blacks are raising their voices in criticism; he knows that the Tuskegee teachers and students are restive; and it seems to me that he profoundly knows that his own success is being accompanied by mounting victories of antinegro legislation; for all his success and all his placation he knows about lynching and raises one last plea against it. He ends his book with an account of his triumphant welcome in Richmond, the capital of his native state, yet anyone sensitive to the narrative will feel Washington's anxious wonder whether he may have been as secure under the sidewalk as he is on top of it.

In citing this fear in the book, I am once again forced to distort the nature of its presence. The inertial style cannot and does not express it dramatically but contains it constantly. That, it seems to me, is the mastery of the inertial style. To speak of Washington's mastery may again provoke a smile. But my point in using the word is that Washington is a master. His whole book is devoted to coming up *from* slavery, not up against it. Slavery is the deep ground of his experience; to reject it totally would remove all possibility of becoming a master of the self—and self-mastery is what much of Washington's book is about. It is the iron discipline that he pursues, and it is the basis on which he builds a school and is its master. He becomes the master speaker who aspires to total control of his audience; the description of that control he leaves to white reporters, whose description of his galvanizing presence he almost self-servingly enters in the text.

It would be easy to misconstrue the figure of Washington as master. By converting it into a metaphor, I could jump on the bandwagon with Washington's innumerable critics and say that Washington is playing the role of white master on the old plantation, getting along with the white society of former masters, and making his students the same old black laborers on the new Tuskegee plantation. I have heard it said and I cannot quite unsay it. For Washington is deeply related to the old white world. He is a slave son of an unknown white father from that world; and even George Washington, the white father of freedom whom Washington "adopts" once he is free, did own slaves—a paradox which Henry Adams contemplated with almost paralyzed dismay.

The fact remains, however, that Booker Taliaferro Washington, if not all black, defines himself as black, not white. He determines to remain in a society which will aggressively see him as black. If the name he takes is white and the civilization which he is set on acquiring for himself and for his people is white, these are to be acquisitions, not being; they are property, not identity. They constitute a self to be moved and built, both in Washington's life and in his book. If it is possible to say that this model self is white, I think it equally possible to say that the white model self is Washington's very slave. It is simple, fiercely reduced in its outlines, kept rigidly in line, and controlled with an iron discipline. It has enormous dynamic energy which can only be implicitly seen.

The inertial style makes Washington seem like an old man, rather than a relatively young man. He was at most forty-five when it was published; he was only twenty-five when he went to Tuskegee. It is hard to believe, this youth so given over to age, this drive which moves so slowly. Yet it is just this slow and steady movement which is the black being of Washington—the being that he retained for himself, yet represents for his people. He does not create the motion; it has been created by the force which ended slavery. It is slow, but it is relentless: it is both a force and a fact—the emotion of identity and the motion of history—which cannot be stopped. Since it is everywhere present it cannot be revealed.

To have said so much may not prove that *Up from Slavery* is literature. I certainly cannot prove it so to anyone disposed to exclude it from the shelf of our "major" works of art. I do believe that it is a wonderful parallel text to Henry Adams's *Education*, just as I believe that it is a remarkable counterpart to Du Bois's *The Souls of Black Folk*. Du Bois's style is at once intellectual and poetic, yet what gives his book its dynamic power is his full awareness that it is just this style which has cut him off from the souls of his people; his imagination and his achievement are to direct the very language which has taken him away from those souls—and is taking him away with every sentence he writes—across the gulf of his separation to reach behind the veil.

That soul which Du Bois so poetically seeks to recover is what Washington has retained all the time. In discussing his practice as a public speaker, he observes that, for all the rules of speaking one can master, "none of these can take the place of *soul* in an address." But that is a statement, not a revelation. There is a passage which touches closer to the inertial heart. Describing his anxiety as he eats the fine dinner after which he is to give a speech, he writes:

> I rarely take part in one of these long dinners that I do not wish that I could put myself back in the little cabin where I was a slave boy, and again go through the experience there—one that I shall never forget—of getting molasses to eat once a week from the "big house." Our usual diet on the plantation was corn bread and pork, but on Sunday morning my mother was permitted to bring down a little molasses from the "big house" for her three children, and when it was received how I did wish that every day was Sunday! I would get my tin plate and hold it up for the sweet morsel, but I would always shut my eyes while the molasses was being poured out into the plate, with the hope that when I opened them I would be surprised to see how much I had got. When I opened my eyes I would tip the plate in one direction and another, so as to make the molasses spread all over it, in the full belief that there would be more of it and that it would last longer if spread out in this way. So strong are my childish impressions of those Sunday morning feasts that it would be pretty hard for any one to convince me that there is not more molasses on a plate when it is spread all over the plate than when it occupies a little corner—if there is a corner in a plate. At any rate, I have never believed in "cornering" syrup. My share of the syrup was usually about two tablespoonfuls, and the two spoonfuls of molasses were much more enjoyable to me than is a fourteen-course dinner after which I am to speak.

Think of the teachers of college English who could show Washington how to improve that passage. They could show him how, by reducing the number of words and by cutting out the repetition, he could eliminate the slightly awkward manner of his description. Yet that awkwardness seems to me Washington's very hold on the experience. It is the slow but desperate possession of a bare something which the fear of speaking has enabled him to take hold of. How little is there, yet how much: the present anxiety, the wish for the lost past which nonetheless *cannot* be forgotten, and then the memory itself—with its expectation, its anxiety (in the tightly closed eyes), its habitual disappointment (implicitly revealed in the effort to make the small amount bigger), and then the molasses, caused to move by the moving plate which the child moves, then moving in slow inertial expansion.

That passage may not be greatly moving in its effect, but it is slowly moving. The memory has not been enhanced, but it cannot be forgotten. Max Thrasher could no doubt have enhanced it, but he took Washington's dictation. It was not Washington who died after the book was done (he survived for fourteen years); it was Thrasher. He died of peritonitis at Tuskegee in 1903.

HOUSTON A. BAKER, JR.

[Booker T. Washington's Mastery of Form]†

The "changing same" is Amiri Baraka's designation for the interplay between tradition and the individual talent in Afro-American music.[1] Invoked in reference to the Harlem Renaissance and Afro-American modernism, the phrase captures strategies that I designate as *the mastery of form* and *the deformation of mastery*. Such strategies come most decisively to the foreground of black intellectual history with the emergence of Booker T. Washington as a black man who possessed (in his own words) "a reputation that in a sense might be called National."[2] The event that produced this reputation occurred at the moment I postulated earlier as the commencement of Afro-American modernism—September 18, 1895. The event, which lasted just ten minutes, was Washington's delivery of the opening address at the Negro exhibit of the Atlanta Cotton States and International Exposition. I designate Washington's speech as the point at which an agreed upon (by those whites in power, or by those empowered by whites in power) direction was set for a mass of black citizens who had struggled through the thirty years since emancipation buffeted on all sides by strategies, plans, hopes, and move-

† From Houston A. Baker, Jr., *Modernism and the Harlem Renaissance* (Chicago: U of Chicago P, 1987), 15–22, 25–36. Reprinted with the permission of the author and the University of Chicago Press.

1. See Amiri Baraka (LeRoi Jones), *Black Music* (New York: William Morrow, 1967).
2. Booker T. Washington, *Up from Slavery*, in *Three Negro Classics*, ed. John Hope Franklin (New York: Avon, 1969), p. 140 [94]. All citations to Washington's work refer to this edition and are hereafter marked by page numbers in parentheses. [Norton Critical Edition page numbers appear in brackets—*Editor*.]

ments, organized by any number of popular, or local, black spokespersons, without before 1895 having found an overriding pattern of *national* leadership or an approved plan of action that could guarantee at least the industrial education of a considerable sector of the black populace.

The immensity of the Tuskegee orator's ability (quite cannily won) to take the stage at Atlanta and speak into existence a program, policy, and platform that offered guiding premises and discursive strategies has been remarked by many. But the specifics of his captivating power before a turn-of-the-century audience have not, I think, been fully appreciated. His most influential set of public utterances is contained in *Up from Slavery* (1901), his autobiography and a work that dramatically portrays patterns that I call the mastery of form. Before considering the autobiography's discursive strategies, however, a definition is in order.

* * *

For the present, I shall use the term "form" to signal a symbolizing fluidity. I intend by the term a family of concepts or a momentary and changing same array of images, figures, assumptions, and presuppositions that a group of people (even one as extensive and populous as a nation) holds to be a valued repository of spirit. And the form most apt for carrying forward such notions is a *mask*.[3]

It is difficult to convey notions of *form* and *mask* in the exact ways that I would like, for the mask as form does not exist as a static object. Rather it takes effect as a center for ritual and can only be defined—like form—from the perspective of action, *motion seen* rather than "thing" observed. I shall make an attempt to convey the notion of mask as form, however, by summoning a familiar imagistic array, a long-standing group of concepts and assumptions that serves as a spiritual repository for a quintessential American ritual. The form, array, mask that I have in mind is the *minstrel mask*. That mask is a space of habitation not only for repressed spirits of sexuality, ludic play, id satisfaction, castration anxiety, and a mirror stage of development, but also for that deep-seated denial of the indisputable humanity of inhabitants of and descendants from the continent of Africa. And it is, first and foremost, the mastery of the minstrel mask by blacks that constitutes a primary move in Afro-American discursive modernism.

The spirit of denial in the minstrel mask is nowhere more defining of a national spirit than in the United States. The mask, for generations on end, has been so persuasively captivating, so effectively engaging in its

3. The critic Henry Louis Gates, Jr. has produced an intriguing essay on masking and dialect in Afro-American expressive traditions. As in the past, I find myself in accord with his speculations. The essay is entitled "Dis and Dat: Dialect and the Descent" and appears in *Afro-American Literature: The Reconstruction of Instruction*, ed. Dexter Fisher and Robert B. Stepto (New York: Modern Language Association, 1978), pp. 88–119.

seeming authenticity, that an astute intellectual like Constance Rourke can actually take it as an adequate and accurate sign of a "tradition" of "Negro literature" predating the "cult" of Afro-American expressivity she found so wearying in the 1940s.

But if Rourke seems too credulous about the authenticity of representations of Afro-America that took place behind the minstrel mask, she is nonetheless capable of a fine analytic dissection when she allows herself to be subjected to what one might call the *sound* emanating from the mask. She records her reaction as follows:

> Early blackface minstrelsy revealed indeed the natural appropriations of the Negro from the life about him: but the persistent stress was primitive, the effect exotic and strange with the swaying figures and black faces of the minstrels lighted by guttering gas flames or candlelight on small country stages or even in the larger theaters. Within this large and various pattern lay a fresh context of comedy, plain in the intricate, grotesque dancing as the minstrels "walked jaw-bone" or accomplished the deep complications of the "dubble trubble" or the "grapevine twist." A bold comic quality appeared which had not developed elsewhere in American humor, that of nonsense. With all his comic wild excesses the back-woodsman never overflowed into pure nonsense; the Yankee did not display it. Perhaps the Negro did not invent the nonsensical narratives told in song on the minstrel stage, but the touch is akin to that of Negro fables in song; and nonsense in minstrelsy shows a sharp distinction from other humor of the day.
>
> A little old man was ridin' by,
> His horse was tryin' to kick a fly,
> He lifted his leg towards de south
> An' sent it bang in its own mouth—
>
> . . . .
>
> The note of triumph, dominant in all early American humor, appeared in these reflected creations of the Negro, but not as triumph over circumstance. Rather this was an unreasonably headlong triumph launching into the realm of the preposterous.[4]

What Rourke compresses into the space of this lengthy quotation is the psychodrama of the minstrel mask.

If the inhabiting spirit of the mask is, as Rourke suggests, one of nonsense, misappropriation, or mis-hearing (a misconstrual fundamental to American minstrelsy), then the results are as bizarre (and, surely, as appealing) as witch burning or lynching, to suggest other embedding American rituals. The Afro-American writer William Melvin Kelley

4. Constance Rourke, *The Roots of American Culture and Other Essays* (New York: Harcourt Brace, 1942), pp. 269–70. The essay in which the passage appears is entitled "Traditions for a Negro Literature."

brilliantly conflates the motions of the minstrel show's ritual with lynching and exorcism in his novel *A Different Drummer* (1962). Threatened with lynching by a southern mob that is enraged because the Negroes of the region have followed an exodus led by Tucker Caliban (O, happily named protagonist!), Kelley's Reverend Bradshaw is suddenly identified as "our last nigger" by one of the mob. Having made this identification, the group decides that before they kill Bradshaw, they should present him—in a bizarre and archetypally American reversal of the *prisoner's* last wish—with a final request: "Do you know 'Curley-Headed Picaninny Boy'?" they ask. Bradshaw nods, and the narrator comments:

> Of course he knew, everybody knew it; it was a song liberal-minded third-grade music teachers in New York, Chicago, Des Moines, San Francisco, and all the towns in between had their pupils sing to acquaint them with Negro culture; in Cambridge it was sung whenever anyone with a guitar who prided himself as a folk singer got together with a group of people who considered themselves folklorists; it was known all over the country, had been sung for a long time. And Dewey [the youthful Harvardian of Kelley's tale] realized that Bradshaw's nod had signified a knowledge of something else; he knew now and could understand why the Negroes had left without waiting or needing any organizations or leadership.[5]

The whites are enraged when Bradshaw, a Harvard alumnus, sings the song with a British accent and proves inept at minstrel dancing. "You stink!" they exclaim, and drag him off to die.

Combining Kelley's and Rourke's figurations of minstrelsy results not only in a sense of the absurdity implicit in the mask, but also in a notion of minstrelsy's prevalence. To be a *Negro*, the mask mandates, to be a *Negro* one must meld with minstrelsy's contours. (And what a reversal the black entertainers Bert Williams and George Walker effected when they advertised themselves as "Two *real* Coons.") Such a concurrence casts one headlong into the realm of nonsense. The minstrel mask is a governing object in a ritual of *non-sense*. The brand of non-sense to which minstrelsy gives force is best described, I think, by Susan Stewart's observations on "ready-made systems" of nonsense. She writes:

> At times nonsense will effect a traversal that depends upon the availability of a given, or ready-made, system from common sense. The common-sense system provides the closed form within which nonsense effects its rearrangements or substitution of elements. One such use of the play of rearrangement within closed fields is the mnemonic device. Here a structure is used to incorporate all the elements of what is desired to be remembered. For example, there is the mnemonic for the colors of the rainbow (red, orange,

5. William Melvin Kelley, *A Different Drummer* (New York: Avon, 1969), pp. 195–96.

> yellow, green, blue, indigo, and violet), "Roy G. Biv," which appears in *Ulysses*, and another mnemonic for the same elements, "Read Over Your Greek Books in Vacation." The mnemonic is knowledge centered in itself; it has no meaning outside of its use. It is purely "a device," for it does not "count" on its own.[6]

By misappropriating elements from everyday black use, from the vernacular—the commonplace and commonly sensible in Afro-American life—and fashioning them into a comic array, a mask of *selective* memory, white America fashioned a *device* that only "counts" in relationship to the Afro-American systems of sense from which it is appropriated. The intensity of the minstrel ritual, its frantic replaying to packed and jovial houses, is a function of the "real" Afro-Americans just beyond the theater's doors, beyond the guttering lights of the mind's eye. The device is designed to remind white consciousness that black men and women are *mis-speakers* bereft of humanity—carefree devils strumming and humming all day—unless, in a gaslight misidentification, they are violent devils fit for lynching, a final exorcism that will leave whites alone. Which all returns us to the "mastery of form." For it was in fact the minstrel mask as mnemonic ritual object that constituted the *form* that any Afro-American who desired to be articulate—to speak at all—had to master during the age of Booker T. Washington.

* * *

Thirty-two years after the Emancipation Proclamation, Booker T. Washington changed the minstrel joke by stepping inside the white world's nonsense syllables with oratorical mastery. *Up from Slavery* offers a record and representation of Afro-America's mastery of form. Early in the text we discover that Washington understands the constraints that define Afro-American *sound:*

> As the great day [of emancipation] drew nearer, there was more singing in the slave quarters than usual. It was bolder, had more ring, and lasted later into the night. Most of the verses of the plantation songs had some reference to freedom. True, they had sung those same verses before, but they had been careful to explain that the "freedom" in these songs referred to the next world, and had no connection with life in this world. Now they gradually *threw off the mask;* and were not afraid to let it be known that the "freedom" in their songs meant freedom of the body in this world. (P. 39, my emphasis) [15]

Playing *behind* a pious mask is as central to the narrator's characterization of black quarters as the renaming that he describes: "In some way a feeling got among the coloured people that it was far from proper for

6. Susan Stewart, *Nonsense: Aspects of Intertextuality in Folklore and Literature* (Baltimore: Johns Hopkins University Press, 1978), pp. 186–87.

them to bear the surname of their former owners, and a great many of them took other surnames" (p. 41) [16].

A liberating manipulation of masks and a revolutionary *renaming* are not features commonly ascribed to the efforts of Booker T. Washington. Yet the narrator's clear awareness of the importance of such strategies appears at the very opening of *Up from Slavery*. What causes one to bracket (in an almost phenomenological manner) such liberating strategies is the way the narrator keeps culturally specific information hushed to a low register beneath his clamorous workings of the minstrel tradition.

His working of minstrelsy's nonsensical stereotypes begins, most outrageously, when he recalls his mother: "One of my earliest recollections is that of my mother cooking a chicken late at night, and awakening her children for the purpose of feeding them. How or where she got it I do not know. I presume, however, it was procured from our owner's farm" (p. 31) [8]. *Up from Slavery* is barely begun. We are two pages into the narrative when we are confronted by a "chicken-stealing darky"—as mother. How soothing and reassuring such a formidably familiar image of "Negro behavior" must have been to Washington's white readers! Such portraiture was bound to overshadow the type of epic discourse that marks a subsequent observation such as this one:

> This experience of a whole race beginning to go to school for the first time [during Reconstruction], presents one of the most interesting studies that has ever occurred in connection with the development of any race. Few people who were not right in the midst of the scenes can form any exact idea of the intense desire which the people of my race showed for an education. *As I have stated*, it was a whole race trying to to go school. Few were too young, and none too old, to make the attempt to learn. (P. 44, my emphasis) [19]

The repeated announcement of the subject in the passage, pre-fixed by the phrase "as I have stated," comes so hard upon the opening epic intentions that it appears the narrator *knows* that no one in his white audience will listen to sounds of an epic. In order to ensure attention, therefore, he must employ strategies such as repetition—or the summoning to the stage of comic, unprepared, and grossly pitiable darkies.

"Bring up the shines, gentlemen! Bring up the little shines!" is the way Ellison's school superintendent in *Invisible Man* captures the necessities of Washington's situation.[7] And, indeed, the following lines from *Up from Slavery* come like a kick in the stomach and stand in blatant contrast to the epic note already introduced:

7. Ralph Ellison, *Invisible Man* (New York: Random House, 1952). The words are part of the first chapter of the novel and are important white code phrases for the classification of the protagonist and his peers in the "Battle Royal" scene and in the later Brotherhood scene in which the protagonist delivers a fiery speech in a boxing arena.

> It could not have been expected that a people who had spent generations in slavery, and before that generations in the darkest heathenism, could at first form any proper conception of what an education meant. . . . The ambition to secure an education was most praiseworthy and encouraging. The idea, however, was too prevalent that, as soon as one secured a little education, in some unexplainable way he would be free from most of the hardships of the world, and, at any rate, could live without manual labor. (P. 71) [40]

One of the utterly extraordinary things about this passage is the way it revises the tone characterizing a first epic view of blacks turning toward education at the dawn of freedom. The invocations of "heathenism" and "slavery" become comprehensible, however, when one realizes that the passage appears in a chapter entitled "Reconstruction."

Any southern spokesperson—and this was, *preeminently*, the role that Washington occupied—who would be kindly received by a southern audience at the turn of the century had to set forth a dim view of black Reconstruction politics. Washington's narrator not only plays the role of a judiciously southern, post-Reconstruction racist but also supplies a preposterous character direct from minstrelsy to play the darky role in this condemnatory drama:

> I remember there came into our neighbourhood one of this class [Negro teachers who could do little more than write their names], who was in search of a school to teach, and the question arose while he was there as to the shape of the earth and how he would teach the children concerning this subject. He explained his position in the matter by saying that he was prepared to each that the earth was either flat or round, according to the preference of a majority of his patrons. (P. 72) [41]

The continuation of such "darky jokes"—of what I call *sounds* of the minstrel mask—flows from the mother as chicken thief (our origins in "jes some sich mis'chief, boss") through a condemnation and mockery of Afro-American professionals in the chapter on Reconstruction. In its drama of condemnation, this chapter also presents a deceived body of Afro-Americans who reside in the nation's capital and have been victimized by their removal from southern "country districts." These urbanites have suffered the false guidance of higher education, yielding to wastefulness and sin. "I saw," says the narrator, "young coloured men who were not earning more than four dollars a week spend two dollars or more for a buggy on Sunday to ride up and down Pennsylvania Avenue in order that they might try to convince the world that they were worth thousands" (p. 76) [44]. In harmony with white Northern sentiment, the narrator wishes that "by some power of magic . . . [he could] remove the great bulk of these people into the country districts [of the South] and plant them upon the soil, upon the solid and never deceptive foundation of Mother Nature, where all nations and races that have ever succeeded have gotten their start,—a start that at first may be slow and toilsome, but one that nevertheless is real" (p. 77) [44–45].

Epic gives way to pastoral; a black *nation* is displaced by a deceived urban sector in need of redemption. Implicit in the drama of condemnation is the real theme of the piece: the aspirations that characterized a *federal* period of Reconstruction (metonymically signaled by the District of Columbia) must be relinquished. More realistic goals are necessary to meet incumbencies of a new *regional* (the New South) era in which blacks will cast down their buckets where they are and seek advice and counsel from southern whites.

The narrator plays out this discursive drama in ways clearly identifiable as masterful *strategies of attraction*. His cullings from a bizarre white assemblage of distorted syllables gathers force and frequency as he moves beyond Reconstruction. There is, for example, his presentation of the ignorantly comic darky whose political sagacity is recorded as follows:

> "We wants you to be sure to vote jes' like we votes. We can't read de newspapers very much, but we knows how to vote, an' we wants you to vote jes' like we votes. . . . We watches de white man, and we keeps watching de white man till we finds out which way de white man's gwine to vote; an' when we finds out which way de white man's gwine to vote, den we votes 'xactly de other way. Den we know we's right." (P. 88) [53]

Surely this is a voice heard only in the theater of minstrel madness, just as the inhabitants of the "country districts" that Washington presents are grievous caricatures. Witness the man whose help he solicits to renovate a henhouse: "When I told . . . [the] old coloured man who lived near, and who sometimes helped me, that our school had grown so large that it would be necessary for us to use the hen-house for school purposes, and that I wanted him to help me give it a thorough cleaning out the next day, he replied, in the most earnest manner: 'What you mean, boss? You sholy ain't gwine clean out de hen-house in de *day*-time?' " (p. 98) [61–62]. The old man is surely akin to the pathetic old "An'ty" who hobbles into a room at Tuskegee and, despite her obvious poverty, offers Washington six eggs: " 'Mr. Washin'ton, God knows I spent de bes' days of my life in slavery. . . . I ain't got no money, but I wants you to take dese six eggs, what I been savin' up, and I wants you to put dese six eggs into de eddication of dese boys an' gals' " (p. 99) [62].

There are other examples in Washington's autobiography of the narrator's self-conscious adoption of minstrel tones and types to keep his audience tuned in. These tones and types, as I have suggested, are reassuring *sounds* from the black quarters. Although the narrator may be stunningly capable of standard English phraseology, crafty political analyses, and smooth verbal gymnastics that move him through an amazing invocation and half-invention of a pastoral Eden at Tuskegee (replete with the founder and his wife figured as a godlike Moses and a tireless helpmate Eve), there can be no worry that the Negro is getting "out of hand." For at all the proper turns, there are comforting sounds and figures of a minstrel theater that we know so well—"Look away! Look away! Look Away! Dixie Land."

Given that *Up from Slavery* has sometimes been considered merely an imitative version of Horatio Alger or of Andrew Carnegie's *Gospel of Wealth* (1889), how can one justify an emphasis on self-conscious design—on a culturally specific and canny rhetorical appropriation that I call the mastery of form? One possible answer to this question can be formulated in structural terms. In Washington's work more than forty of two hundred total pages are devoted to oratorical concerns. In chapters entitled "Two Thousand Miles for a Five-minute Speech," "The Atlanta Exposition Address," and "The Secrets of Success in Public Speaking," Washington's work becomes a *how-to* manual, setting forth strategies of address (ways of talking black and back) designed for Afro-American empowerment. The narrator provides one explanation for his success as a public speaker:

> If in an audience of a thousand people there is one person who is not in sympathy with my views, or is inclined to be doubtful, cold, or critical, I can pick him out. When I have found him I usually go straight at him, and it is a great satisfaction to watch the process of his thawing out. I find that the most effective medicine for such individuals is administered at first in the form of a story, although I never tell an anecdote simply for the sake of telling one. (P. 161) [111]

Surely Washington's narrator—a man who describes his life as unrelieved work and who is more enamored of biography and fact than of fiction and games—never tells a story "simply for the sake of telling one." No, his mind is undoubtedly always fixed on some intended gain, on a *mastery* of stories and their telling that leads to Afro-American advancement. The most scandalous instance of his deeply intentional play on minstrel form is coextensive with patterns set in motion early in the narrative. It occurs in fact in the Atlanta Exposition Address—an address transcribed in the autobiography as an embedded document.

A white farmer tells Washington on the day before his Atlanta talk that he will have to please an audience composed of white northerners, white southerners, and blacks. "I am afraid," says the farmer, "that you have got yourself into a tight place" (p. 144) [97]. But Washington's speech is an overwhelming success with black and white alike. It includes tributes to northern philanthropy, gratitude to southern patriarchs, and prescriptions for Afro-American accommodation in an age of Jim Crow. It also includes the *sound* of minstrelsy. Listen:

> Starting thirty years ago with ownership here and there in a few quilts and pumpkins and *chickens (gathered from miscellaneous sources)* . . . (P. 149) [101]

SCANDAL is the only designation for the appearance of such a *sound* (a chicken-thieving tonality) in the first address presented in the South by a black man considered a *national* leader. Extricating himself from a "tight place" and finding room for an authentic voice seem to occasion the scandalous for an Afro-American speaker.

Rather than going straight at a possibly somnolent white southern audience in Atlanta—and at lovers of minstrelsy throughout the nation—Washington strikes a "straight lick with a crooked stick." He turns minstrel nonsense into what he believes is the only available good sense, or, sense intended for a common black good. The efficaciousness of his "public speaking" is captured in another of the embedded documents in *Up from Slavery*. "I will be very glad," reads the document, "to pay the bills for the library building as they are incurred, to the extent of twenty thousand dollars, and I am glad of this opportunity to show the interest that I have in your noble work." The letter is signed "Andrew Carnegie." Further evidence of the success of *Up from Slavery's* rhetorical mastery is offered by the changed status of Tuskegee revealed at the close of the work. Commencing in a stable and a henhouse, the school is transformed during the course of the narrative into a handsomely endowed and architecturally attractive oasis of skills and morality in the midst of southern "country districts." One implicit lesson of Washington's narrative, therefore, is that public speaking—indeed, the Afro-American's ability to find a voice at all—is a function of the mastery of form. Like Billy Kersands stretching the minstrel face to a successful black excess, or Bert Williams and George Walker converting nonsense sounds and awkwardly demeaning minstrel steps into pure kinesthetics and masterful black artistry, so Washington takes up types and tones of nonsense to earn a national reputation and its corollary benefits for the Afro-American masses.[8] He demonstrates in his manipulations of form that there *are* rhetorical possibilities for crafting a voice out of tight places. What, then, of chicken stealing and the mother? The narrator continues his earlier report with these words:

8. The names of Kersands, Williams, and Walker are those of black men who possessed enormous theatrical talent (Williams was in fact a genius of pantomime and comedy) but who found themselves with but one role to play on an American stage—that of minstrelsy. Converting confinement into the birth of genius, they effectively subverted minstrelsy through their original and energetic "plays" within the form. For an account of these performers, see Langston Hughes and Milton Meltzer, *Black Magic: A Pictorial History of the Negro in American Entertainment* (Englewood Cliffs, N.J.: Prentice-Hall, 1967).

> Some people may call this [my mother's action] theft. If such a thing were to happen now, I should condemn it as theft myself. But taking place at the time it did, and for the reason that it did, no one could make me believe that my mother was guilty of thieving. She was simply a victim of the system of slavery. (P. 31) [8]

It seems we must conceive Washington's appropriation of the minstrel image (so intimately linked with the mother and so casuistically explained) as theft. It is in fact a Promethean cultural appropriation, since he surely took images that fueled the minstrel theater and used them to draw attention to the contours, necessities, and required programs of his own culture. The mother's act thus offers instruction in (and nourishes) a cultural voice won from slavery's victimization and silencing. And *Up from Slavery* as a whole projects a model for the mastery of form that serves as type and figuration for the Afro-American spokesperson. In his provision of the model, Washington—offspring and descendant of slavery's misappropriations—achieves an effective modernity. His "speaking manual" is a sign and a wonder. It emerges from a mass of southern black folk who sought ways beyond factionalism, uncertainty, oppression, and minstrel nonsense that marred their lives during thirty uneasy years from emancipation to the dawn of a new century.

WILLIAM L. ANDREWS

The Representation of Slavery and the Rise of Afro-American Literary Realism, 1865–1920†

The most famous metaphor of slavery in the history of Afro-American literature appears in the climax of the *Narrative of the Life of Frederick Douglass, an American Slave,* in which Douglass reconstructs the significance of his struggle with the slave-breaker, Edward Covey, on a hot August morning in 1834. Triumph over Covey, known as "the snake" among his slaves, became Douglass's "glorious resurrection, from the tomb of slavery, to the heaven of freedom."[1] A little more than a half century after Douglass's *Narrative* was published, the most infamous metaphor of slavery in the history of black American literature appeared in the first chapter of Booker T. Washington's *Up from Slavery.* When we "look facts in the face," Washington states, "we must acknowledge

† From *Slavery and the Literary Imagination*, ed. Deborah E. McDowell and Arnold Rampersad (Baltimore: Johns Hopkins UP, 1989), 62–64, 68–80. Reprinted by permission of the publisher.

1. *Narrative of the Life of Frederick Douglass, an American Slave, Written by Himself,* edited and with an introduction by Houston A. Baker, Jr. (New York: Viking Penguin, 1982), 113.

that, notwithstanding the cruelty and moral wrong of slavery, the ten million Negroes inhabiting this country, who themselves or whose ancestors went through the school of American slavery, are in a stronger and more hopeful condition, materially, intellectually, morally, and religiously, than is true of an equal number of black people in any other portion of the globe."[2] The disparities between these two metaphors are striking. The antebellum writer says slavery was like a tomb, in which he languished in what Orlando Patterson would call "social death" and from which he was resurrected only by rebellious effort.[3] The postbellum writer, on the other hand, compares slavery to a school, in which he and his fellows received, rather than lost, social purpose and from which they graduated not by violence but by sanctioned behavior like industry and dutifulness. I do not call attention to this difference between Douglass and Washington in order to question the reliability of one or the other as historian of slavery. The metaphorical shift between the two most influential slave narratives in American literature urges a more important inquiry, I believe, into the dynamics of Afro-American literary, rather than sociopolitical, history.

Throughout the nineteenth century and well into the twentieth, autobiographies of former slaves dominated the Afro-American narrative tradition. Approximately sixty-five American slave narratives were published in book or pamphlet form before 1865. Between the Civil War and the onset of the depression, at least fifty more ex-slaves saw their autobiographies in print, to a large extent eclipsing in their own time the influence, if not the memory, of their antebellum predecessors. Yet with the exception of criticism on *Up from Slavery*, there has been little investigation into what I shall call the postbellum slave narrative, nor has there been any serious study of the large number of black autobiographies in the late nineteenth and early twentieth centuries that were written in the shadow of the postbellum slave narrative, especially Washington's.[4] It is imperative to read the slave narrative tradition wholly, however, if we wish to reckon with the significance of the crucial shift in the metaphor of slavery that highlights the Douglass and Washington texts. If we read the Afro-American autobiographical tradition from 1765 to 1920 in toto, we can see that major parameters of this tradition—such as the representation of slavery—underwent revision, not only according to the differing perspectives of individual writers but also in relation to the changing social and political priorities of successive generations of freedmen and freedwomen.

The slave narrative took on its classic form and tone between 1840

2. *The Autobiographical Writings*, vol. I of *The Booker T. Washington Papers* ed. Louis R. Harlan and John W. Blassingame (Urbana: University of Illinois Press, 1972), 222–23.
3. Orlando Patterson, *Slavery and Social Death* (Cambridge: Harvard University Press, 1982), 38–45.
4. For a brief, introductory look at the subject, see my "Forgotten Voices of Afro-American Autobiography, 1865–1930," *A/B: Auto/Biography Studies* 2 (Fall 1986): 21–27.

and 1860, when the romantic movement in American literature was in its most influential phase. Transcendentalists like Theodore Parker welcomed antebellum slave narratives (and Douglass's in particular) into the highest echelon of American literature, insisting that "all the original romance of Americans is in them, not in the white man's novel."[5] Douglass's celebration of selfhood in his 1845 *Narrative* might easily be read as a black contribution to the literature of romantic individualism and anti-institutionalism. Ten years later Douglass's second autobiography, *My Bondage and My Freedom*, deconstructs his 1845 self-portrait with typical romantic irony. The idea of heroic slaves like Douglass resurrecting themselves from graves of the spirit by forceful resistance to authority undoubtedly appealed to an era fascinated by the romantic agon, the life-and-death contest of the spirit of revision against all that represses it.[6] But after the Civil War, few ex-slave autobiographers recounted their lives in the manner of Douglass. The stunningly different treatments of bondage and selfhood in *Up from Slavery*, for instance, signal a new wave of revisionism in postbellum Afro-American literature, instanced in the reaction of later slave autobiographers to what they perceived as romanticized interpretations of the pre-emancipation past, whether by black or white writers. By the turn of the century, slave narrators viewed slavery and its significance to the advancement of black people in an increasingly pragmatic perspective, delineated most effectively in *Up from Slavery*. This immensely influential slave narrative articulates a quasi-literary realism whose rhetoric, conventions, and cultural import need to be examined if we are to reckon adequately with the effort on the part of turn-of-the-century black novelists to make fiction address matters of fact.

* * *

The pragmatism of the postbellum slave narrator stems primarily from his willingness to interpret and evaluate slavery according to its practical consequences in the real world of human action. * * * The postbellum narrator rarely appeals to such ideals or to the righteous indignation that let his antebellum predecessor condemn slavery so categorically. Instead he asks his reader to judge slavery simply and dispassionately on the basis of what Booker T. Washington liked to call "facts," by which the Tuskegean meant something other than empirical data. In *Up from Slavery*, as in many other postbellum slave narratives, a factual evaluation of slavery exploits what William James would later call the "practi-

5. Theodore Parker, "The American Scholar," in *The American Scholar*, ed. George Willis Cooke, vol. 8 of *Centenary Edition of Theodore Parker's Writings* (Boston: American Unitarian Association, 1907), 37.
6. For further discussion of the relationship of mid-nineteenth-century black American literature to romanticism, see William L. Andrews, "The 1850s: The First Afro-American Literary Renaissance," in William L. Andrews, ed., *Literary Romanticism in America* (Baton Rouge: Louisiana State University Press, 1981), 38–60.

cal cash-value" of the word, its significance in the present day.[7] What slavery was in the past is not so important as what slavery means, or (more importantly) can be construed to mean, in the present. A factual view of slavery, for Washington, is concerned less with a static concept of historical truth, frozen in the past, than with the need for rhetorical power in the ever-evolving present. To the postbellum slave narrator, particularly Washington, slavery needed to be reviewed and reempowered as a concept capable of effecting change, of making a difference ultimately in what white people thought of black people as freedmen, not slaves. The facts of slavery in the postbellum narrative, therefore, are not so much what happened *then*—bad though it was—as what *makes* things, good things, happen now.

Looking the facts of the present (more than the past) in the face, Washington could justifiably call slavery a school in which black Americans had learned much about the necessity of hard work, perseverance, and self-help as survival skills in their difficult passage in the antebellum South. The fact of turn-of-the-century American "scientific" racism, which stereotyped "the Negro" as degraded, ignorant, incompetent, and servile, demanded that slavery be re-presented anew, not as a condition of deprivation and degradation, but as a period of training and testing, from which the slave graduated with high honors and even higher ambitions. Given the changed socio-political circumstances, it is not surprising to find the postbellum slave narrator treating slavery more as an economic proving ground than an existential battleground for southern black people. The slave past, if effectively represented, could provide the freedman and freedwoman with credentials that the new industrial-capitalist order might respect. By the turn of the century, blacks were realizing their need for a usable American past on which they could build.[8] They could also see that southern whites needed to be reminded of who had built the Old South and who could help to build a New South as well.[9] The agenda of the postbellum slave narrative thus emphasizes unabashedly the tangible contribution that blacks made to

7. William James, "What Pragmatism Means," in *American Thought: Civil War to World War I*, ed. Perry Miller (New York: Holt, Rinehart, and Winston, 1954), 169.
8. Much of the despair registered in the slave narratives of the late antebellum era stems from their writers' conviction that American history was not progressive because slavery held the process of American social and political evolution in thrall. In search of historical precedent for their message, most antebellum slave narrators buttressed their narratives in mythical history as recorded in the Bible, which showed how God had delivered the people of Israel from their bondage. Only after emancipation did the slave narrative incorporate a historical consciousness that chronicles progressive change at work in contemporary America. In the late nineteenth century, as black socio-political prospects declined, the postbellum slave narrator often turned for consolation back to the slave past, partly to remind himself and his readers of how far the race had really come, and partly to recover something valuable and sustaining to his present struggles.
9. Washington's Atlanta Compromise address evokes the sentimental image of the slave "whose fidelity and love you have tested in days when to have proved treacherous meant the ruin of your firesides" not simply to pander to white stereotypes but to exploit them in an argument that pictures the freedmen and freedwomen as builders, not destroyers, of the South in the past and the future (p. 100). Washington was by no means unique among postbellum slave

the South, in and after slavery, in order to rehabilitate the image of the freedman, not the idea of slavery, in the eyes of business America.

Although in some ways a typical postbellum slave narrative, *Up from Slavery* stands out today, as always, because of its articulation of an accommodationist strategy that, though by no means original, Washington managed to identify as his own.[1] What we would call accommodationism, however, is what the Tuskegean would have termed realism. What are the sources of real power in the real world? asks the writer of *Up from Slavery*. In the antebellum slave narrative, as I have already noted, the answer is almost unanimous. Knowledge is power, and the fundamental source of knowledge is literacy, the ability to open one's mind to the words of others and to liberate other minds with a text of one's own. As an ex-slave and an educator, Washington pays lip service to the importance of reading in his own life and in the training of his people. But in his preferred persona as pragmatic student of power, he demotes men of the word and elevates men of action to the putative leadership of his people. The irony of the preeminent black speaker and writer of his day identifying himself as a man of real acts, not mere words, should not prevent us from recognizing the literary significance of Washington's antiliterary thesis. *Up from Slavery* is, in its own quiet and indirect—should I say sly?—way, a manifesto of a quasi-literary realism that attempts to restrict the traditional sovereignty of the black wordsmith by chaining the signifier to a preexistent signified and thus making the word merely reflective, rather than constitutive, of reality.

Washington's realism entails a radical distinction between deeds and words. "The actual sight of a first-class house that a Negro has built is ten times more potent than pages of discussion about a house that he ought to build, or perhaps could build" (p. 253). Action, Washington insists, produces things; discussion, by contrast, produces only more discussion. "Instead of studying books so constantly, how I wish that our schools and colleges might learn to study men and things!" (p. 30). The men Washington studies are, of course, white men of action and substance, like Andrew Carnegie, Collis P. Huntington, and William McKinley. In stark contrast with them are black men of words—in particular, southern politicians, preachers, and educators. These men, Washington argues, have too often made speaking and writing a refuge from doing, from working productively for the good of the race. As he surveys the recent history of his people, he finds that politicians stirred up in the people only an "artificial" desire to hold public office; preach-

narrators in stressing the constructive role of slaves in building the Old South and making possible the aristocratic tradition of which the New South liked to boast. See, for instance, John Quincy Adams, *Narrative of the Life of John Quincy Adams, When in Slavery, and Now as a Freeman* (Harrisburg, Pa.: By the Author, 1872), 46–47.

1. See August Meier, *Negro Thought in America: 1880–1915* (Ann Arbor: University of Michigan Press, 1963), 85–99.

ers inspired in literate black men only a self-serving "call to preach"; teachers merely pandered to "the craze for Greek and Latin learning" (p. 40) among pathetically ignorant blacks. Instead of doing tangible good, all this preaching and teaching and speech-making created in the minds of rural southern blacks a pernicious notion, namely, that an alternative resource of power existed to what Washington called the "real, solid foundation" (p. 44) of black advancement, the agrarian life. Even Washington had to acknowledge that the black community had traditionally revered the man of the word as "a very superior human being, something bordering almost on the supernatural" (p. 40) in the case of those who understood the mystery of foreign languages. Such men seemed not to require "the solid and never deceptive foundation of Mother Nature" (p. 44–45), that is, a grounding in the life of "the soil," to exercise power and excite envy among southern blacks.[2] Washington's fear was that the example of Afro-American men of the word would encourage young blacks to believe that the route to black power was not hand-to-mouth, from act to word, but rather just the reverse, from performing word to reforming act. Washington pays inadvertent tribute to these black masters of the speech-act by noting that they "live by their wits" instead of by their hands and that the white South regards them with a perplexed and uneasy suspicion.

Few can read *Up from Slavery* today without recognizing that Washington also lived by his wits and in a consummate manner. A former political stump speaker and student of the ministry, Washington clearly understood the power of the word in the mouth of an artful and ambitious black man. "I never planned to give any large part of my life to speaking in public," he blandly remarks, adding, "I have always had more of an ambition to *do* things than merely to talk *about* doing them" (p. 91). Yet no black man could have built Tuskegee Institute without knowing that action proceeds from speech and that speech is itself a most potent form of action. Washington acknowledges that he authorized the erection of Porter Hall, the first building on the Tuskegee campus, before he had the money to pay for it. He relied on his charm and good name in the community to secure loans to complete the edifice. He had no capital at all when he conceived of putting up a second building, but, as he offhandedly comments, "We decided to give the needed building a name" (p. 81) anyway. Naming the building Alabama Hall proved, of course, a shrewd political maneuver that helped to ensure the continuation of the state funding on which Washington depended so much in the early years. This speech-act alone, so reminiscent of the talismanic power of naming in the slave narrative tradition, belies Washington's insistence that words merely publicize deeds. Thus, even though he

2. "I remember that the first coloured man whom I saw who knew something about foreign languages impressed me at that time as being a man of all others to be envied" (p. 40).

claims that he always "had a desire to do something to make the world better, and *then* be able to speak to the world about that thing" (p. 35; emphasis mine), Washington had the wit to see that speaking makes doing possible and that reality is contingent on language, not the other way around.

Nevertheless, in an effort to subvert the "almost supernatural" status of the man of words in the black community, the author of *Up from Slavery* presents himself as a naturalist, arguing that only from a rootedness in "nature" does he derive the "strength for the many duties and hard places that await me" (p. 121) in the real world. Washington is not talking about communing with Nature in some romantic fashion. His need is more immediate and tangible: "I like, as often as possible, to touch nature, not something that is artificial or an imitation, but the real thing" (p. 121). Hence it is no surprise to find Washington depreciating belles-lettres and enthusing over newspapers as "a constant source of delight and recreation." Obviously, fiction, poetry, and drama are artificial and merely imitative of "the real thing." Only one kind of storytelling can satisfy Washington's appetite for realism, namely, "biography," for which he claims "the greatest fondness." Why he should prefer biography to all other kinds of reading is plain enough: "I like to be sure that I am reading about a real man or a real thing" (p. 120). But the way Washington prefaces his predictable desire for the "real thing"—"I like to be *sure*"—suggests that he knows that readers of biography do not always get what they expect or want, nor does biography always assure its readers of their ability to distinguish between the real and the artificial. Maybe this is one reason why Washington is at such pains in writing his own biography to portray himself as a plain and simple man of facts, "the real thing" among autobiographers, a man who represents himself as no more than what he is. Washington *knows* the prejudice in his white audience against black men of words as truth-tellers; this is a major reason why he claims he is a man of acts and facts.[3] By repeatedly declaring his "great faith in the power and influence of facts" and his conviction that one can touch the real thing in biography, Washington acts to shore up the foundation of *Up from Slavery*, which we can see is not so much grounded in real things as in linguistic demonstrations of realism.

Capitalizing on the postbellum slave narrator's pragmatic revision of the facts of slavery, *Up from Slavery* promulgates a concept of realism which challenges the traditional status of the sign in the Afro-American narrative tradition. By claiming a radical distinction between action and speech and by disclaiming language as anything more than a referential medium, Washington denies the performative dimension of representa-

3. White suspicion of the veracity of slave narrators is almost as old as the slave narrative itself, which is one reason why there are so many authenticating documents in *Up from Slavery*. See Robert B. Stepto, *From Behind the Veil* (Urbana: University of Illinois Press, 1979), 3–31.

tion. The consummate rhetorician, he tries to pass for a realist, we might say, since this lets him keep his agenda masked behind a semblance of nonrhetorical *vraisemblance.* If Washington could define the terms by which realism would be judged in Afro-American writing, then he could consign literary representation to a *re*active status in Afro-American culture, thereby robbing it of the expressive power that the word had held in the black community since the antebellum era. The rise of Tuskegee realism then, foregrounded by the postbellum slave narrative and reinforced by numerous autobiographies of Washington's protégés, imitators, and admirers, discounts the hard-won victory of antebellum narratives like *My Bondage and My Freedom* and *Incidents in the Life of a Slave Girl,* texts that liberated black narrative from an alienating and objectifying focus on the sign as a referent to an object—slavery—rather than a subject—the questing consciousness of the former slave. Tuskegee realism, ever respectful of Washington's much-heralded "gospel of the toothbrush," sanitizes the mouth of the speaking subject until it attains that acme of "unselfishness" which is, in Washington's eyes, the hallmark of every successful man of action.

Neither the rise of pragmatism in the slave narrative nor the articulation of Tuskegee realism in *Up from Slavery* exerted a profound impact on the idealism of the protest fiction that dominated much late nineteenth- and early twentieth-century black belletristic prose in America. Protest romances from Frances Ellen Watkins Harper's *Iola Leroy* (1892) to Du Bois's *The Quest of the Silver Fleece* (1911) answer the call that Pauline Hopkins delivered in the preface to her novel *Contending Forces* (1900): "We must ourselves develop the men and women who will faithfully portray the inmost thoughts and feelings of the Negro with all the fire and romance which lie dormant in our history."[4] The problem with devoting the novel to romances of racial uplift, however, was that this could easily play into the hands of Tuskegee realism. Washington would have been happy to see the novel in its place, as a defensive, (merely) inspirational reaction to unjust realities.[5] The way to combat Tuskegee realism was not to justify romance, however well intentioned. Black wordsmiths needed to decertify—literally, to make *un*certain—the "real, solid foundation" on which Tuskegee realism claimed its hegemony. This is what happens in two prominent fictive texts of this period, Charles W. Chesnutt's *The Conjure Woman* (1899) and James Weldon Johnson's *The Autobiography of an Ex-Colored Man* (1912).

As fictive autobiographies, both of these books exploit the anxiety that Washington expressed about biography as a representation of "a real man or a real thing." *The Conjure Woman* purports to be a collection of

4. Pauline Hopkins, *Contending Forces* (1900; reprint, Carbondale: Southern Illinois Press, 1978), 14.
5. Hazel Carby points out that when Washington saw a novelist like Hopkins as a threat, he took forceful action—by buying the organ, *The Colored American Magazine,* in which her novels were first serialized.

dictated slave narratives transcribed by a white entrepreneur from Ohio. However, by mediating his intention through Uncle Julius McAdoo's narratives and the conflicting interpretations of them offered by the Ohioan and his wife, Chesnutt made it hard for many readers to tell what the man behind all these masks really meant. Reviewers who did not know that Chesnutt was an Afro-American (neither Chesnutt nor his publishers mentioned this fact when *The Conjure Woman* came out) extrapolated from the text an implied author who, though a Northerner, had thoroughly immersed himself in the local color of the South and had written to entertain his white readership with the quaint customs and folklore of the southern Negro. Comparatively few reviewers perceived a "dark side" and tragic note in Chesnutt's representation of the slavery past.[6] The disparity between the two implied authors attributed to *The Conjure Woman* demonstrated that the real is not a constant but a function of words like "Negro" and "white" which are themselves but traces of racial *différence* in the cultural text of the racist American reading community.

Even more destabilizing of black biographical reality is Johnson's *Autobiography of an Ex-Colored Man*. Published anonymously, the novel was designed by its author to be taken as a real, not a fictive, work. Most reviewers, as well as a large part of the black reading community,[7] were taken in by the *vraisemblance* of the novel, which, if one were to analyze it in detail, reads almost like a catalog of the stock in trade of nineteenth-century realism. What distinguishes the ex-colored man as a persona is not his storytelling but his leisurely digressions from the facts of his life into the realm of social and cultural commentary. His breadth of experience, his criticism of whites and blacks alike, and his almost Olympian detachment from racial loyalties give him an objectivity toward the whole race question that sounds almost Tuskegean. Moreover, Washington would surely have concurred with the ex-colored man's regretful judgment of his having passed for white as a selfish and socially unproductive act. An even more obvious invocation of the Tuskegee line comes at the end of the novel, when Washington himself makes a cameo appearance representing all the "earnestness and faith" of a progressive race, as contrasted with the self-protective cynicism of the ex-colored man.

What do these apparent endorsements of Tuskegee realism mean, however, if the narrator who makes them is not a "real man"? Does the fictiveness of the narrator invalidate the authority of what he says? Does fictive language have less—or perhaps more—performative potential

6. I base these generalizations on the critical response to *The Conjure Woman* which I found on my perusal of the scrapbooks of contemporary press clippings and reviews of that book housed in the Chesnutt Collection of the Fisk University Library, Nashville, Tennessee.
7. In his autobiography, Johnson recalls a dinner party at which he met a man who obliquely confessed to having authored *The Autobiography of an Ex-Colored Man*! See *Along This Way* (1933; reprint, New York: Viking, 1968), 238–39.

than natural language?[8] Did Johnson invent a fictive character like the ex-colored man out of a belief that such a vehicle could actually represent certain facts more fully and freely than an actual man? If so, is this a testimonial to the strength of the Afro-American novel or the weakness of Afro-American autobiography? However we answer these questions posed by the problematic "author-function" of *The Autobiography of an Ex-Colored Man*, we can see clearly enough that the novel does not leave unscathed many of the assumptions about realism—how to recognize it, how to read it—that Washington held dear.[9] If Johnson wrote the ex-colored man's story with no other purpose than to unveil the cultural conventions that predisposed his readership to believe an "autobiography" by a doubly phony white man over a novel authored by a real black man, namely, Johnson himself, his effort must be considered a signal success in the history of Afro-American autobiography, as well as fiction.

The pragmatic reassessment of slavery and the rise of Afro-American realism illustrate a process of revisionism at work in black narrative of the late nineteenth century that exempted virtually nothing in the past from being remade anew. Whatever black reality *was* historically, whatever one generation of black narrators said it was, their successors refused to be bound by it. First pragmatic slave narrators, then the Tuskegee realists, and then novelists like Chesnutt and Johnson insisted on their right to reappropriate the signifying potential of black reality and, through what we might call deconstructive acts, prepare the discursive ground once again for a new assay of the basis on which a usable truth could be constructed. From the perspective of the New Negroes of the Harlem Renaissance, Johnson had only begun to probe the deeper resources of subjective consciousness in *The Autobiography of an Ex-Colored Man*; Chesnutt had only glimpsed the import of black folk culture in the magical realism of *The Conjure Woman*. Nevertheless, in their revisionistic attitude toward prevailing notions of the real, and in their emphasis on reality as a function of consciousness mediated through language, these were enabling texts. They not only pointed new directions for the Harlem Renaissance; they bore witness to the postbellum slave narrators' determination to keep the past alive and meaningful to the present. In short, the work of Chesnutt and Johnson helped preserve Afro-American realism as a literary tradition, a bridge between the antebellum and modern eras, that makes Tuskegee available for the Invisible Man to reinvent and enables the transposing of the "apparently incoherent" slave songs of Douglass's *Narrative* into the *Song of Solomon*.

8. I use the terms "fictive" and "natural" as Barbara Herrnstein Smith uses them in *On the Margins of Discourse* (Chicago: University of Chicago Press, 1978), 15, 21–25.
9. I use the term "author-function" as Michel Foucault defines it in "What Is an Author?" in Josué V. Harari, ed., *Textual Strategies* (Ithaca: Cornell University Press, 1979), 141–60.

Booker T. Washington: A Chronology

1856	Born in Franklin County, Virginia, son of Jane, a slave, and an unknown white man.
1865	End of the United States Civil War; abolition of slavery. Moves to Malden, West Virginia, with mother and siblings.
1872–1875	Attends Hampton Normal and Agricultural Institute, graduating with honors in 1875.
1875–1877	Teaches school in Malden, West Virginia.
1877	End of Reconstruction era in the South.
1878–1879	Attends Wayland (Baptist) Seminary, Washington, D.C.
1879–1881	Teaches at Hampton Institute.
1881	Opens Tuskegee Normal and Industrial Institute, Tuskegee, Alabama, on July 4.
1882	Marries Fannie Norton Smith, of Malden, West Virginia (d. 1884).
1883	Birth of Portia Marshall Washington; Supreme Court overturns Reconstruction Civil Rights Act of 1875.
1885	Marries Olivia A. Davidson, of Tuskegee, Alabama (d. 1889).
1887	Birth of Booker Taliaferro Washington, Jr.
1889	Birth of Ernest Davidson Washington.
1892	Marries Margaret James Murray of Nashville, Tennessee.
1895	Delivers address at the opening of the Cotton States and International Exposition at Atlanta, Georgia.
1896	Supreme Court upholds segregation in state law in its *Plessy v. Ferguson* decision; receives honorary Master of Arts from Harvard University.
1900	Launches National Negro Business League in Boston; publishes *The Story of My Life and Work*.
1900–1901	Secretly organizes court case testing Louisiana state constitution's grandfather clause.
1901	Publishes *Up From Slavery*; dines with President Theodore Roosevelt at the White House while consulting about political appointments in the South.

1903	Receives $600,000 endowment gift from Andrew Carnegie.
1903	W. E. B. Du Bois writes "Of Mr. Booker T. Washington and Others," a critique of Washington's philosophy and methods, in *The Souls of Black Folk*.
1906	Atlanta Race Riot.
1909	Founding of the National Association for the Advancement of Colored People.
1911	Publishes *My Larger Education;* assaulted by a white man in a New York City apartment building.
1912	Publishes *The Man Farthest Down*.
1913	Writes to President Woodrow Wilson deploring new federal segregation policy.
1915	Dies on November 14 at Tuskegee, Alabama.

Selected Bibliography

This bibliography does not include those works from which the excerpts above have been taken.

MAJOR WORKS BY BOOKER T. WASHINGTON

Harlan, Louis R., et al., eds. *The Booker T. Washington Papers*. 14 vols. Urbana: U of Illinois P. 1972–89.

Washington, Booker T. *The Future of the American Negro*. Boston: Small Maynard. 1899.

———. *My Larger Education*. New York: Doubleday Page. 1911.

———. *The Story of My Life and Work. Autobiographical Writings. The Booker T. Washington Papers*. Ed. Louis R. Harlan. Urbana: U of Illinois P. 1972.

———. *Up From Slavery*. Intro. by Langston Hughes. New York: Dodd, Mead. 1965.

———. *Up From Slavery*. Intro. by William L. Andrews. London: Oxford UP. 1995.

MAJOR BIOGRAPHIES OF BOOKER T. WASHINGTON

Harlan, Louis R. *Booker T. Washington: The Making of a Black Leader, 1856–1901*. New York: Oxford UP. 1972.

———. *Booker T. Washington: The Wizard of Tuskegee, 1901–1915*. New York: Oxford UP. 1983.

Mathews, Basil. *Booker T. Washington, Educator and Interracial Interpreter*. Cambridge, MA: Harvard UP. 1948.

Scott, Emmett J., and Lyman Beecher Stowe. *Booker T. Washington: Builder of a Civilization*. Garden City, NY: Doubleday Page. 1917.

Spencer, Samuel R. *Booker T. Washington and the Negro's Place in American Life*. Glenview, IL: Scott Foresman. 1955.

GENERAL HISTORICAL AND LITERARY STUDIES

Anderson, James D. *The Education of Blacks in the South, 1860–1935*. Chapel Hill: U of North Carolina P. 1988.

Andrews, William L. *To Tell a Free Story: The First Century of Afro-American Autobiography, 1760–1865*. Urbana: U of Illinois P. 1986.

Bruce, Dickson D., Jr. *Black American Writing from the Nadir: The Evolution of a Literary Tradition, 1877–1915*. Baton Rouge: Louisiana State UP. 1989.

Foster, Frances Smith. *Witnessing Slavery: The Development of Ante-Bellum Slave Narratives*. 2d ed. Madison: U of Wisconsin P. 1994.

Franklin, John Hope and Alfred A. Moss, Jr. *From Slavery to Freedom*. 7th ed.New York: Alfred A. Knopf. 1994.

Hawkins, Hugh, ed. *Booker T. Washington and His Critics*. 2d ed. Lexington, MA: D. C. Heath. 1974.

Logan, Rayford W. *The Betrayal of the Negro from Rutherford B. Hayes to Woodrow Wilson*. New York: Collier. 1965.

Thornbrough, Emma Lou, ed. *Booker T. Washington: Great Lives Observed*. Englewood Cliffs, NJ: Prentice Hall. 1969.

Toll, William. *The Resurgence of Race: Black Social Theory from Reconstruction to the Pan-African Conferences*. Philadelphia: Temple UP. 1979.

Wells, Ida B. "Booker T. Washington and His Critics." *The World Today* (April 1904): 518–521.

Williamson, Joel. *The Crucible of Race: Black-White Relations in the American South since Emancipation*. New York: Oxford UP. 1984.

CRITICISM ON *UP FROM SLAVERY*

Barton, Rebecca Chalmers. *Witnesses for Freedom: Negro Americans in Autobiography*. New York: Harper and Row. 1948.

Butterfield, Stephen T. *Black Autobiography in America*. Amherst: U of Massachusetts P. 1974.

Dudley, David L. *My Father's Shadow: Intergenerational Conflict in African American Men's Autobiography*. Philadelphia: U of Pennsylvania P. 1991.

Gibson, Donald B. "Strategies and Revisions of Self-Representation in Booker T. Washington's Autobiographies." *American Quarterly* 45 (September 1993): 370–393.

Hedin, Raymond. "Paternal at Last: Booker T. Washington and the Slave Narrative Tradition." *Callaloo* 2 (Oct. 1979): 95–102.

Olney, James. "The Founding Fathers—Frederick Douglass and Booker T. Washington." In *Slavery and the Literary Imagination*. Eds. Deborah McDowell and Arnold Rampersad. Baltimore: Johns Hopkins UP. 1989. 1–24.

Stepto, Robert B. "Lost in a Cause: Booker T. Washington's *Up from Slavery*." In *From Behind the Veil: A Study of Afro-American Narrative*. Urbana: U of Illinois P. 1979. 32–51.